REASON IN RELIGION.

BY

FREDERIC HENRY HEDGE.

"Keine vertrautere Gabe vermag der Mensch dem Menschen anzubieten als was er im Innersten des Gemüthes zu sich selbst geredet hat."

Schleiermacher.

BOSTON:
WALKER, FULLER, AND COMPANY
245, Washington Street.
1865.

SECOND EDITION.

BOSTON:
STEREOTYPED AND PRINTED BY JOHN WILSON AND SON,
No. 15, Water Street.

CONTENTS.

INTRODUCTORY.

Book First.

RELIGION WITHIN THE BOUNDS OF THEISM.

Book Second.

RATIONAL CHRISTIANITY.

REASON IN RELIGION.

Introductory.

I.

BEING AND SEEING.

INTRODUCTORY.

I.

BEING AND SEEING.

PHILOSOPHY has observed that human consciousness is most distinct on the surface of life, and grows dim and confused as it reaches toward the interior. The reason alleged is, that individuality, the subject of consciousness, is merely phenomenal; and that, where the phenomenal ceases, individual existence is merged in the universal life.

The fact is certain, the explanation questionable. I rather believe that individuality is real and radical, and that the limitation of consciousness on the inner side is due to the fact, that consciousness depends on external impressions: its condition is re-action on a world without; it is the differentiation of self from all beside, and therefore loses its distinctness in proportion as all beside is withdrawn; that is, toward the interior of our being.

There is, in all men, something deeper than themselves, — than the conscious self of their experience. It is the elder, aboriginal self, which no consciousness can grasp. Who remembers the time when first he began to say "I," and found himself a conscious unit, distinct from all others? If we attempt to trace the history of the soul, its beginning is lost in a period of blank unconsciousness, beyond all scrutiny of memory or imagination. Blind mystery envelops our origin, as it does our end. No man quite possesses himself. The self which he seems to possess is growth from a root which bears him, not he it.

Springing from this unknown root, our being carries an unknown factor which modifies all its action. Our thinking, as well as our doing, obeys its influence. It is written, "As a man thinketh, so is he." We may reverse the proposition, and say with equal truth, "As a man is, so he thinketh." His thinking is the product of his being; consequently, the gauge and exponent of his being. It is his being translated into thought, — his being intellectually expressed. According as he is wise or foolish, his opinions will be true or false: they will be right or wrong according as he is good or evil.

The character in religion determines the creed. Character has been defined "the educated will." But the will — the conscious, personal will — is not the only factor in this product: there is something in it of the radical self. And something of the radical self there is in every creed which is genuine, and not mere subscription to the *placita* of a Church. The true creed of a man is his character confessed.

Or does any one suppose that belief is independent of character? — that a man can be one thing, and think another? We sometimes talk as if truth were a secretion of the brain, entirely unaffected by moral conditions; as if one could lay hold of spiritual truth, without spiritual insight, by mere dint of logic: or as if spiritual insight were the product of some organic arrangement, mechanical in its operation, and quite as likely to go right with a vicious character as with a righteous one; just as a watch may keep equally good time whether worn by a sinner or a saint.

This I believe to be a very false view of the action of the mind in this relation. The intellect is nothing distinct from man. It is man himself in one of his functions. As the man, so the function, so the product of that function. As he is, so he thinketh.

I say nothing of positive science. I do not deny that one who is morally depraved may be a good mathematician or a good physiologist. These are regions of truth beyond the jurisdiction of religion, and independent of moral conditions; excepting always the general influence which character has on all the action of the mind. I am speaking of truth in morals and religion, when I say that the character determines the belief. Truth of spirit is essential to the right apprehension of spiritual truth. To know the truth, it is necessary to will the truth, and to *be* the truth.

This connection between being and seeing implies two things: 1st, A perverted nature cannot see the truth; 2d, A (morally) sound nature, seeking without bias, will see the truth.

1st, A perverted nature cannot see the truth. A man must be in harmony with it by moral and spiritual affinity, in order to apprehend it. There are facts which seem to contradict this proposition. It is notorious, that very depraved men sometimes profess a very pure theology; at least, a very Orthodox one: whereas, according to this view, they ought to be infidels and atheists. I leave out of question the hypocrisy which consciously and deliberately assumes the disguise of religion to lull suspicion or to palliate crime. Such characters are not very common in our day, and are wholly foreign from our theme. I speak of bad men who actually receive, or think they receive, the religion they profess.

But, observe, there is a wide difference between reception and conviction. Various degrees of persuasion are comprehended in the term "belief." Most of them stop short of genuine conviction. In fact, there are few, the world over, who can be said to have positive convictions in religion, if we understand by convictions the results of personal investigation or personal intuition. The religious tenets of most men are accidents; that is, they are impressions derived from the ecclesiastical atmosphere in which the holders of them happen to live. Or they are social conventions, adopted unconsciously, as it were by contagion. Or they are traditions inherited by education. A man is said to "believe" a doctrine imbibed in this way, although he has never come into real mental contact with it, — has never subjected it to the action of his own mind, — has never looked it fairly in the face. He is said to believe what he has never questioned. The fact is precisely the reverse. A man can never truly believe what he has not at some time questioned. In this sense of unquestioning reception, a very depraved man may hold very Orthodox opinions. Nay, the more depraved he is, the more tenacious of such opinions he is likely to be; the more zealous in defence of the Orthodoxy in which he was bred; the more disposed to annex to it an outlying Orthodoxy exceeding that in which he was bred, and to clothe himself in extra folds of rigorous doctrine; actuated, it would seem, by the notion that a rigorous creed atones for a vicious life. For the Protestant world inherits from the Church of Rome the idea, that God is pleased with Orthodoxy, and that every article which a man adds to his creed, so it have the sanction of the Church, is a step toward heaven.

It is nothing uncommon for very unscrupulous people — tradesmen of doubtful integrity, intriguing politicians, unprincipled men in public life and in private — to maintain with earnestness a stringent Orthodoxy. Not from hypocrisy, not with any intent to deceive; but partly in the hope of being justified by their belief, and partly in order to atone to themselves for conscious depravity. They would balance laxity in practice with severity in doctrine, and thus maintain a moral equilibrium in their life. It is the same principle which led the gay women of the court of Louis XIV. to become devotees with advancing years; putting on "the ornament of a meek and quiet spirit" as outward charms decayed, and replacing the varnished attractions of personal beauty with the still available "beauty of holiness." It is the same principle which leads worldly men and women, in later time, to seek refuge in the bosom of Romanism and to expiate a reckless life by religious austerity.

In such cases, there is no genuine conviction; no true interior knowledge, but mere profession. It may be sincere, so far as intention goes, but based on no actual personal experience of the truth. Only they have sight of spiritual verities, who arrive at them through spiritual experience. Only the true soul can know the truth.

2d, A sound nature, seeking without bias, will see the truth.

Here, again, we encounter a fact which seems to contradict the supposed connection between the intellectual and the moral in man, between character and creed. There are cases of men of pure character and blameless life, who have been infidels in religion. If it be true that the character determines the belief, it would seem that every pure and honest mind must receive, if not the doctrine of the gospel, at least the essential truths of universal religion; and that all who reject these must be morally depraved. But such is not the fact. At least, there are many and significant exceptions. Epicurus, the arch-atheist of antiquity, is said to have lived a blameless and beneficent life at the head of a company of friends who professed to seek private satisfaction as the sure and only good. Spinoza, who is usually regarded as the arch-atheist of modern time, is allowed by his bitter opponent, the unscrupulous Bayle, to have been upright, kind, and strictly moral; which, says he, "may seem strange, but, in reality, ought not to surprise us any more than that men who believe in the truth of the gospel should lead an irregular life." Hume, the inveterate sceptic of English philosophy, is characterized by Adam Smith as generous, charitable, and urbane. Shelley, the zealot antagonist of Christian Orthodoxy, seems to have been possessed with the purest spirit of Christian love. How shall we explain such cases, in which it would appear that pure minds and sound natures had no perception of the truth?

It must be remembered, that what we know of these men, for the most part, is not their belief, but their negations. We see that they reject the established religion as a whole: we do not always see what equivalent they received in its place. But we know, from the nature of the human mind, that some equivalent they must have had; some secret convictions; some spiritual insight; something in the nature of religious faith, however imperfect and ill-defined. For man is not so constituted as to do without faith. These unbelievers have been repelled by some apparent absurdity, or some revolting impiety, in the popular creed. In warring against that, by a natural tendency of the human mind, they have been led to reject the entire system of religious belief of which it seemed to be a necessary part. Or perhaps it is the form in which the popular conception, or a false philosophy, has clothed the doctrines of religion, that they reject; and, rejecting that, they appear to reject the essential truth so embodied. Be this as it may, where the life is pure it is so through belief, and not through unbelief; through the influence of truth, and not through falsity or error. If the life of these unbelievers was true, some true perception must have sprung from it, some religious conviction must have accompanied it. Is there a reputed atheist whose heart is true and whose life is righteous? I say that man believes in God, in a spiritual centre, however his conception of divine wisdom and love may differ from the popular conception, or the theological dogma which bears that name. He believes in a moral law, and a necessary and everlasting distinction between right and wrong, however his standard of moral obligation may clash, in some particulars, with the commonly received ecclesiastical code. He believes in an Infinite Good, in eternal spiritual realities, however he may dissent from the popular view of the life to come.

Hear the confession of one who was counted an atheist in his time, and is still so regarded by most theologians: "Experience had taught me," says Spinoza, "that all which life commonly offers is worthless and vain. I therefore determined to know if there were any genuine good which might be attained, and with which the soul, abandoning every thing else, might be content; the discovery and appropriation of which would yield a continual and supreme satisfaction. That which mankind, if we judge from their actions, regard as the highest good, is either wealth, honor, or sensual enjoyment. The pleasure derived from these is delusive, and only an infinite and everlasting good can impart pure joy to the soul. Therefore I resolved to collect myself, that I might lay hold of this supreme good." And what was the supreme good in his apprehension? "The supreme good," he continues, "consists in becoming partaker of a more excellent nature, and in realizing the intimate relation which connects the individual soul with the universe of things."

And so this remarkable man, a Jew by birth, but excommunicated from the Jewish synagogue for his opinions, lived a life of strict seclusion, devoting himself to meditation and inquiry concerning the deepest mystery of things, refusing lucrative offices which were tendered to him, and maintaining his frugal existence by mechanical labor.

Thus we see that the nominal unbeliever may cherish in his heart a sublime faith which explains the moral anomaly of his life. But we deceive ourselves, if we suppose that such cases are frequent; and that even this negative purity of life (for usually it amounts to nothing more) is a common accompaniment of what is called infidelity. Such combinations are exceptions, not the rule. If we search for the saints of history, — for the moral heroes, the men and the women who stand pre-eminent in moral excellence, choice examples of heroic virtue, — we find them, not in the ranks of unbelief, but among the disciples and among the confessors of a given religion.

If speculative unbelief is sometimes associated with purity of life, practical unbelief, on the other hand, is inseparably connected with moral corruption. By practical unbelief, I mean inward aversion; alienation of the heart from spiritual truths which, however, may not be contradicted by the understanding, and which are outwardly acknowledged by formal compliance with the uses of the Church. I have spoken of depraved men who seek to atone for their vices by their Orthodoxy. There are men who are not depraved in that sense of the term; who are guilty of no misdemeanors; whose life is regular, their manners irreproachable; but whose hearts are selfish and filled with vicious affections, — envy, hatred, and lust; — there are such, I say, who formally assent to the truths of religion; who never entertained a speculative doubt; who never dreamed of questioning the creed of their communion; who deem such questioning impious, and burn with righteous indignation against all who so question, all so-called infidels; but who no more believe in that creed with a genuine appreciative faith than they believe in Brahmanism. Their theological creed is one thing; their practical belief, another and a very different thing. Ecclesiastically, they subscribe to the Athanasian Creed, or the Apostles' Creed, or the Thirty-nine Articles, or the Westminster Catechism; but, if they would confess the secret conviction of their hearts, their creed would be, "I believe in one supreme and all-sufficient good, — the good of riches, the good of honor, the good of enjoyment. These three are one good; the same in substance, equal in value and satisfaction. I believe that the chief end of man is to get gain and lay up much good for many years. I believe that religion is the necessary safeguard of life and property, and must be maintained with strict conformity and punctual observance. I believe in success. I believe in respectability. I believe that the respectable are the children of God and shall inherit the kingdom prepared for them from the foundation of the world; but the needy and the vagabond, the profane rabble, shall be cast into outer darkness, where there is wailing and gnashing of teeth."

It is commonly supposed, that the understanding is competent, in and of itself, with no aid but its own inductions, and no method but its own law, to discover and establish the truths of religion. This supposition is contradicted by the history both of science and religion. The understanding possesses no such capacity; otherwise, the truths of religion would long since have ceased to be matters of debate. What the understanding is competent to decide, it does decide beyond the possibility of question. If by its own methods, in its own right, it could decide these questions, there would be no more difference of opinion concerning them than there is concerning the properties of a circle or a triangle. There are no open questions in mathematics. There is but one theory in astronomy, in mechanics, in any department of inquiry of which the understanding is an adequate judge. Accordingly, recent philosophers have excluded from their survey of human knowledge all ideas of God and spirit, — whatever transcends the facts of sense and the methods of the understanding, as without the pale of legitimate inquiry. To all the revelations of faith and feeling they oppose their so-called "positive philosophy."

The truths of religion are not discovered by the understanding: they are not laid hold of by scientific inquiry. The understanding has no God, no spiritual high calling, no immortal destination. Whoever would know of these things must arrive at them by a different way: he must follow the dictates of faith; he must obey the law written in the heart; he must live in them and for them. To the mere understanding, the world is as intelligible and as satisfactory without a God as with one. If the only use of belief in a God were to furnish a theory of the material universe, to account for the origin of things, — by means of a "First Cause" and a supermundane, creative Power to aid the understanding in the solution of its problems, — humanity could do without this idea, which, after all, does not solve the problem of existence to the intellect, but only replaces it by a new one, and gives us, instead of an inexplicable world, a more inexplicable God. If the understanding were the only or principal source and organ of truth, mankind would have lived to this day without God in the world, and would never have felt the want of the Being whom we so name; would never have felt the inadequacy of a world without a God. But there are other faculties and functions in man; other sources of perception and conviction than the understanding; and other necessities and cravings than those which the understanding can supply. There are moral and spiritual sentiments and aspirations, — the sense of duty, of moral obligation and accountableness; the longing of the soul for an infinite good; the loyalty of the affections to an invisible Supreme; faith, devotion, hope. These demand a God and providence and grace, a spiritual world, and everlasting life.

The greatest philosopher of the last century employed the penetrating analysis of the keenest powers that ever dealt with metaphysical problems, in a critical examination of human ideas and belief, with a view to ascertain what portion of our supposed knowledge could be absolutely legitimated by scientific demonstration. He could find no logical foundation, no critical authority, for those ideas with which religion is conversant, — the sublimest convictions of the human mind, — God, infinity, eternity. And he wrote a book, in which he denied to these ideas any basis in pure reason, any scientific value. But our philosopher was too wise not to perceive, that convictions so deeply rooted, so universally diffused, so inseparable from human nature, could not be mere illusions, but must have some other basis besides tradition and popular prejudice. He saw that man needed a God, and he saw that the need implied the reality. He therefore applied his analysis next to the moral and practical part of man's nature ; and he found the ideas of God and eternity to be legitimate inductions of the moral sense, truths logically resulting from the feeling of moral obligation, — the law written in the heart. That law, he concluded, must have a lawgiver ; that obligation, a sanction ; that consciousness, an object : there must be a God to answer these conditions, to explain the facts of the soul. And he wrote another book, affirming, as truths of practical reason, what the speculative reason had denied.

That part of man's nature which science calls into action is not the whole man. Spiritually, intellectually even, it is a very small part of us, and however respectable, however wonderful in its capacity, is comparatively limited and transient in its application. A man may be very able and very eminent as a scientist, immensely learned, astonishingly acute ; and yet be a poor creature tried by the true criterion and highest standard of humanity. He may be a mere child in spiritual attainments and spiritual insight ; a stranger to all the deeper experiences of the soul ; morally meagre, lank, hungry, destitute. With great activity of brain, there may be an utter want of interior life.

Far be it from me to undervalue the work of the understanding, or to speak disparagingly of the scientific mind in its own legitimate province and function, or to cast contempt on scientific pursuits. Who can help revering the power which possesses and rules this world of ours like a second terrestrial god,—that power to which Nature, in all her realms, is subject and tributary; to which the deeps below and the deeps above yield up their secrets; which makes to itself eyes, that, transcending the limits of natural vision, discover new worlds in the heavenly spaces, millions of miles removed, or detect them near by, in a globule of water or a grain of sand;—the speculative faculty which methodizes the heavens with its unerring calculus, and predicts the position of a planet in some far-removed time;—the practical faculty which utilizes the waste of Nature; which harnesses the idle vapor to the axle of a carriage, or chains it to the oars of a ship, and traverses earth and ocean by aid of this ethereal agent; which converses with distant lands in electric whispers of instantaneous communication; which disarms the surgeon's lancet of its terrors, and transmutes the agonies of the flesh into tranquil dreams? Who can help admiring these things and triumphing in these triumphs?

Nevertheless, this power which spans the heavens and subdues the earth has no interest or part in the highest objects of human life and the noblest aspirations of the human soul. It has no experience and no vision and no surmise of the real and eternal. The devout heart is conscious of a higher calling and worthier aims than the scientific mind; and many an unlearned but faithful doer of God's will converses with sublimer topics than "star-eyed science" has ever scanned. To science belongs the material universe, with its heights and its deeps, its earths and its suns, its stuffs and its shows. Still, the material universe is but a sprinkling of dust upon the spiritual All which encloses it; at best, a transient vision, a temporary showing of God to the finite mind. It had a beginning, it will have an end; and the science which explores it must share with it its date and its doom. But faith and duty have the spiritual and real, — absolute Being, for their sphere and portion. The knowledge which they acquire is not relative and accidental, but essential and unchangeable; for, in it, Being and Knowing are one.

II.

"NATURAL AND SPIRITUAL."

II.

"NATURAL AND SPIRITUAL."

> "There are not two worlds, but one and the same, embracing all, even that which vulgar thought conceives as opposite, — Nature and Spirit."
>
> SCHELLING.

THE popular religion is Manichean. It is so not only in its pneumatology, where it has the warrant of its sacred books, but also in its ontology, where it has no such warrant. It assumes, in the current antithesis of Nature and Spirit, a duality of which its scripture knows nothing.* The doctrine crept into the Church from an extra Christian source, and belongs to another system. A distinction is recognized by philosophy, ancient and modern, between soul and spirit. The soul is common to man with the brute; the spirit is that which distinguishes him from other animals. This distinction, in the hands of theologians, became oppugnance: a difference of degree became battle-array of hostile forces. Instead of "natural" and "supernatural," the two were conceived as natural and contranatural.

* St. Paul distinguishes between animal and spiritual, — τὸ ψυχικόν and τὸ πνευματικόν. Our version improperly renders the former term "natural." Hence the popular dualism. There is nothing of this dualism in the doctrine of Christ, who so penetrated what we call Nature with his spiritual vision as to see only spirit there, and who was so domesticated in what we call the spiritual world, that to him it was as natural as earth and sky.

Nature was put in antagonism with spirit, that is, with God; and St. Augustine, who did more than any other to mould the anthropology of the Christian Church, and who never outgrew his Manichean antecedents, taught that all which is good in man is contrary to nature, and that all which is natural in man is Satanic; making the human a mere arena for the demonstration of hellish and divine powers.

So ingrained in the language of religion is this dualism, that the popular theology is ineradicably infected, the popular mind irrecoverably bewildered, by it. Writers in defence of Christianity declare it to be "against the grain of human nature," and fancy that they exalt it by this declaration. What could infidel say more damaging to the cause of Christian truth?

As a classification of the facts of life whereby one class of phenomena and functions is distinguished from another, the antithesis of natural and spiritual, although inadequate, might pass as loose phraseology. But to make of the rhetorical antithesis an ontological antagonism, to say that nature and spirit are mutually oppugnant, is to put contradiction in the Godhead; or, what is the same thing, to affirm two Gods.

What we mean by nature, when we speak of it as an active power, is God. And "that which is natural,"— vegetable and animal, day and night, summer and winter, growth and decay, — are divine operations, processes ordained and conducted by God. And, what we mean by spirit, — is it not the same God? And "that which is spiritual,"— truth and goodness, conversion, grace, — are these not also divine operations, processes, acts? Are they not also of the very God who made day and night, and the earth and the stars? Further than this we cannot go. We have no experience and no revelation which reaches behind the phenomena; no revelation other than that of the one Creator and Spirit. We only know that all phenomena have one origin at last; that the same all-present and all-teeming Power works equally in the soul and in the sod, is manifest, however diversely, in the life of a saint and the life of a plant; that the God who makes grass to grow in the field makes love and goodness to spring in the heart; that the Father of spirits is the sparrow's Father too, and the Father of the lilies of the field; that the sovereign Will, which, in one of its aspects, we term the law of gravitation, in another is the law of duty which impels the Christian and the Christ.

Nature and spirit are not opposite, but one; related to each other as genus and species, or as parts of one whole; the same arch-power in different characters and functions. It matters little how we theorize about them, so long as we acknowledge in nature and spirit a common fountain and a radical affinity thence arising. We may call nature unconscious spirit, and spirit conscious nature; or we may regard them as parallel independent manifestations. However we may speculate, the essential fact remains. Both meet in one source; both reflect one image. All that is natural is spiritual "in its ascent and cause;" all that is spiritual is natural "in its descent and being."

If for "natural" we substitute "material," we have, it might seem, a more legitimate antithesis. But, even then, the terms should be conceived as expressing different stages of being, not contrary powers. Matter is nature at rest; spirit is nature in action. Throughout nature, there is a tendency and an effort to become spirit, a struggling-up into liberty and consciousness. From shapeless masses to the salient crystal, the beginning of intelligible form; to the growing plant, the beginning of organism; to the sentient animal, the first revelation of conscious soul; to rational man, the highest and last revelation of spirit; — the progress is still from stage to stage of natural life. We say of the plant, it lives. Previous to that, through all the stages of the mineral kingdom, — earths, metals, jewels, — Nature had slept. But now, with the plant, she awakes from her torpor, and looks about her. From the dark bosom of insensate matter emerges a soul. Intelligence looks out from the full-blown flower; instinct shows itself in the natural adaptation of the seed to the soil. With the brute creation, nature attains a higher level, — becomes more active and free. Deeper instincts, sensation, affection, begin to appear. Then finally, in man, the same nature appears as spirit: it becomes reflective, self-conscious, moral. The sense of obligation, aspiration, reverence, charity, faith, devotion, are its finished fruits.

In this progressive unfolding of itself from what we call matter to what we call spirit, nature does not cease to be nature as it rises and ripens. The flower is not less natural than the earth from which it springs; the animal, not less natural than the plant; and the perfect man with all his aspirations and his virtues, the prophet, the saint, is not less natural, but more so, than plant and brute; more natural because more developed and complete.

And now, within the region of the human, what do we mean, what can we mean, by the "natural" and the "spiritual" man? I say, the natural and the spiritual man are the same man in different manifestations and stages of growth. They differ from each other as the garden-plant differs from the same plant in its native state. We say of fruits and flowers which derive their character from the culture bestowed upon them and without that culture could not be what they are, — we say they are not natural but artificial products. In one sense, we are right: they are not *original* nature. And yet they are natural. For "nature is made better by no means, but nature makes that means." The very culture bestowed on flower and fruit is an operation of nature. In all that he does in the way of cultivation, man employs the aid of natural agents and laws. Whatever *he* produces, therefore, is a product of nature. So, too, the spiritual — our virtue, our religion — is, in this sense, a natural product. As the plant is created a flower-and-fruit-bearing creature, so man is created a moral and religious creature: he has a capacity of moral and religious life, as the plant has a capacity of floral and pomal life. In either case, culture is required to bring out that capacity; and whatever that culture produces is natural. No measure of holiness, no work of grace, can exceed nature. Whatever height of goodness the saint may attain in his upward progress, he can arrive at nothing of which the germ and the promise were not laid in his constitution. He can arrive at nothing that is not natural.

This view does not overlook the immediate action of Deity on the soul. It does not overlook or deny what is technically called the operation of divine grace. Whoever believes in God as a present, immanent, diffusive Power, not as an isolated, incommunicable individuality, will recognize a divine agency in those influences which regenerate human nature, renewing the selfish, earth-bound soul, and establishing the empire of truth and goodness in man's will and life. All such influences are God working in us to will and to do. To question a divine agency in the education, or in the conversion and renewing, of the human soul, is to question a fact to which the consciousness of every Christian man or woman will bear witness. But what right have we to say that there is any thing unnatural in this kind of influence, — any thing which distinguishes it from other divine operations, except the direction which it takes, and the consequences in which it results? What process or product of nature is there in which the agency of the same God is not concerned? Not to speak of great things, of suns and systems, and the earth with its seasons, take the humblest product of a summer's growth; take the berry by the wayside, the clover in the field. These creatures exhibit the immediate action of God in every period and circumstance of their being. The juices of the earth, the beams of the sun, the summer showers which conspire to unfold their little life, which round their bodies and paint their cheeks and put sweetness in all their cells, — what are these but so many agencies and aspects and acts of the universal Being who is equally present and equally active and equally perfect in the clover and the berry, and the soul of man? If, then, Divinity is required to call forth and perfect the produce of the field, which to-day is, and to-morrow passes away, how much more is such agency required to unfold the moral life which never dies? We may call this agency in the one case a process of nature; in the other, an operation of the spirit: but these phrases do not alter the identity of the agent. Because the effects are different, is it not therefore the same God? "There are diversities of operations; but it is the same God who worketh all in all."

A process of nature is also a work of grace, and a work of grace is also a process of nature. We no more degrade the agency in the one case by giving it that name, than we exaggerate it in the other. What but a miracle of grace is each returning spring, unlocking myriad doors of life, flooding the landscape with glory and joy, everywhere bursting into flower and song, evangelizing the new-born earth with summer beauty and harvest hopes? The heart is not satisfied with ascribing all this to the different position of the sun in the ecliptic, and the action of cold mechanical laws. Piety sees here the immediate presence and grace of God; and long ago, before the revelation in Jesus Christ, had learned and sung the great truth, "Thou sendest forth thy spirit; they are created: thou renewest the face of the earth." And so, on the other side of the antithesis, the purest manifestations of divine grace do not disdain to exhibit themselves in natural processes; and, even of him whose life was the advent of grace and truth on the earth, it is written, that "the child grew, and waxed strong in spirit," and "increased in wisdom and in stature, and in favor with God and man." The operation of God's spirit in the regeneration of a human heart but unfolds a life-germ inborn in that heart, and is therefore a natural process, as much so as the growth of an apple or an apple-tree. The tree may never bear, and man's spiritual life may never mature; but there it is: there is the faculty, there is the root. Whatever springs from that faculty and that root is a natural product.

This view is something more than philosophic speculation: it is theologically and practically important in its bearings on human duty and destiny. If we say that natural and spiritual are contrary and incompatible, we affirm that religion is unnatural, contranatural; that man must become denaturalized, must become inhuman, before he can become religious, — before he can lead a religious life. And this, I grieve to say, is virtually the doctrine of a large portion of the Christian world. The doctrine taught by Augustine, and revived by Calvin, is, that human nature, as such, is adverse to religion; that Christianity and human nature are related to each other, not merely as root and fruit, or as stock and graft, but as fire and water, or as heaven and hell. Human nature, as such, according to this doctrine, is incapable of holiness: nature must be supplanted by grace. Until that revolution is accomplished, all that man does, however angelic in appearance, is sinful and devilish; and, after that change has taken place, the righteousness that follows is no product of human nature, but grace excluding human nature, and acting in its stead. All this has been inferred from that saying of St. Paul, — or been thought to be sanctioned by that saying, — "The natural man receiveth not the things of the spirit of God." I cannot so interpret the apostle's language. For "natural" let us say "animal;" and the real meaning will be found to be this, — Man, as an animal, with only so much of mental life developed in him as belongs to his sphere in the animal scale, cannot receive the truths of the gospel: he cannot be a Christian. A further development is needed for that. Even as animal, man develops a certain degree of mental or spiritual life: he is capable of society and civil government, but not of religion, not of conscious communion with God, not of worshipping in spirit and truth. To attain that is the new birth by which man becomes what Paul calls "spiritual," as distinguished from animal. One is represented by Adam; the other, by Christ. But both are one and the same man, — the same human nature in different stages of development. First that which is animal; then that which is spiritual.

Human nature, as such, is not hostile to religion; but a hostile principle, as we all know, may spring up in it. There is a possible adversary in human nature as well as a "Lord from heaven." In man, as we find him, for the most part, there are opposite tendencies: a principle of self and a principle of love; an upward and a downward tendency. But both of these tendencies are equally natural: the one is as proper to man as the other. Both are constituent elements of humanity. Man's calling is to subdue the one, and unfold the other.

Here, then, is the true antagonism. Not nature and spirit are contrary, but the worldly (or carnal) and the heavenly mind. "The carnal mind," it is written, "is enmity against God." Yet even here we have to distinguish between the carnal mind in its proper essence, and those to whom that mind may be ascribed, — between worldliness intrinsically considered, and worldly men. It is my belief, that worldliness is seldom so predominant as utterly to extinguish the moral and religious life. The most worldly-minded have some religious experiences; some aspirations, some gropings, at least, sufficient to attest the fellowship of the Spirit, though not sufficient to regenerate the life. Could you look into the heart's recesses of this unregenerate worldling; this eager, driving man of business, to whom, if you speak of the "highest interest," he straightway thinks of his ten per cent; of this hack-politician, who trades in principles, and would sell his country for some paltry office in the gift of Government; of this bloated sensualist, whose face is a record of no spiritual experiences, but of spirituous draughts and unctuous repasts, — could you penetrate the interior of such characters, you would find, that, even there, in those wastes and deserts of the soul, the Holy Spirit is not quite extinct; you would find even there some faint flicker of the everlasting Light, feeble though it be as the last gleam of departing day on some desolate crag, which reddens without reclaiming its ungracious barrenness. I have seen in Catholic lands a wayside chapel which seemed to be divested of all sacred associations, — exposed as it was to public desecration, and covered with the dust of daily travel; but, entering, I found, in a quiet niche, a votive lamp, which the piety of another generation had kindled, and which the present generation would not suffer to go out. And I thought, how many a man of affairs, who stands in the thick of public life, and is well-nigh smothered with the dust of the world, may have in his heart some quiet corner where the lamp of life which a pious mother once kindled there burns feebly indeed, but still burns, and may, by God's grace, flame forth one day into fervent devotion!

The worldly mind, in its proper essence, is enmity against God; but men of the world are not all worldly. The deepest tendency of every being is Godward; and when all the layers of life are removed, and all other images erased from the heart, the image of God will be found there, inwrought and indelible. And when all the experiments of life have been tried, and all other satisfactions exhausted, the heart will still thirst for "the living God" with longings insatiable.

BOOK FIRST.

Religion within the Bounds of Theism.

I.

THE RETREATING GOD.

BOOK FIRST.

Religion within the Bounds of Theism.

I.

THE RETREATING GOD.

THE eldest of religious ideas remains to this day the most indemonstrable, the most undefinable. For unknown ages, religion has said "God" with intense conviction of some arch-reality answering to that term, and has wondered and trembled and triumphed in the contemplation of that reality; yet science, at this moment, is no nearer the truth of that idea, no better prepared to affirm it on independent grounds, no more ready to say "God" from any discovery or experience of its own, than when it first opened the book of Nature. In that book, as leaf after leaf was turned over, Science found order, law, intelligent method, beneficent arrangement; but a Being distinct from nature, in whom those qualities inhere, it found not, and cannot find by its own legitimate methods.

Attempts have been made to prove the existence of God from nature. Whatever apparent success has attended such efforts is due to an antecedent faith already possessed of the God whom it sought. The first glance at nature reveals him to faith; the most intimate acquaintance with nature will not reveal him to science. There is no way to God through the understanding, which knows only to arrange and elaborate what the senses supply. He who, by the very hypothesis of his being, underlies both the senses and the understanding, and is himself the light by which they see, must needs be inscrutable to both. He eludes investigation, not by foreignness and distance, but by intimate nearness. No candle can show us the daylight; we cannot go behind our own consciousness; we cannot see behind our eyes. "I am nearer to thee," he says in the Persian oracle, "than thou art to thyself."—"The roads leading to God are more in number than the breathings of created beings. . . . The eyes of purity see him, and the lustre of his substance; but dark and astounded is he who hath sought him by efforts of the understanding." Hussein was asked the way to God. "Withdraw both feet, and thou art with him, — one from this world, the other from the world to come."

When we say he is inscrutable, it is not in the sense of latency, as a jewel of the mine is inscrutable, but in the sense of reconditeness, as light and life are inscrutable, which yet are the most patent of sensible facts. Our knowledge of God is constituted by faith and conscious experience. If we attempt to verify that knowledge by demonstration, it disappears. The moment we approach God with scientific tests, "he hideth himself." And his hiding is his own transcendent light. As science advances, God retires from the commerce of the understanding into mystery more and more impenetrable. Do we seek him in the realms of space? Science rebukes that quest as preposterous. How can he be nearer to one point of space than another, of whose idea omnipresence is a prime constituent? What lurking-place, what local retreat, what private chamber in the heights or the deeps, can we assign to God? With powers of perception that could look creation through, we should come no nearer the secret of his presence. We need not be told that the fancied throne above the heavens, which figures in the poetry of ancient devotion, is a crude and childish conceit; but, for scientific purposes, what does it avail to take up the word of philosophy and talk of the one sole Substance, the all-animating Life? The being of God is brought no nearer by such phraseology. For who, in any creature, can detect the final secret of its life, or discover by analysis any thing more essential and divine than life itself, as it passes before our eyes? No experiment will disclose the root and substance by which an object subsists. Science explores the secrets of nature, and hopes, by removing veil after veil of material form, to come upon the innermost hidden life, — the soul or substance which those veils conceal, — to reach the radical essence of things. But science finds only qualities, — form, color, size: the substance in which those qualities inhere is undiscoverable. The most powerful microscope, the most active chemistry, detects only qualities. Science, through all eternity, will discover nothing else.

If, on the other hand, we say, as Jesus taught us, "God is a spirit," we have the statement which best satisfies rational faith, but not one which serves any better as a demonstration of God to the understanding. All that the understanding can know of spirit is negative; that it is not body, and has none of the properties of body, — no parts nor form nor color, density or weight. The thing itself which we designate as spirit, in its positive essence, is unknown, is inconceivable.

In whatever way, by whatsoever terms, we state our idea of the being of God, the substance of that being for ever eludes, not only the test of scientific inquiry, but all intellectual conception. As substance, God is not only inscrutable, but inconceivable.

Is he, then, more apparent, or more traceable, as agent and cause? Do we seek him, in that capacity, in the processes of nature? We find there only our own inferences, — confirmations of a preconceived idea. We see what we call design, adaptation of means to ends, which proves intelligence. But intelligence in nature is one, and the God of religion is another. It is not logic, but faith, that builds the inferential bridge between the two. I said science is no nearer to God, no more apprehensive of the truth of that idea, now, than when the study of nature commenced. I might rather say, that science is further estranged from that idea, less cognizant of the being of God, less ready to affirm him, now than then. Science hides the agency of God in a multitude of secondary agents, which multiply the more, the more we become acquainted with the constitution of things. In the infancy of knowledge, every thing was referred directly to God as the sole and immediate cause of every existence and every event. If a nation was visited with pestilence or blight, it was the Lord that sent them; and there ended the inquiry. There was nothing more to be said on the subject. If a comet or eclipse appeared in the heavens, they were quite spontaneous occurrences, with no antecedent but the arbitrary will of God. Every blessing and success was a special providence, entirely aside of the necessary sequence of events. In the progress of intellectual culture, it has come to be understood that every event has its necessary antecedent in time, and forms a necessary link in a chain of events which extends indefinitely before and after, beyond the knowledge and surmise of man. Every effect which we witness or experience in nature or ourselves has its necessary cause in something that went before; is itself the cause of something that is to come; is part of a process of which no man knows the beginning or the end. In the view of faith, the one divine Cause, the immediate will of God, is present and active at every stage of this process, — is the real agent by which that effect was produced. In the view of faith, there is but one Cause: those which we call secondary causes are no causes at all, but only accompanying conditions. But this is not the aspect which the facts present to science, holding by visible agents, investigating natural laws, and tracing the necessary operation of cause and effect in the natural world. Where science finds an invariable connection between certain antecedents and certain consequents, where it finds that, one particular thing preceding, another particular thing invariably follows, it affirms the former to be the origin or cause of the latter.

Thus, without any conscious atheistic design, it is the tendency of science to put God out of view. Science does not formally deny the agency of God; but it is not the business of science to take knowledge of it.

On the contrary, its business is, if possible, to get on without it; i.e., to discover for every phenomenon in nature some natural, finite, intelligible agent, without resorting to the supernatural. A resort to the supernatural is a confession of ignorance which it is the interest and business of science, so long as possible, to avoid. In other words, it is the interest of science, so far as possible, to banish the supernatural; that is, to banish God from the actual world. This is not said in disparagement of scientific men, who are often devout believers. And surely no class of men have greater reason to be so! They may heartily believe in God; they may acknowledge his agency in nature; they may acknowledge all nature to be his work and method and manifestation: but this acknowledgment is out of school. As scientific investigators, it is their business to find natural causes for every fact and event; to supplant the supernatural, so far as possible, with known, appreciable, natural agents. Where religion says "creation," science says "development." It refers the genesis of things to the operation of natural laws, by which the earth, and all the planets, suns, and stars have shaped themselves, in the lapse of ages, out of the shapeless, igneous mass that furnished the raw material of their being, and by which all the tribes of animated nature, with man at their head, have been evolved, in their order, from certain vesicles and rudimental germs of organic life. Now, the agency of God, in the view of faith, is as much required to conduct this process, and to furnish the elements out of which this development proceeds, as it would be to form each creature by itself, with a special act of creative skill. But this is not the scientific aspect of the subject. Science puts God out of view, and substitutes law instead. A personal agent in the processes of nature is not apparent to scientific investigation.

If law and design and intelligent order are no demonstrations of God to the understanding, neither are the tokens, as we regard them, of providential care, — the marks of divine beneficence, the bounty of Nature, the joy of which all beings partake according to the measure of their capacity and kind, — demonstrations of God to the understanding. The understanding recognizes good in nature, — genial sunbeams, refreshing showers; the smiles of heaven, the wealth of earth; the beauty of flowers, the deliciousness of fruits. But the understanding sees also evil in nature, — evil and suffering so manifold, so vast, so irremediable, that mere logic could never reconcile its existence with the doctrine of one God of boundless wisdom, power, and goodness, of whom and by whom all things are. Faith alone can vindicate that doctrine against the contradiction of this enormous woe. And even faith, in most religions, has had recourse to the supposition of an evil principle to meet the difficulty which theism encounters in this aspect of things.

Passing from nature to the moral world, shall we seek for the agency of God in human life? Shall we seek him as ruling and overruling Providence? An essential part of faith in God is faith in divine providence. No belief is more precious to the human heart, and none perhaps more needful, than faith in a special, providential agency interposing succor in seasons of peril and distress. But this sacred idea, this cherished conviction, without which religion can hardly exist, the understanding refuses to verify. The understanding cannot find, in the cases which are cited of such interposition, any special and extraordinary agency exerted to secure a particular end. The event so signalized in the view of faith is found to have, like every other event, its natural antecedent, and to stand in intimate, unbroken connection with the constant order of human things. The guiding power in such cases, though extraordinary in our experience, is not found to be extraordinary in itself. It flashed intensely upon our feeling; but, when sought by the understanding, it hides itself in the ordinary, fixed series of agencies and functions by which all the processes of nature, and all the events of life, are conducted and brought to pass. God came nearer to our consciousness in this instance than in others; but the understanding finds here also no unveiled Divinity. It is still the same hidden, secret force, the same inexplicable, inextricable web of cause and effect; no thinner, no more transparent, at this point than at others in our experience of life.

There are cases in which our impatience craves the special action of God's providential government, not for our own, but for others' and Humanity's sake, — cases which seem to us to cry aloud for divine interposition, in the way of protection or of retribution, to avert some impending evil or avenge some outrageous wrong; cases in which we feel, that, if we had the power, we could not refrain from exerting it in such a cause. "Oh for an hour of Omnipotence!" sighs the outraged heart, in view of triumphant wrong. When the liberties of a people are assailed with unrighteous usurpation; when the union and existence of a nation are threatened by rebellious treason; when the God-defying evil-doer prospers in his wickedness, — it seems to us that a merciful and just God cannot look on, and see the mischief grow and the crime succeed, the good suffer and the righteous perish, without stretching forth the arm of his power to smite and to save. But when did Providence ever visibly respond to such demand? The interposition comes not: God hides himself when most we need and invoke his aid. "My God! my God! why hast thou forsaken me?" is a cry which elicits no theophany, and wrings no audible response from the heavens, — not even when uttered by the Son of man. The answer is found in the heart alone, — the trusty heart; the brave, strong heart; the deep, unfathomable heart, that flings its wondrous self into the balance, and outweighs a world of woe.

History is full of apparent injustices. We see calamities piled on the head of the good; we see treacherous and bloody men prosper to the last. A Huss, a Cranmer, a Sidney, a More, we see perish at the stake or beneath the axe; while the judges and kings who condemn them die quietly in their beds. We see a Richelieu, guilty of every vice, licentious, cruel, tyrannical, loaded with riches and honors, crowned with every gift of fortune, reaching an age of more than fourscore years without reverse; while men like Raleigh and Vane are doomed to a felon's death. Christ is crucified, and Barabbas set free. Had the Son of man but come down from the cross, every knee had bowed; but he came not down. A righteous God does not interpose with visible retributions to avenge his violated laws, or to rescue and protect his faithful servants. Nor is the world so arranged by any principles inherent in its constitution, and invariable in their operation, as to bring only good to the good, and only evil to the wicked. The most we can say is, that the good, on the whole, are more likely to prosper, and the wicked to fail; and that, not from any providential interference for or against, but through the inherent strength of the former and the fatal disability of the latter. Further than this, the moral government of God, which forms so essential an article of faith, does not approve itself, does not reveal itself, to the understanding. God, in his character of moral governor and judge, as in every other predicate affirmed by religion, is inaccessible to all attempts of the understanding to verify his attributes.

So, whether we seek him in the realms of space, in the processes of nature, or in human life, God hides himself from the curious intellect, more inscrutable now, in the full age of the human understanding, than in its childhood; retiring ever farther, the farther we advance in culture and knowledge. To the early world, he seemed separated only by distance of space. The imagination enthroned him on mountain-tops or above the clouds. It was deemed not impossible that he might appear to the human eye in a human form, and converse with mortals face to face. But science, which has scaled all heights and sounded all deeps, has dispelled this illusion, and, while extending indefinitely the bounds of creation, can find no room for a local God. He is separated from us now, not by distance of space, but by the impossibility, in our intellectual enlightenment, of forming any image of his being which reason does not immediately rebuke as incongruous. To the intellect, he is removed by the impassable gulf which yawns between the finite and the infinite, between every organized nature and uncreated mind. He hides himself the more, the nearer we seem to approach him in intelligence. Other mysteries disappear like spectres of the night before the spreading illumination of science; but this one mystery deepens and deepens with increasing light.

And let us be glad that it is so; that this aboriginal mystery remains, inviolable, impregnable, unsearchable still; that while the profane intellect is removing the veil from so many a wonder which its marvellousness had endeared to our early faith, and letting daylight in upon so many a recess long consecrated to our imagination by embowering shade, here still is a veil which no human intellect will ever lift; a covert where wonder and awe, and faith, their offspring, may repose for ever; an idea on which the mind, retreating from the shallowness of human knowledge, may rest, and be sure that no plummet cast by mortal thought or immortal inquiry will ever sound that infinite deep. Man needs this mystery for the health of his spirit, as he needs for his physical well-being the sweet intercession of overshadowing night. He needs the relief of shade for his mental eye as well as for his bodily. Religion needs mystery, and cannot exist without it. Without mystery, it degenerates into mere mechanical philosophy; into arithmetical calculation; into ethical systems that may serve to smooth the outward life, but exert no quickening power on the soul. The tree of life, like the plants of the earth, needs darkness for its roots; while its fruit-bearing branches rejoice in the light. It is good to know that there is a mystery which no inquisition of science can detect, and no reach of intellectual vision comprehend; that the highest created intelligence, searching, soaring, sounding through eternity, can never attain to a theory of God which shall cover all the dimensions and define all the attributes and exhaust all the secrets of his being. A God whom the intellect might fathom would be no God to us. Let us understand this; let us freely admit it, — admit the futility of all attempts to demonstrate God to the understanding, to prove him from the marvels of nature, to establish the fact of Godhead by induction. Let us freely concede to the atheist, to the positivist, the inadequacy of such demonstration, the inconsequence of most of the reasoning employed for this end.

There is no danger that science will ever unclasp man's hold of this primal truth, or seduce the general heart from the Being more assured to us than our own; the Being whose certainty is the basis and guaranty of all certainty beside.

God withdraws from the speculating intellect. He will not be laid hold of with scientific inquiry; but shut the eye of speculation, and the heart soon finds him who is personally related to every soul. Let every soul bless the never-to-be-known, — grateful, like the prophet in the rock-cleft, for even the vanishing skirts of the mystery in which the Eternal hides, reverently adoring where we cannot comprehend; content to follow where we cannot fathom; happy if we are able to walk by faith where neither man nor angel can ever walk by sight.

At the funeral of Ferdusi, says his biographer, the Scheikh Aboul Kasem refused to repeat the customary prayer, because the deceased had sung the praise of the Magi. The following night, he saw, in a vision, Ferdusi in Paradise, in a blaze of glory. Being asked how he came to be thus exalted, he replied, "It was because of that one verse of mine in which I sung the unsearchable God: 'Thou art the highest and the deepest. I know not what thou art. Thou art all that thou art.'"

Religion would press science into her service, and compel her to testify of theism. But science has her own appointed way of serving the truth: she furnishes her own incidental and involuntary illustrations of Deity, and will not be subsidized by religion, nor render the kind of testimony which religion demands. Science is no theist: her business is to seek the causes of things in the universe of things, and not to appeal to supermundane power. Her mission and that of religion, as ministers of truth, are essentially one; but the methods and immediate objects of the two are entirely distinct, and neither should usurp the other's function. The end of science is knowledge; that is, intellectual possession: the end of religion is worship; that is, intellectual renunciation. The aim of the one is conquest; the aim of the other is surrender. Both, in different ways, are a search after truth. But in ways how different! Science seeks with the senses, with the understanding, with computation and deduction, with analysis and hypothesis. Religion seeks with the trusting heart and devout aspiration. Science would fathom all the realms of being, would stand face to face with the final fact, and write her *eureka* on the core of creation. Religion is content to bow low before an Unknown, Unknowable.

Such being the divergence of their nature and function, it is not to be expected that science and religion will ever unite in one perception. It is not to be expected that religion will attain to scientific demonstration of her convictions; it is not to be expected that science will ever appropriate those convictions as scientific truth. It is possible that a higher synthesis may one day unite them in a new and better bond than the old infructuous union which theology has sought to enforce: meanwhile, let each pursue its separate way. Let science have her rule in the heights and the deeps, wherever she can reach, and establish her sway. Let her reconstruct the genesis of nature, lay over again the courses of the planet, and lean her ladder against the stars. But, after all, it is faith that builds the house where life and honor love to dwell. All great works, all noble births, all that is most precious and saving in life, — scriptures, temples, hymns, — all beautiful arts, all saintly and heroic lives, all grand and sublime things, are her offspring. When faith languishes, civilization droops, empires perish. When faith revives in some new advent of the Spirit, new empires start into life. The course of ascending history is tracked by her benefactions; of history descending, by her hurts. Her monuments, in distant lands and ages past, are honored in their decays and draw the wondering eyes. These are the things which men traverse earth and sea to behold, — the pyramids that still point heavenward after the lapse of four thousand years, the stupendous aisles of Philæ, the unerring sculptures of Athens, the sacred dust of Palestine, the newer marvels of Christian Rome. All these are the offspring of faith: they consecrate the world. Curiosity traces them out in every remote corner of the globe. Science waits upon them with eager ministries; traffic and travel are accommodated to them; railroads are built to convey pilgrims to their sites; at their crumbling altar-stones, devotion rekindles her fires.

Shall men wander so far to behold what faith has done in time past, and despise the power of faith in the present? That wonder-working power which laid the entablature of Denderah, and sprung the arches of Cologne, is no antique, no recluse of the middle age, no native of Egypt or Rome, but cosmopolitan and modern as the sun. God her father, and Humanity her mother, survive all change; and the constant offspring works hitherto, and will work.

II.

THE ADVANCING GOD.

II.

THE ADVANCING GOD.

IT belongs to the nature of God, or, what is practically the same thing, it belongs to our idea of God, that he should make himself known. Our idea of God includes the Creator. An uncreative God is no God, since God is conceivable only as the correlate of a finite world. But creation — especially the creation of conscious, intelligent beings — implies conscious intelligence in the Creator. And, if God be supposed self-conscious, he must be supposed to will the reflection of himself in intelligent minds.* Or, to rest our thesis on more practical ground, if God be that moral Sovereign whom we suppose, it follows that the subjects of his rule must be made acquainted with the Lord of their allegiance.

The necessity of revelation is thus grounded in the very idea of God.

Assuming, then, that God, by his nature, is self-revealing, and must make himself known to intelligent beings, what will be the method and conditions of that

* This statement perhaps is too condensed. God, conscious of his perfection, must will the recognition of that perfection in intelligent beings, as their ideal and way to a blessed life, — that being the only supposable end of the moral creation.

revelation? In what way can we suppose that God will declare himself, his will and his truth, to man? Let any one figure to himself a demonstration that would satisfy all mankind of the being and attributes of God, — of such a God as theism represents, — what will he propose? Shall we say that some stupendous prodigy would best accomplish that result? — some exhibition so far transcending human power and skill, that all who beheld it should be forced to confess a superhuman agent; therewith, some clear, emphatic annunciation of the truth to be received? — an apparition in the sky, with accompanying voice out of the heavens? — a scroll cast down upon the earth, or tablets, received amid lightnings and thunders on some mountain-top, inscribed with the lessons of Deity? Somewhat after this fashion would be, I suppose, the first conception of a revelation from God. Such, in fact, was the Hebrew idea. But closer attention will convince every one who reflects on the subject, that no such portent could serve as a permanent communication, valid to all generations, from God to man. Its efficacy, at the most, would be confined to the sphere in which it occurred and to those who witnessed it, or their immediate offspring. Beyond that sphere, and beyond the experience of eye-witnesses and the children of eye-witnesses, it would soon become an incredible tradition, a legendary myth, an old wives' fable, which the critical understanding, unable to adjust it with other experiences, would unfailingly set aside.

Or, if we suppose the revealing portent to be a stated permanent wonder, it would soon cease to be a wonder at all; it would take its place among the forms and processes of daily nature, and be regarded with no deeper attention, and no livelier emotion, than sunrise and sunset or the rainbow or the moon's phases. For what indeed is universal nature, — this ancient frame of earth and sky, with its stated wonders, its solemn shows, its serviceable forces, its unfathomable deeps and golden fires, its august days and refulgent nights, — what is it but just that portent, — a present and pressing demonstration of the living God? What stronger demonstration can there be? what prodigy more astounding? If they believe not in sunrise and sunset, in summer and winter, in earth and sky, neither will they believe though an angel stood in the sun, and proclaimed the fact of Deity, or though the stars were constellated into runes that should spell the sacred name. No prodigy can reveal God, for the reason that prodigies can only appeal to the senses; and the strongest demonstration of God to the senses is already given in the universe as it passes before our eyes.

Yet this demonstration has never sufficed to convey the knowledge of God to minds unenlightened by other revelation. We know how, age after age, the earth, as it traversed the annual round, had clothed itself with annual splendors; how bloom and hoarfrost had chased each other around the belted globe, and sunrise and sunset balanced their pomps, and the heavens declared the glory of God; how day unto day had spoken his word, and night unto night had shown his wisdom; and yet how many ages had elapsed before that word was understood, or that wisdom perceived? And we know how small a portion of the race, comparatively speaking, has even yet seized the idea of God, — of the only God. It is plain that the senses have no knowledge of God, nor, through the senses, the understanding; although,—the idea once started in the mind, both sense and understanding may nourish and confirm it. By no prodigy does God reveal himself, nor by any external demonstration.

Revelation is not external, but internal. Internal in the first instance; then, in a secondary sense and degree, it may become, as personal or ecclesiastical authority, external.

The first revelation of God is a revelation to the moral sense. For what is it in God that is nearest to man, and which man is most concerned to know? Not his creative power, not the fact of creatorship, but the moral archetype, the moral ideal, which, received by the conscience, becomes the moral law. If God were merely omnipotent force or transcendent skill; if all that could be said of him were, that "he can create and he destroy," or that the universe is his handiwork, it would matter little whether we knew him or knew him not; it would matter little whether the universe were conceived as the product of a single will or of many wills, or whether as a self-existent power. What it really concerns us to know of God, is, not that he made the worlds, but that he is justice and truth and holiness and love. And of this the evidence is not external, but internal. Nature does not furnish it. Nature knows nothing of holiness,—has no perception, exhibits no trace, of the moral law. "The depth saith, It is not in me; and the sea saith, It is not with me." Man would never have inferred it from the visible creation, until it was first revealed to him by a voice within.

Some elect individual of rare endowments and exceptional moral nature, living in the midst of polytheisms and wild superstitions, reflecting on the facts of consciousness, perceives in himself a law which impels him, in spite of inclination and passion, to choose the right and refuse the wrong. This law he refers to the Author of his being, and concludes that the Author of his being is not mere power and cunning, but a holy Will, a moral Governor and Judge. This is the first revelation of Godhead; for, until God is known as moral ideal, he is not known at all. Whatever bears the name of Deity previous to that, is fetish or myth, and lies without the pale of theism and revelation.

In the mental process which I have described, it is not necessary, nor is it possible, to draw the line between the spontaneous action of the individual mind, and the action upon it of the mind of God, — between reflection and inspiration. The vulgar idea of revelation as a purely external communication supposes in the human subject no other agency than obedient reception of some truth or command conveyed from without by an audible voice or visible sign. It is not enough, in the view of this idea, that Moses experiences within himself an impulse which he interprets as divine commission; it is not enough that he is thus, by the witness in the heart, divinely called. God must appear to him externally; he must hear a voice; he must see an apparition which represents God in person. Christian thought has outgrown such fancies. All direct revelation is internal; and, in that revelation, reflection and inspiration combine. The mind is not a passive recipient, but an active, co-operating power. In every original intuition of the mind, there is something divine, and in all inspiration there is human co-agency, voluntary effort, intense thought, meditation musing till the fire burns.

When therefore certain truths are said to be revealed, or given by inspiration of God, we are not to understand that they are given, so to speak, bodily; that they are put into the mind, or breathed into the mind, from without, in distinct propositions. We are to understand, rather, a state of mental exaltation, a quickening of the mental faculties, whereby the prophet or seer arrives at perceptions beyond the reach of ordinary powers or ordinary states of mind. This mental exaltation, this quickening of the powers, is inspiration, the divine Spirit co-operating with and re-enforcing the action of the mind. And this is revelation; the *unveiling* of hidden truth by quick prophetic insight; the intuition of the Spirit that "searcheth all things, even the deep things of God."

The prime condition, the one indispensable prerequisite, of all revelation is sincerity, entire surrender of the mind to the leadings of the Spirit. The truth comes only to such as seek it with perfect simplicity and singleness of purpose, without pre-occupation, without conceit. Only to such does God reveal himself. On the other hand, these elect souls, these seers and prophets, may be supposed to be specially endowed and qualified by God to become the oracles and organs of spiritual truth. With the strictest propriety, therefore, they are said to be "called," or, considered in relation to their fellow-men and their earthly work, to be "sent," by God.

If, now, it be asked how revelation is to be discriminated from mere philosophic speculation, I answer, First, by its practical character, its sensuous, popular handling of the deepest questions and dearest concerns of the soul. The truths of revelation are no metaphysic conceptions, no labored inductions, no analytic subtleties, no abstract reasonings, which can only be expressed in abstruse, scholastic phraseology, but plain, emphatic enunciations of truths concerning God and man, duty, destiny, and human well-being; such as the humblest and most uncultured can appreciate and appropriate, and turn to use. Plato and Plotinus, Spinosa and Hegel, speak only through the medium of books to scholars, — here and there a scattered few. Moses and Paul, through the oral circulation of their word, address themselves to kindreds and nations. Philosophy concerns itself with intellectual and theoretical aspects and relations; revelation, with practical. All its utterances have a moral bearing: they point to some practical use, some work to be performed, some saving discipline, some rule of life, some peril to be shunned, some evil to be put away, some prize to be secured, some heavenly consolation. God in revelation is presented in no theosophic formulæ, — as abstract Deity, Soul of the world, the one universal Substance, or however speculation may strive to express the divine nature, — but in personal, practical relations; as Father, Ruler, Judge. Not the God of speculation, but the God of experience, personally present, and personally related to every soul.

Another criterion of revelation, distinguishing it from mere philosophy, is authority, — the authority it gives to the Teacher who first declares its truths, the authority with which those truths are clothed, as uttered by him. It was said of Jesus by his contemporaries, that he "spoke as one having authority, and not as the scribes," — not as the learned and philosophic of his time. They felt that here was something more than learning or cleverness or mental ingenuity. In these utterances, there was no casuistry or cunning, and no dialectic prowess, but real insight, direct intuition of the truth; hence, rightful assurance, and the weight which that assurance unfailingly gives. Jesus, says Rénan, did not argue with his disciples; he did not preach his opinions; he preached himself. This is the impression which revelation makes, and revelation only, in that degree. The character, no doubt, is a part of this effect. The moral pre-eminence which marks the true prophet, his sanctity of life, is one ingredient in his authority. I can hardly conceive of a high degree of spiritual insight associated with great moral defects. But moral excellence, as seen in the manners and the life, is not the true or chief source of this authority. One can easily imagine great purity of life, a character unblemished, and abounding in all the virtues, without much insight, and, consequently, without authority. It would not be difficult to name individuals, among the saints of history, whose life was blameless, and whose virtues unsurpassed; but whose opinions, notwithstanding, carry no weight,—who have no authority in matters of belief. I find no fault in St. Francis of Assisi, or Charles Borromeo, or Philip Neri; but their views and convictions on spiritual topics would not influence my faith. Moral superiority there must be in the organs of revelation; but moral superiority, in this connection, means something more than blameless manners and a virtuous life. It means a superior nature: it includes intellectual power, but intellectual subordinate to moral. It is nearly related, if not identical with, what, in its intellectual manifestations, in poetry and art and the conduct of affairs, we call genius. It includes that, but with it unites a moral intensity which genius lacks. It is genius adopted by the Spirit of God into heavenly fellowship, and consecrated to heavenly uses.

In a rude and uncritical age or population, the prophet who appears as the organ of revelation will be a reputed worker of miracles. Whether he actually perform them or not, he will have the credit of miraculous works. For this, in the popular judgment which deifies material power and exalts material phenomena as God's chief witnesses, is the test of revelation, the only authentic proof and warrant of divine authority. "What sign showest thou?" and "Show us a sign from Heaven," is the popular demand. On the contrary, in an age of scientific culture, of critical investigation, the reality of such performances will be disputed; and not only so, but the very allegation of miraculous works, in the judgment of some, will discredit the revelation and the prophet of whose truth and claims they are cited as proofs.

The two positions, — the popular and the scientific, — it seems to me, are equally erroneous. To say that revelation is impossible without miracle, or that miracle is the only valid proof of revelation, is inverting the divine order. It is subordinating the greater to the less. The prophet's intuition of the truth is more than any feat which he may perform in the world of sense. Truth is a right relation between the human and the divine. To see the truth is to see God; to live the truth is to be like God: and he who effects that vision and that likeness performs the greatest of all works, greater than healing the sick or raising the dead. And if it be urged that the latter is a necessary condition of the former; that the prophet, in order to make his word seem truth, and secure its entrance into the mind, must exhibit superhuman power; that so only can he draw the requisite attention to himself and his mission; that, granting the superhuman power and granting the miraculous work, it is God that speaks in the prophet's word, and without this, only man, — I reply, in the first place, that, so far as the word is true, it is God that speaks in any case; for all truth is of God. And, again, I maintain that a candid examination of the history of religion will show, that, where miracles were claimed, the belief in the prophet preceded the belief in the miracles, and furnished its chief support; and that the opponents and unbelieving who rejected the prophet's word were not convinced by his wonderful works. "But, though he had done so many miracles before them, yet believed they not on him."

But then, to deny the possibility of miracle, — that is, of any thing out of the ordinary course of human experience, of any thing that may not be explained by laws yet discovered, or paralleled with ascertained facts, — appears to me equally unphilosophical. What right has science to dictate a negative judgment of this question? what right, from all that is known, to determine all that can be? Who will presume to draw the boundary-line of the possible? "The laws of nature cannot be violated." Granted; but who claims that miracle is a violation of the laws of nature? And what are the so-called "laws of nature" but our own generalizations of observed facts? And what is the so-called "constancy of nature" but the statement, in objective terms, of the limitation of our experience? And who, moreover, has had such private advices from the Author of nature as to warrant the conclusion, that all the laws of nature have been discovered, and all the laws of spirit? and that, perchance, some unknown law may not subsidize, and so seemingly contradict, some known one, as the law of projectiles seemingly contradicts the law of gravitation? "A miracle cannot be proved." Granted. Does it therefore follow thence that a miracle cannot be? I receive no truth and no prophet on the ground of miracles; but I can believe in a wonder-working Power. I can believe that the man of God, in closer alliance with, and so partaking more largely of, the one sole Power that moves and makes this world of shows, may effect results impossible to men of ordinary vision, and unprecedented in human experience. To believe the contrary, seems to me not very rational and not very cheering. I can conceive, that the prophet, through the might of the Spirit, shall work miracles; and, to many, the miracles will be a confirmation of his mission. But they will not be performed for that sole purpose: they will be the natural working of a spirit in league with God, intent on beneficent ends, and overcoming natural obstacles by the willing of that faith to which nothing is impossible. I cannot conceive, that the prophet should parade his wonders for the mere purpose of drawing attention to himself, that he should say in effect, "Behold! I do this and that feat which to you were impossible; therefore what I tell you is true." The Son of man repels, as a devilish suggestion, the idea of amazing the world by throwing himself from a pinnacle of the temple.

Finally, revelation and philosophy are differenced by their respective results. Philosophy founds schools; revelation, churches. Philosophy discusses; revelation prophesies. The one has professors; the other, confessors and martyrs. The one is represented by lectureships; the other, by sacraments. The one utters treatises; the other, Bibles. Through these, its peculiar products, revelation assumes a secondary phase and becomes external, — what we call a religious dispensation. Such are Mosaism, Islamism, Christianity. This is revelation in the usual popular sense, and the only revelation known to the mass of mankind. Direct, internal revelation, in any degree, is a rare experience. A revelation so emphatic and intense as to issue in a Church, as to furnish the ground of a new dispensation, has been the experience of a few individuals only in all time. The mass of mankind must receive their religion at second hand, and receive it on historical authority, as they receive the greater part of all their knowledge. The accredited prophet, the Church, the Bible, and even perhaps the favorite preacher, the catechism, the creed of their sect, are revelation to them. Thus the founders of religions acquire a mediatorial character: they become interpreters of heavenly mysteries, the medium of communication from God to man; in some cases, themselves the God of the popular religion.

So strong a disposition there is in man to interpose a middle term, a third person, between the Supreme and the human soul.

In this way, then, God makes himself known, and becomes a fact to human intelligence. Not by prodigy or portent, in whirlwind or in fire, but through the still small voice of the moral sentiment in man, he advances from the unimaginable secret of his being into such cognition as the finite mind can have of the Eternal. On some retired soul, intensely musing, far back in the unknown past, first dawned the great Idea which fills and rules this earthly sphere; the idea whose birth in the human mind was the birth of an intelligible, spiritual world from the dark, wild chaos of polytheism; the idea which alone gives being a plan, creation a purpose, a meaning to life, to holy aspiration an adequate goal. Once risen on the world, the quickening, saving idea did not set; but, when it waxed dim, in the dim, confused ages of nature-worship and priestly oppression which compose the cycles of primeval history; fresh inspiration was breathed upon it, new musing souls rekindled its beam, new revelations confirmed the old; — new revelations and better, clearer, fuller, as human progress opened the mind, and reflection deepened with advancing life. For revelation is a thing of degrees; the God of Abraham, of Isaac, and of Jacob, though sacred and dear as the morning-star of theism, is not the God of the Isaiahs, still less the God who is a spirit, to be worshipped in spirit and truth.

The revealing word was always in the world; the

receptive mind, not always. "He came unto his own, and his own received him not." But, finally, they *did* receive him, — some with such power and fulness as to be, in the high apostolic sense, the "sons of God." And those who received the light in its fulness dispensed it to others: they became the lights of their time, — sages, prophets, servants of God, to whom and through whom "he revealed his secret." From them issued streams which outlived them; which passed into sayings, laws; which became institutions, became churches, became fixed traditions, descending from generation to generation. And all such traditions, however hardened and sapless with the lapse of time they become, attest some former inspiration which flooded the soul, as the fossil-shell on the mountain-side attests the swelling of the waters in some foregone spasm of the globe.

The fruit of revelation is tradition; but revelation itself, in its origin and essence, is spiritual insight. The different terms express two different aspects of one fact. Spiritual insight is the human aspect; revelation, the divine. But spiritual insight is something far different from induction or ratiocination. The knowledge of God is not a conclusion of the understanding, but an intuition of the moral sense. Theism never originated in that way. The being of God would never be inferred from the constitution of things, without the idea pre-existing in the mind.* There is no natural

* The uttermost that legitimate induction can establish, on this basis, is intelligent Power, — the so-called "First Cause" to which speculation refers the creation of the world. But that intelligent "First Cause" is not the God of religion. There is nothing in it of ethical or religious import. The argument from design may suggest a Designer, but can never amount to

religion, in the sense of a theism, born of the understanding; but the being of God is given in the moral nature of man. There, if anywhere, the Eternal reveals himself from time to time, in successive communications, to such as are able to divine his secret.

Revelation is a thing of degrees; yet all revelation is essentially the same. All revelation is in man and through man. It is not an unearthly voice speaking to us out of the clouds: it is not an angelic apparition; but always the voice of a brother man that instructs and exhorts. And that voice is not the revelation itself, but only its witness and declaration. The true revelation is internal. The only effectual knowledge of God is the private experience of the individual soul. The earliest prophet of Jehovism saw this and confessed it, appealing from his own written law to the elder tables of the heart: "For this commandment is not hidden from thee; neither is it afar off. It is not in the heavens, that thou shouldst say, Who will go up for

---

demonstration of a God. Cicero, arguing against the atheism of Epicurus, affirms it to be just as credible that the letters which compose the "Iliad," if thrown promiscuously into the air, should come to the ground arranged in that order, as it is that the world was made by chance. The argument from design has never been better stated; but Cicero was no monotheist, and Cicero's doctrine, such as it was, created the argument, not the argument the doctrine. The Esquimaux told the missionary, that he had often reflected how a *kadjak*, or canoe, with all its tackle, does not come of itself, but requires to be constructed with much care and skill; and how a bird is a far more wonderful contrivance than the best *kadjak:* and yet the bird is no man's workmanship. I bethought me, he said, that a bird proceeds from its parents, and they from their parents; but there must have been some first parents. Whence did they proceed? I concluded that there must be some one who is able to make them and every thing else, — some one more knowing and powerful than the wisest man. So reasoned the Esquimaux; and yet he had never arrived at the idea of God. A cunning artificer, surpassing the cunning of men, but no God.

us to heaven, and bring it down to us, that we may hear it and do it? Neither is it beyond the sea, that thou shouldst say, Who shall go over the sea for us, and bring it to us, that we may hear it and do it? But the word is very nigh thee, in thy mouth and in thy heart, that thou mayest hear it and do it."

III.

THE REGENT GOD.

III.

THE REGENT GOD.

ALL who believe in the being of God believe in a divine Providence of some kind in the natural as in the moral world; but opinions vary as to the nature and method of its action. Some believe it a rule of fixed laws, established in the beginning, inherent in nature, and self-acting. Others believe it to be partly a rule of fixed laws, and partly an immediate action of the divine will. Others still believe it to be wholly the immediate action of the divine will. The first of these opinions makes Providence to consist of a pre-adjustment of the universe, dating from the first commencement of its existence, and so complete as to comprehend every agency and every event, — the world's entire history from beginning to end. It makes the world a perfect machine, — a machine directed by God, who bears the same relation to it that an engineer does to the engine which he invented and superintends. The second makes Providence to consist in occasional interposition, where the course of nature, as it is called, i.e., the ordinary agencies at work in the world, the regular order of events, would otherwise fail to accomplish the desired ends, or where those agencies would result in consequences to be avoided. It makes the world a machine, but not a perfect one, — a machine which requires regulation, adjustment, alteration. The third makes Providence to consist in those very agencies which compose the order of nature and the regular course of events, — a present, immediate, continuous action of Deity in every event that takes place. It makes the world no machine at all, but a living organism pervaded by the spirit of God, a constant and immediate expression of the divine mind. I propose to examine these different theories, with a view to determine the true idea of divine Providence in human affairs.

1. The first is the theory of those who suppose that the world is governed by general and fixed laws, — laws impressed upon the universe in the beginning of creation, — by which it now pursues its course and fulfils its functions. They suppose that the act of creation embraced a plan or scheme of operation, which the universe, once set in motion, has followed ever since, as a piece of human mechanism fulfils of itself the functions intended and provided for in its construction. Every event that takes place is the necessary consequence of these laws, and could not be other than it is. The theory does not suppose that every event was specially willed by the Author of the universe: only the laws and processes which produced it are so willed. The laws of the universe are not aimed at particular cases, but at general results. In other words, the world is governed, not by partial, but by general laws. The action of these laws will sometimes result in disastrous consequences to individuals, especially when

applied by man to his purposes, — when human free-agency comes in as one of the factors in determining the course of events. But these disasters, it is argued, are rare exceptions, and do not materially affect the beneficent design and operation of these laws. They are designed to produce, and do produce, the greatest possible good on the whole. They could not be other than they are without diminishing the amount of good in the world. Any change in the constitution and government of the universe, by which these disasters could be avoided, would cause more evil than it would cure. The vast preponderance of good in the world demonstrates the wisdom of the present arrangement, and, in spite of occasional, unavoidable exceptions, vindicates the general beneficence of divine rule by fixed and universal laws.

The objection to this theory is, that it separates God from his works and makes him, instead of a present, living, inworking power, at the most, a mere director and overseer of past creations. It supposes a God intensely active at one time, and comparatively inactive ever since; exhausting his activity in one original effort of creative power, then ceasing from creation, and taking up his millennial rest. It places him far away in the past, and gives us in effect a universe without a God. For what need of a God, a present, living God, or what room for one, if laws will suffice for the world's governance? — if the world once created and put in motion, and furnished with the requisite agencies and adaptations, will thenceforth govern itself, obeying, with automatic regularity, the impulse imparted, and the laws assigned, to it by one original fiat of creative power? The world, in this view, is a soulless, unconscious mechanism, cast off by its master, whose care of it was exhausted in its first production, and thenceforth left to take care of itself. Suppose that this view of creation could satisfy the understanding; suppose it sufficient to account for the order of events, and explain the phenomena of nature and of life, — it can never satisfy the heart. The heart demands a present God, — a God who is never far from any one of us; it demands the immediate presence and constant care of a heavenly Father; it demands, when it looks upon nature, to feel that God is there, not in his laws only, but in conscious and perpetual action; not in the sense of a Wisdom and a Goodness, embodied in arrangements contrived and perfected long ago, as the mind of an artificer may be said to present in the work of his hands, but in the sense of a Love co-present to every aspect of nature, and a Will inworking in every event that takes place. It demands, in human life, to know that it is not abandoned to hard, inevitable laws, and processes that act with unconscious necessity, but to feel the guiding hand of the Shepherd God, in whom is no want. The heart rejects the theory of pre-established laws: it demands an immediate, personal Providence.

But neither is this theory, rightly considered, sufficient for the understanding. It is based on a notion, which, however plausible it may seem at first view, is not only incapable of demonstration, but will be found, on a closer inspection, to be very questionable. It borrows the idea of a self-acting universe from those contrivances of human workmanship, which, once set in motion, by the interaction of mechanical forces will retain that motion, and perform certain functions, for a given time, without the aid of any other agency than their own mechanism. If human skill can construct a machine which will act thus by laws and forces inherent in itself, then infinite Wisdom, it is argued, may construct one which will do the same, on an infinitely larger scale, for all time; — the material universe is such a machine. But the analogy fails in one important particular. Man makes the machine, but he does not make the laws and capacities by which it acts. He avails himself of laws and capacities that are given in the substances he employs. And what are those laws and capacities? They are nothing inherent in the substances themselves; they are not attributes of matter. To call them so, may suffice for practical purposes; but it does not satisfy reason. Matter, by definition, is passive and incapable: it does not act of itself, but is acted upon. Laws and capacities are not attributes of matter, but of intelligence. In reality, the machines of man's make are not self-acting, but are acted upon by intelligence; and that intelligence is God. All the forces of the material world are only methods of divine action; and what we call the *laws* of the material world are only a phrase to denote the regularity and usualness of that action. When I say that the law of gravitation causes a body thrown into the air to return to the ground, I do not express a property of bodies, but a simple fact, — a fact which the term "gravitation" designates, but does not explain; of which no explanation can be given but the immediate volition of God. Thus the inference drawn from human contrivances in favor of a self-acting universe is a fallacy. The idea of such a universe has no foundation in analogy, or in any thing we know of the nature of things.

2. The second theory of Providence supposes it to consist partly in pre-established, general laws, and partly in occasional interpositions of divine power for the sake of certain ends not included in the original plan of creation, and which general laws would not have accomplished. The latter method is called a particular Providence; the other, a general one. Those who believe in such interposition find examples of it in remarkable escapes from danger, in instances of special good-fortune, or in signal retributions — "judgments," as they are called — incurred by evil-doers. This hypothesis is even more objectionable than the first. It adds to the notion of pre-established laws and a self-acting universe, which we have seen to be groundless, the greater difficulty of ineffectual contrivance. It supposes, like the other, a mechanized nature; but supposes an imperfect mechanism, — a mechanism which fails to accomplish all that should be accomplished, which requires constant addition, correction, and improvement. It supposes a Contriver whose contrivances come into collision with his own will, a God whose providence is in conflict with his own works. Moreover, it gives the providence of God the appearance of arbitrariness and partiality. If here one is rescued from peril, why is another, equally deserving, permitted to perish? If one sinner is overtaken with divine retribution, why does another, equally guilty, escape unharmed? In supposing Providence more active in some cases than in others, putting in here, quiescent there, it virtually

supposes that God does some things, and not others; that some events are the products of his agency, and others not: and the query arises, If this is of God, why is not that of God? If helpful here, why help-denying there? If the world is specially guided by divine power in parts, why is that power not uniformly active? We are right in speaking of special providences; if by that term we designate striking providences; if we merely express our own feeling of their import to us, if it is understood that the specialty refers to our own personal experience, and not to the will of God. When, in any instance, we have experienced a signal felicity, and feel ourselves peculiarly blest, the devout mind is peculiarly impressed with a feeling of providential care and love. To our gratitude, such blessing is a special Providence; and we do well to emphasize it as such. At the same time, we ought to understand, that, so far as the divine government is concerned, every event that befalls is equally providential. To suppose that some things are more so than others, is to charge God with a fitful and partial rule, instead of a uniform care and government over us.

3. We come, then, to the third hypothesis, which supposes Providence to consist in the everywhere present, uniform, and direct action of Deity; which supposes it to be the sum and substance of all these agencies, processes, and laws which we call Nature, and by which the material universe moves and subsists. According to this theory, there is no power in nature, or in works of man's device, but God; no law but divine volition; no process but divine performance. Gravitation is one mode of Providence; magnetism,

another; electricity, another. Providence is attraction and repulsion, cohesion and explosion, flood-tide and ebb-tide, sunrise and sunset, motion and rest. All the energies of nature are methods of divine activity, and all the phenomena of nature are phases of the one eternal Presence. According to this view, whatever chances is willed,—the mischance as well as the looked-for and desired result, the failure as well as the fulfilment, the disaster as well as the success, the foundered and unreturning vessel as well as the safe arrival, the earthquake which shatters a city as well as the sunrise which blesses a world: according to this view, the unlooked-for escape is providential; but equally providential the loss and the death. Whatever chances is willed; and whatever is willed is right.

This is the theory of Providence which my own feeling inclines me to embrace,—the only theory which approves itself to my judgment, as satisfying equally mind and heart. It satisfies the understanding by its simplicity. It avoids the paradox of an active universe and an inactive God, of intense activity at one time and quiescence ever after, of a sabbath longer than the term of labor. It avoids the perplexity of two divinities,—Nature and God; of self-subsisting energies and forces; of attributes without an adequate substance; and, lastly, of a double Providence,—one for every-day use, and one for special occasions. It offers a plain, distinct, and decided view of God's connection with the natural world,—his agency in, and his government over it. It presents an idea of Providence, which, if any object to it on other grounds, must be allowed, at least, to be unambiguous, well-defined, and perfectly intelligible, — a Providence at once universal and particular, uniform and unceasing; not coming in and going out, now here and now there, as occasion may require, but everywhere present and all time active, and everywhere and all time one and the same, — a Providence, in fact, which is nature itself in all its aspects and ways. This theory satisfies the heart by bringing God nearer to us. It shows him equally near at all times, and equally active and equally beneficent * at all times, in all things. It dissipates the hard and comfortless doctrine of a government of general laws, which, acting with fatal and remorseless necessity, pursue their course and fulfil their functions, blindly regardless of individual necessities; and which, though productive of general good, are often fraught with individual evil. It makes God the special guardian of each individual, as if that individual were Providence's sole and peculiar charge, and the universe made and managed expressly for his behoof. It realizes to each one with gracious emphasis, as a personal experience, the beautiful word of the Psalmist, "The Lord is my shepherd: I shall not want." It spiritualizes the universe, instead of mechanizing it. It gives us a full world, instead of an empty one; instead of brute matter, insensate forms and unconscious forces, the living Presence, the conscious Spirit, the pervading God. The universe is transfigured to him who considers it in the light of this doctrine. "The dead, inert mass which choked up space has vanished, and instead thereof flows

* This statement presupposes the moral character of God as a being whose purpose is the good of his creatures.

and waves and rushes the eternal stream of life and power and deed. All is quick, all is soul, and gazes upon us with bright spirit-eyes, and speaks in spirit-tones to the heart."* In the eye of this hypothesis, the universe is not a past product of creative effort, which, once produced, subsists thenceforth by mere conservative power, but a present, momentary, continuous production. The action by which it subsists is not a preservation of some former work, long since created and complete, but an ever-new creation. The universe is new-born continually, — birth everlasting out of the bosom of self-existent, original being. The old types remain; but the substance is new evermore, — an eternal generation from the Lord; life welling forth in measureless efflux, fresh from the heart of the living God; a beginningless, endless procession of self-communicating Love.

Informed with this view, I can never be alone in the world; for the world itself is the presence of God to my mind and heart. Wherever the moment may find me,—in the thronged highway, in the closet's retirement, in pathless deserts, on the rolling deep, — the benign Presence confronts me face to face. Wherever I turn my feet, wherever I turn my thought, I encounter the besetting God. He is my sun, and he my shade. The morning comes, he floods me with his light; in the evening, the heavens are all eyes, through which he gazes as a pitying Father on his child. If I say, "Surely the darkness shall cover me," I look within, and there I meet him "in eternal day." Every process

* Fichte, "Bestimmung des Menschen."

in nature is the going-forth of the Everlasting on his messages of love, and every event in my experience is a message of love fulfilled in me.

If any one object to this view, that, in shunning the one extreme of a far-away, isolated God, — a God who dwells apart from his works in solitary self-sufficingness, — it runs to the opposite extreme of pantheism, I can only say, I have no desire to repel the plea. I accept the charge of pantheism, not in the cheerless, impious sense of a God all world, and a world instead of God, but in the true and primary sense of a world all God; i.e., a God co-present to all his works, pervading and embracing all; a God, in apostolic phrase, "in whom and through whom are all things." If this is pantheism, it is the pantheism which has ever been the doctrine of the deepest piety: it is the pantheism professed by devout men in every age of the world. It is the pantheism of Berkeley when he speaks of "finite agents imbosomed in an infinite Mind." It is the pantheism of Newton when he speaks of "a Being pervading space, who, present to all things, sees and embraces all things present within himself." It is the pantheism of David when he says, "Thou hast beset me behind and before."—"If I ascend into heaven, behold! thou art there; if I make my bed in the under-world, behold! thou art there." It is the pantheism of Paul when he says, "In him we live and move, and have our being."

To embrace this truth with a faith proportioned to its blessed import, to believe it truly and to feel it wholly, is the best result of practical wisdom, as it is the distinguishing trait of pious souls. To feel around us the everlasting arm in all time of peril, to know and adore the present God in all time of distress, to discern and to follow the guiding "Shepherd" in every strait, is the high privilege of manly faith. Such faith is strength in weakness, refreshment in sorrow, hope in death. So instructed and so panoplied, we shall "not fear the power of any adversary," nor sink despairing under any fate. We shall bide undaunted our season of peril, and fearless tread the dark valley. When the blows of adversity fall thick and fast on our devoted heads, we shall bear, with strength proportioned to our day, the spoiling of our goods, the loss of our beloved, the disappointment of our hopes; — most comforted then when most afflicted, most trusting then when most severely tried, most hopeful when most stricken, most calmly blest when at length we have learned effectually the hard but fruitful lesson of unconditional, undoubting submission to the Power which passes alike comprehension and control.

"Submit, in this or any other sphere,
Secure to be as blest as thou canst bear;
Safe in the hand of one disposing Power,
Or in the natal or the mortal hour.
All nature is but art unknown to thee;
All chance, direction which thou canst not see;
All discord, harmony not understood;
All partial evil, universal good."

IV.

THE ANSWERING GOD.

IV.

THE ANSWERING GOD.

In our prayers and addresses to the unseen Power, faith takes it for granted that the suppliant is heard; that the prayer is not a cry into empty space, a breathing wasted on the desert air; that there are really two parties in all such exercises, — the soul that prays, and the God who hears. Faith supposes this, or prayer would be the most unmeaning mockery, and, with honest, simple souls, would soon cease altogether.

And yet, if we consider it, what a daring assumption, to suppose that the Infinite takes note of individual supplications! When we think what countless myriads of suppliants are proffering their petitions, it may be, at one and the same moment, and, it may be, for contradictory favors; in such wise that to grant the requests of one party would be to deny the requests of the other; as where, in the conflict of armies, individuals on both sides pray for success in battle; or where religionists of different faiths entreat the divine blessing, each on their separate cause, and desire the prevalence of their respective churches; — when we think of this, it baffles the understanding to conceive that the infinite God should give special heed to the prayers of individual finite beings. On the other hand, the belief of this is so essential to religion, that the two must stand or fall together. Religion, in any sense characteristically distinct from philosophy, poetry, or art, is impossible without worship; and worship is hardly possible without prayer; and prayer would soon cease without the belief in a Being who hears and heeds supplication, if he does not always grant the request.

And happily, the power of the understanding to conceive is not the measure of spiritual truth. The understanding knows nothing of the existence of God by any insight or function of its own; and, if the understanding were the only guide and the only avenue of truth to man, no prayer would ever go up from mortal lips, and no Godward thought or desire would ever arise in mortal breasts. The understanding views every thing in the light of its own laws, which weigh and measure the material world, and reduce all the processes of nature and life to arithmetical calculation. Happily there is something else in the world beside measure and weight, and the multiplication-table, and cold, mechanical laws. What a world it would be in which every thing went by dead-weight; where all could be calculated, — so much always in a given time; so much, and no more, with given means! — a world in which there should be no surprises, no incalculable factor ever interposed among the measurable forces that work the machine and work out the results of every-day life, no inspiration in man, no reserved power in nature, no residue of spirit or supplemental grace in God. Such is the world in which the understanding lives and moves; a piece of mechanism of limited capacity, in which there is nothing spontaneous, in which every act is predetermined, and piety itself the result of inevitable laws. In such a world there is evidently no place and no legitimate ground for prayer. The world is a machine set agoing with the prime creation, and all the processes of nature and human history are mechanical functions: there is nothing for it but to take what the mill of all-work may grind for us, and ask no questions. Instead of a present God with whom our spirits may commune, and whose spirit responds to our seeking, we must rough it as we can with driving-wheel and fly-wheel, — memorials of a God who lived long ago, — and trust that the power may not fail, nor the gearing foul, in our short day.

The world which faith inhabits is otherwise constituted. In that world, God is the present Will by whose momentary action it exists and proceeds, — a Will in immediate contact with our wills; and prayer, in that world, is a real power; and human life, instead of the blind play of shaft and piston, is growth from a seed, susceptible of momentary modification through the action of that power of prayer on that present, living Will.

For those who live always and altogether in that world, there needs no other proof than their own faith that prayer is heard by the Being addressed; that their souls are in actual communication with God, and God with them, through this medium. But faith is not equally active at all times. Doubts of the objective efficacy of prayer will sometimes obtrude themselves on otherwise believing souls. Do we breathe our petitions into empty space? or do they light upon some listening

Presence? Do they reach their destination in some sympathizing, infinite Spirit, — some divine Person, who, shrouded in unfathomable but not inaccessible mystery, receives and considers the supplication addressed to him? It is a question between theism and atheism.

There are moments in life when some pledge is desired of divine communication, — some demonstration of a real, responsive relation between the soul and the Supreme. A man is hesitating, let us suppose, between two sides of a given alternative: he has to choose between two courses of conduct, between doing or not doing a certain thing, between taking or not taking a certain position. His decision involves consequences of vast moment to himself and others. Reasons are weighty on both sides, for and against. He is in a strait betwixt two. Unable or unwilling to decide of his own wisdom, he craves direction from the All-wise. Let God decide: let the burden of responsibility rest with him! His will be done! But what is his will concerning the matter in debate? How shall the suppliant, seeking divine guidance, be apprised of it?

Individuals, in such cases, resort to different measures, or satisfy themselves with different tests, according as different ages and faiths, or differences of individual constitution, may incline.

The Hebrew Gideon, fifth in that line of military dictators known in our Bible by the name of "Judges," felt himself divinely called to free his people from the ravages of the Midianites who invaded their borders and laid waste the land. Before entering on this difficult and dangerous enterprise, he required to be assured of the truth of his calling by some visible token which should justify and supplement the inspiration of faith, and be a God-given pledge of success. "If now I have found grace in thy sight, show me a sign that thou talkest with me.". . . "If thou wilt save Israel by my hand, as thou hast said, behold! I will put a fleece of wool in the floor; and if the dew be on the fleece only, and it be dry upon all the earth besides, then shall I know that thou wilt save Israel by my hand as thou hast said." According to the story, the sign was vouchsafed: the fleece, in the morning, was wet with dew, and the earth around was dry. The chief still wavered. Natural causes might explain the wonder. Another trial was required. Let the miracle now be reversed. "Let it now be dry only upon the fleece, and upon all the ground let there be dew. And God did so that night; for it was dry upon the fleece only, and there was dew on all the ground."

I enter into no explanation of this story. My concern is not with Gideon's fleece, but with the impression on the mind of the suppliant, — with the feeling which led him to desire this external authentication of his mission. The same feeling has impelled men in every age to look for demonstrations of the will of Heaven in some visible or audible sign. The Greeks had recourse to oracles, which consisted in the utterances of a kind of delirium, supposed to be a medium of divine communications. The Hebrews consulted the sparkle of jewels, or were counselled by voices in the air. The Romans drew auguries from the entrails of victims and the flight of birds. Decision by lot is a common resort in cases of doubtful choice. When, after the death of Judas Iscariot, the disciples of Jesus proceeded to fill his vacant office, of two individuals who seemed to be equally fitted for the function, they prayed the Lord to designate by lot the one whom he had chosen. And, when the lot fell upon Matthias, they doubted not that the Lord had directed the event in accordance with their prayer.

Chance readings in sacred or cherished books have also been accepted as signs from heaven. St. Augustine, at a critical moment of his life, resolved that the passage on which his eye should first light, on opening a copy of Paul's Epistles, should determine his future course. He opened and read, "Make no provision for the flesh to fulfil the lusts thereof," and forthwith embraced a life of devotion. How many good Christians, the world over, have sought and received counsel, suggestion, consolation, inspiration, from accidental words of Scripture! The soldier on the eve of battle, opening his pocket Bible in the tent, chances on the passage, "A thousand shall fall at thy side, and ten thousand at thy right hand; but it shall not come nigh thee." And he thinks, on the field the next day, in the thickest of the fight, that he bears a charmed life. The preacher on shipboard, in imminent peril as he fancies, opens at random, and reads, "Thou shalt not die, but live and declare my statutes." He feels that God has spoken to him in those words, and the tempest loses its terrors. There are few devout persons who have not at some moment of their lives experienced what seemed to be an immediate communication of God to their souls, — who have not felt that God spoke to them individually by some written word or sign addressed to the eye or ear or, it may be, some dream which they so interpreted, or some internal experience which they could not, or would not, explain in any other sense than that of the immediate action of God on their mind. The prepared soul finds a divine communication in every word or event that touches it effectually and savingly in its hour of need. Wherever it finds God especially near, it feels itself found and addressed by him.

But reason still questions, Can there be a direct communication with God, and of God with us, as man converses with man? Can there be any token or demonstration to the senses or the understanding of such communication? Can there be, in the nature of things, any credible sign that God talks with us, or hears and heeds our prayer? — that he is really a party, an active, conscious party, in this supposed communication with Deity in prayer? — that the conscious action is not all on one side, — on the side of the soul? Can there be any proof of this that will stand the test of criticism?

Here are two distinct questions. The possibility of a real communication between the human and divine is one question. The possibility of any proof to the understanding, of such communication, is another. The first is substantially, as I have said, a question between theism and atheism; between God and no God, in the proper sense of the term; between a personal God and any other conception to which we may choose to apply that sacred name. Mutual communications between the human soul and a personal God follow necessarily, if truly and devoutly sought on the human side, from the nature of that divine Person. And, if we dismiss from our idea of God the attribute of personality, what have we left but the absolute rule of almighty Power, — the origin and law of universal being? A wise and beneficent rule, if you please, — a rule of which the purpose and issue is the general good, and submission to which is duty and safety, but not a God who receives supplication, or to whom supplication would ever be addressed by rational souls. Prayer, in that case, can mean nothing more than devout contemplation of the universal order, and devout acquiescence therein; grateful recognition of the good received, patient endurance of necessary evil. This, too, is a kind of religion, but not a religion which meets the requirements of faith, or satisfies devout aspiration. It is not enough for me to know that the world is not subject to irrational, lawless accident, but governed, and well governed, and ordered for good. I desire to enter into personal, conscious, mutual relations with the Power that rules; to feel that I, individually, am known and loved by that ruling Power; can reach him with my petitions, so that he shall heed them; that I can commune with a Spirit above the level of the human, and above the order of nature; and that Spirit with me. The idea of a person in the Godhead answers to this demand: it reaches my need with infinite succors. The idea of a personal God carries with it the possibility — nay, certainty — of divine communication to all who sincerely desire, and earnestly and perseveringly seek it.

But when we inquire further, if any sign is possible of the fact and reality of such communication, which shall satisfy the understanding, — any proof impregnable to criticism, — reason answers that such signs are neither possible nor desirable. The region in which these communications take place is a region of faith, and only through faith and to faith are such communications possible. When God speaks to the understanding, it is not of himself, or things spiritual, that he speaks, but of such things only as the understanding, whose function is to methodize sensible impressions, referring them to physical or physiological laws, can receive. Only those truths which admit of mathematical demonstration, or those which follow with logical necessity from incontrovertible premises, are impregnable to criticism. Spiritual truths, however assured to those who receive them, though certain as mathematical demonstration within their proper domain, cannot be proved to the understanding, because the domain itself to which they relate is outside of the sphere of the understanding, or more properly perhaps inside of it; in either view, beyond the reach of that faculty, which deals only with sensible existences and their relations. It is impossible to imagine any outward sign or visible token of divine communications which the understanding will not dispute; for which it will not find another interpretation. The Hebrew warrior doubted the very token he himself had desired: he demanded another, and would, with a little more criticism, have doubted that as well. Visible tokens of divine communication there may be; but faith will always be required to receive them as such. In the view of faith, the answer of prayer in the thing desired will seem a sufficient demonstration of the fact that the prayer is heard, and that the favor received is the natural effect and fruit of prayer. Yet it is impossible to prove to the understanding any real causal relation between the two. A sceptic, disinclined by mental habit to admit the principle involved, will dispose of such cases with the vague and accommodating phrase "coincidence;" which, duly considered, is only a different statement of the fact from another point of view. Coincidence is the external aspect of that for which some interior reason must be supposed. For though things which coincide are not always related as cause and effect, yet where, together with coincidence in time, there is also a mutual fitness and a moral link between the two, a reaching-forth of one toward the other, a natural correspondence between the antecedent and the consequent, it is fair to presume a divine adaptation. Sober thought, independently of faith, will not rest satisfied with an empty name; but, pursuing the inquiry, will see that coincidences are not blind accident, but marks and moments of a pre-established harmony which arranges these parallelisms between the natural and the moral world, and adjusts creation to the faithful soul.

Further than this, it is not to be expected, and not to be desired, that the commerce with God assured to faith should be vouched to the senses by visible signs. One sees at once what a door would be opened to wild superstition and irreverent use, if such demonstrations were vouchsafed, or might be expected whenever and by whomsoever desired; how every event would be subsidized by vain curiosity impertinently questioning the deep things of God; how all nature would be perverted to oracles of private interpretation by importunate souls; and how all barriers between the holy and profane would be broken down. The visionary Rousseau relates, that, in early youth, he sought, by throwing stones at a mark, to ascertain whether he was destined for heaven or hell. A hit or a miss should be a sign from God of life eternal, or everlasting death. No wonder he took care, as he frankly confesses, to stand very near, and to have the mark conveniently broad. Such misapplications might be expected of any supposed license to question God by visible signs. The soul has a right to seek assurance of the presence and participation of God in its conference with him, but not to prescribe the desired pledge, or to dictate the nature of the proof. It stands in the nature of the thing, that the proof must be internal, and the token evident only to faith. Such a token is a sudden inspiration breathed into the mind, or a sudden peace descending on the heart, in answer to the soul's aspiration and appeal; the new strengthening of the will; the new-born courage; the new-born hope. These are the fire from heaven that kindles the flame on the altar, assuring an acceptable offering. What better sign can there be? What surer pledge of a hearing, heeding, answering God?

If there be the personal God whom faith conceives, there must be the personal relations and communications with him which faith supposes and religion craves. Our spirits must be in contact with their kind. Somewhere and somehow there must be an answer to every true prayer. For surely the economies of the moral world are not less exact than those of the natural. In the realm of matter, there is no waste. Not a grain of dust, not a drop of water, not a particle of vapor, can ever be lost to the sphere of which it is a component part. The dew which bathes the summer rose, and glorifies the meadow with its morning sheen, had its origin in what might seem to be the escapes and wastes of the planet. And, when rose and meadow have exhaled their dews at the touch of the sun, the viewless, imponderable vapor is not dissipated beyond recall; it is not all spent on the thankless air; it is gathered and garnered in the chambers of the sky, and returns again in due season, according to its circuit, in orient dews or refreshing showers. And shall not the finer exhalations of the soul, — the prayers which are breathed from the deeps of the breast, the secret vows, the Godward thought, the devout aspiration, — shall not these also return again according to their circuit, and bring their blessing?

V.

THE EXORABLE GOD.

V.

THE EXORABLE GOD.

Faith and unbelief alternate in human history, and shape the world according to their kind. An age of devotion followed by a period of secularism, a period of secularism followed by an age of devotion, inverts the proportions of mortal life. At one time, this earth is but the forecourt of an unseen, heavenly world; the lodge before the garden gates of a spiritual paradise; a mere suburb of the city of God: at another, heaven and the life to come are only a perspective finish, — a kind of artistic background to the earthly world. But, in every age, prayer and religion are one and inseparable: as much as there is of the one, so much of the other.

For this is the one universal thing in religion, common alike to the lowest forms of nature-worship and the most sublime mysticism, more universal than even the belief in God. Religions that have no God, as we understand that term, no Supreme Ruler of the universe, still practise prayer to such forces and demons as they know. However the exercise may vary, and whether performed by mechanism or meditation, whether it consist in the revolutions of a wheel, in manipulating beads, or in the rapt contemplation of the Quietist, prayer is still the essence of religion. The negroes of

Guinea, according to Father Loyer, along with their fetichism, believe in an unseen Power, and pray to it in this fashion, when, in the morning, they have washed in the running stream: "My God! give me this day rice and yams; give me gold and slaves and riches; and grant that I may be active and swift." Compare the frank and childish egoism of such petitions with the prayer of Socrates: "Grant that I may be inwardly pure, and that my lot may be such as shall best agree with a right disposition of the mind!" Compare it with the prayer of St. Augustine: "God grant that my heart may desire thee; that, desiring, it may seek thee; that, seeking, it may find; that, finding, it may love; that, loving, it may be redeemed from all evil!" Compare it with the prayer of Jesus: "That they all may be one, as I, Father, am in thee, and thou in me; that they may be one in us!" Consider these four degrees of supplication, — the prayer for sensual gratification, the prayer for moral excellence, the prayer for God himself as the supreme Good, and, finally, the prayer that all mankind may be partakers of that good, — and learn from these examples the carry and the scope of this act of faith.

Prayer for specific objects, proffered with the hope of influencing the divine Will, is the topic I am now to discuss. In the chapter preceding this, I considered the question, and maintained the fact (in the world of faith), of a real communication with God. The efficacy of prayer — its power to procure the desired blessing — is a quite distinct point. Is God an exorable being? On this question, religion and the current philosophy conflict. Religion assumes the efficacy of prayer as a fundamental postulate. The current philosophy pleads the alleged immutability of God, and the necessary order of events. God is supposed to have pre-arranged every thing, and every thing therefore to be unalterably fixed. Every thing that can happen to me is fore-ordained: so, and no otherwise, must it be with me. All the solicitation I can urge cannot move the Eternal from his fixed purpose, or change the complexion of my lot. Whatever it has seemed good to the All-wise that I should have or be, will come to pass without my asking, and in spite of my entreaty. And whatsoever it has not seemed good to the All-wise that I should have or be, that no asking will procure for me. Why, then, should I pray?

The argument rests on a bare assumption. That God has predetermined every thing or any thing is pure hypothesis, — a theory of God unsubstantiated by any trustworthy authority, incapable of scientific demonstration. Unquestionably, the order of events is a necessary order. Every thing that takes place is the necessary consequence of something which went before it. But, when we say "predetermined," we transfer to God the modes and conditions of the finite mind. We imagine him subject, like ourselves, to the laws and order of time and place, with whom there is neither here nor there, nor before nor after. The order of events is necessary; inasmuch as it is not accidental, but governed by powers, and determined by causes, which act according to immutable laws. But then my will is one of those powers; and prayer, being one of the modes in which my will acts, may be one of the causes which determine the order of events. God is in me as well as out of me. He acts not only on me and for me, but through me. Every movement of my soul is one of his instrumentalities, and prayer among the rest. Therefore it is not unreasonable to suppose, that my destiny and others' destinies may be affected by my prayer.

Another answer to this objection, drawn from the inflexibility of the divine nature and the necessary order of events, is, that no man believes it. No man believes it to that extent, that he is willing to act upon it as a rule of life, which would be equivalent to not acting at all. The objection is just as valid against every other act and effort, as against prayer. If all things are unalterably fixed and must come to pass, so and not otherwise,—whatever we do or omit to do,—then why act at all with a view to any end to be accomplished by our action? But no man is a fatalist to that extent. No man who professes to believe that all things are foreordained abstains from voluntary action on that account. You believe that God has predetermined whether A or B shall carry the day in a popular election: why should you take any steps to promote or prevent that which is fixed by inevitable decree? But you do not hesitate to deposit your vote, and to use such means as you can, to secure the man of your choice. God has predetermined whether or no thieves shall break into your dwelling; but you do not hesitate to adopt the usual precautions. God has predetermined whether or no your farm shall produce; but you do not hesitate to fertilize the soil, and to put it in the best condition for the largest yield. The reason is, you see in these cases, whatever your theory of fixed decrees, a relation of means to ends which invites to action. No man is so persuaded of the fore-ordination of events as not to exercise some voluntary agency of his own in bringing about such as are desirable, and staving off that which he fears. Whatever their theory, men practically believe that events are contingent, and hang in some measure on their volition, — on their voluntary action. In prayer you do not see this relation of means and ends, and therefore you assume that it does not exist; that prayer is unavailing for any practical end beyond the mind of the suppliant. "Our ignorance of Deity," says Plutarch, "manifests itself in two opposite tendencies: one is inordinate superstition; the other, atheism." There are various kinds of atheism. Disbelief in prayer is one kind.

But is the Deity an exorable being? Is the all-wise Disposer of events to be moved by entreaty, determined by the prayer of finite minds? This is not a question on which any one has a right to dogmatize. I only know that the Deity so reveals himself in me; and I also know — who does not know? — that prayer, in imminent necessity, is a universal instinct of the human heart, — an instinct which characterizes man as man, and is common to all faiths and nations. There are few, perhaps none, who would not pray in some cases, however indisposed to prayer in general, by theory or habit, — who would not breathe forth a silent petition in moments of extreme peril. "When the wish within you," says "Asmus," "concerns you nearly, and is very ardent, it will not question long; it will overpower you like a strong man armed; it will hurry on a few rags of words, and knock at the door of heaven."—"I have great respect for the necessary order and connection of events; but I cannot help thinking of Samson, who left the connection of the gate-leaves unchanged, but carried the whole gate off bodily on his shoulders." Philosophy or no philosophy, such is man; such is the instinctive faith of the human soul! This instinct supposes a meaning and efficacy in prayer, without which it would seem to have been implanted in vain. To all theory and reasoning and speculation on the subject, I oppose this inborn, ineradicable instinct of the soul, which, if it does not demonstrate the efficacy of prayer, affords at least a rational presumption in its favor, and, on the whole, is less likely to deceive us than our speculations. It may be objected, that these instinctive prayers for aid in great emergencies are not always answered: they do not always avert the impending evil. The calamity befalls, our prayers to the contrary notwithstanding. It may be so. The prayer is not always answered; but who shall say that it is never answered? Who shall say, that, when unanswered in the thing desired, it is not answered in some other and better way?

As a question of philosophy, I much suspect that philosophy as shallow and insufficient which runs counter to the native instincts of the soul. Philosophy objects, that prayer is founded in low, anthropomorphic views of God. What if it should appear that the current philosophy itself is guilty, and that, in a far greater degree, of precisely the same fault?—that the view of God which that philosophy assumes is the least adequate, the most crude and unphilosophical, of the two? For is it not a mechanical view of divine methods and operations? It regards God as a mechanician; the world as a machine, which, once set agoing, obeys with automatic regularity the impulse imparted to it, — the law in its constitution, — and admits of no change. It places God afar off, apart from the world, which he governs by its own mechanism, interfering only to repair and adjust when the mechanism is out of gear. Is it not more philosophic to think of God as the immanent, all-present Source of life, and the universe as the manifestation of that life? — to think of him, not as apart from his works, but as a Spirit pervading and possessing them and us, — he in us, and we in him, — and prayer as the felt contact of our spirits with his? If this view is the true one, then the question whether God is exorable is already answered. We may boldly say that every genuine prayer affects the Deity in proportion to the faith that is in it. Every genuine prayer is a positive force in the universe of things. The eternal Will — the axis of creation — bows and dips to human entreaty. The world of spirits, subsisting and centred in God, is moved by it as the sea is moved by whatever stirs within its depths. The motion may not reach to the outward, visible result which the prayer contemplates. It may want the requisite force for that consummation. But every prayer, in proportion to the force that is in it, tends to that result. And the force that is in it is the measure of faith which inspires it; which works in it and by it. Faith is the hold we have of the Godhead. Faith is a power which sways Omnipotence. It is no figure of speech, no oriental exaggeration, when Jesus says, "If ye have faith, all things shall be possible to you." It is impossible to set any limit to this power. We may say, without irreverence, that God is constrained by it; inasmuch as itself is divine. In this sense, it was said, "The Spirit itself maketh intercession for us." The Spirit prays, — God acting on God.

I say, then, God is moved, constrained by prayer. I find the philosophy which denies the efficacy of prayer to be shallow and superficial. A more profound philosophy, a more faithful analysis of all the elements involved in the question, will lead to the opposite conclusion. Every sincere prayer is effectual to some extent: it is effectual in proportion to the faith that is in it. The prayer of perfect faith will never fail of its answer.

On the other hand, this perfect faith is itself the inspiration of God, and not to be attained without absolute surrender to the supreme Will.

Faith and prayer relate to each other as inspiration and aspiration, breathing in and breathing out, — the systole and diastole of the soul. In the one, we imbibe the divine life: in the other, we express it. In faith, the Godhead floods the soul as the ocean rushes inland with the swelling tide. In prayer, the soul regurgitates again, and merges itself in the Divine.

The efficacy of prayer depends on the measure of faith. Only that which we ask in full faith are we likely to receive. No rational man believes that he can obtain an accession to his property, success in financial speculation, or any worldly good, by praying for it; because no one who has well considered the discipline and ends of life can feel so assured of the necessity of these things to his well-being as to ask them with perfect faith. A lurking unbelief will vitiate the truth and efficacy of such petitions: they verify the saying, "Ye ask and receive not, because ye ask amiss." Haydon, the painter, prayed for success with his pictures, intent only on the personal advantage to be gained by them, and did not succeed. George Müller prayed for pecuniary succor in his charities, intent on the good of others, and again and again received an answer to his supplications, in pecuniary supplies.

The prayer for even spiritual good may remain unanswered, if, while we perceive with our understanding the need of divine grace, we want that profound conviction and fervent desire which prompt the prayer of faith. Only what we wish do we really pray for; and all our wishes are prayers. There are who pray in set words for the gifts of the Spirit, while the heart's unworded collect solicits the comforts of the flesh. They ask forgiveness of sins, and mean impunity; they ask salvation, and mean prosperity, like the worshipper stigmatized by the Roman satyrist, who offered his prayer in due form to Apollo, but prayed between his teeth to the goddess of thieves: "O fair Laverna! grant me the talent to cheat and defraud without detection, to get the better of all whom I shall deal with, at the same time to appear just and holy before men." It is not inconsistent with the theory of prayer, nor any proof against the principle, that many prayers should fail of their purpose: on the contrary, the theory itself requires that they should. Only the prayer of faith is ever answered to the suppliant.

I have spoken of prayers for specific objects; for this was the topic I proposed to discuss. But the asking of favors is not the whole nor the most important part of prayer. Nor is the value of prayer to be measured by the answer in kind. Its best effect is that about which there is no dispute. There are many states and acts of the mind, beside asking of favors, which partake, in a greater or less degree, of the nature of prayer. Every reference to God in our thoughts, wishes, or actions, is prayer. Every emotion of gratitude for blessings enjoyed, every feeling of contrition for evil committed or duty neglected, every noble aspiration, every good resolution, every resignation to God's decree, every meditation on divine things, is prayer.

There are many who complain that they can form to themselves no distinct conception of the Being to whom prayer is addressed. They have no definite object before the mind. God seems to them so remote, so inconceivable, they cannot lay hold of him by any effort of the imagination, or fancy themselves in real communion with him. But why is it necessary to form a distinct conception of God? Will the prayer be more effectual because addressed to a mental image,—a creature of the imagination? "Beware of idols." All that is necessary is the impression, the conviction, of overruling Power, divine Beneficence, incorruptible Justice, unchangeable Truth, presiding over all the course of things. With this conviction, let the soul go into itself, and consider its belongings, and consider its wants, and breathe its desires; not attempt to form to itself any notion of Divinity, but confine itself to the thing, to the subject of prayer,—its needs, its aspirations, its hopes. Let it rouse and direct itself to worthy ends, under a sense of its relation to the Eternal, its moral responsibilities, its spiritual calling; — that is prayer.

The real difficulty lies behind these metaphysical objections. There is a sluggishness of mind which prevents it from collecting itself in a vigorous effort of self-communion. There is a coldness of heart which makes it indifferent to the supreme Good, — a practical unbelief which shuts the soul against God and the influx of his spirit. If these obstacles were not, there would be no questioning. The spirit of prayer would take possession of the soul, and keep an unbroken communication with the secret God.

The spirit and life of prayer is the consciousness of God, the feeling that we are his, that he is ours, that nothing but the voluntary aversion of our spirits can separate us from him. A feeling of Deity as the power by which we live, the light by which we see, the great Reality in the knowledge of whom is eternal life, and whose participation is the supreme blessing. Where this consciousness lives and burns, there is prayer, though not always expressed in words. For the soul, in its highest devotion, is content to repose in the thought of God, asking nothing, seeking nothing; its whole being concentrated in the one unuttered desire, "Thy will be done!"

There are times, however, when the feeling, if genuine, cannot choose but utter itself in words. The more intense it is, the more apt it will be to seek that vent. "I was dumb with silence," says David: "I held my peace even from good." But, "while I mused, the fire burned; *then* spake I with my tongue."

I conclude with the words of one who, more than any writer of the English tongue, had explored this subject in its breadth and depth, and has written most profoundly concerning it: "Poor and miserable as this life is, we have all of us free access to all that is great and good and happy; and we carry within ourselves the key to all the treasures that Heaven can bestow. We starve in the midst of plenty, — groan under infirmities, with the remedy in our own hands; we live and die without knowing and feeling any thing of the one only Good, whilst we have it in our power to know and enjoy it as really and truly as we know and feel the power of this world. For heaven is as near to our souls as this world is to our bodies. . . . God, the only Good of all intelligent natures, is not an absent or distant God, but is more present to and in our souls than our own bodies; and we are strangers to heaven, and without God in the world, for this only reason, that we want the spirit of prayer, which alone can, and which never fails to, unite us with the one only Good, and to open heaven and the kingdom of God within us. A root set in the finest soil and the best climate, and blessed with all that sun, air, and rain can do for it, is not in so sure a way of its growth to perfection as every man may be who aspires after that which God is ready and infinitely desirous to give him. For the sun meets not the springing bud that stretches towards him with half that certainty with which God, the source of all good, communicates himself to the soul that longs to partake of him." *

---

* Law's "Spirit of Prayer."

VI.

THE OLD ENIGMA.

VI.

THE OLD ENIGMA.

WHOSO interrogates the order of nature from the ground of theism soon stumbles on the world-old problem of Evil,—its origin, reason, and right to be in the scheme of things. The problem states itself thus in our inquiry. If a God created and governs this world of ours,—a God all powerful, wise, and good,—why are these attributes so imperfectly expressed in creation? Why this immense deduction from the good, which a rule of perfect Love, conducted by infinite Wisdom, ought, it is believed, to secure to its subjects? Why does eternal Goodness permit the wide-spread evil with which creation groans? Why this dark shadow which everywhere bounds our capacity, our well-being, our life? If only the guilty suffered, and suffered only in the measure of their guilt, such suffering would seem but just retribution, the wise operations of moral laws. But over and above the evil due to man's free agency,—the woes inflicted by human passion and all the misery incident to mortal folly and crime,—beside all this, which constitutes so large a part of the burdens of humanity, we are persecuted with evil which lies in the constitution of things, elemental plagues, hostilities of nature, national calamities, tempest, blight, physical infirmities, monsters, madness, and all inevitable ills. The universe is full of them. Nature at her brightest conceals beneath that sun-beaming countenance innumerable and inestimable griefs. "All being is in pain," said Paul. "Creation travails."—"The heavens and the earth, and things without life," said Philo, "may be seen to suffer." Philosophers, ancient and modern, Christian and Pagan, have stood perplexed and aghast in the presence of the unveiled enormous woe. One of the most recent denounces the optimism which can see only good in the arrangements of nature, and which deems that this world of ours is the best possible world. "Evil," he says, "is real, colossal, incessant; the world is bad; it is a misery to have been born." "Life is the natural history of sorrow; it is the war of all against all, an internecine strife for ever renewed from age to age, till the crust of the planet shall peel off piecemeal."—"There are miracles of destructiveness in nature,—in the human as well as the brute creation. It is not only in the solitudes of the new world that plants of gorgeous hues delight in putrid miasmata, and drink the death which makes their life; it is not there only that giant oaks are strangled by creeping vines, and die in their grasp. It is not in Australia only that the ant, by a prodigy of suicidal instinct, devours itself, nor only in the ocean-deeps that the young polype nourishes itself with the substance of its sire. Man surpasses all these horrors, and the word of Scripture is for ever true: 'There are those who devour men as they eat bread.'" *

Evil inheres in the constitution of things. The most

* Schopenhauer.

cheerful philosophy cannot blink the fact, however lightly it may esteem it, however hopefully it may reason about it. Evil abounds: what shall we say of it? why tolerated by perfect Love? why uncorrected by almighty Power? how reconciled with infinite Wisdom? This is the question on which age after age has tried its skill, and on which all philosophies thus far have foundered, if the test of philosophic success be an answer at once so luminous and so decisive as to solve every doubt, to satisfy every scruple of reason and piety, and to stop all further inquiry.

The oldest solution of the great problem is also the most natural. It seems to have been the first rude effort of speculative thought in the world's infancy, and formed the basis of one of the most ancient of historic religions. The answer which the Persian gave to the question concerning the origin of evil, was the theory of two Gods, — a holy, just, and benevolent God, who created all that is good and healthful and blessed in nature, all that is fruitful of life and joy; a God whose symbol is light, and whose truest visible type is the sun: and opposed to him a wicked and malevolent God, whose symbol is darkness; who made all hateful and baleful creatures, — whatever hurts and destroys, — and to whom is attributed all the evil that is in the world. A fragment of this Persian faith was introduced through Judaism into Christianity, and still survives in the popular notion of the Devil, who formerly occupied a larger place and played a more important part in Christian systems of theology and philosophy than he does in the modified creeds of our time. Physical as well as moral evil, calamities, and disasters, hail, blight, lightning, wrecks, and hurts of all kinds, were ascribed to him by our ancestors. Luther gravely charges him with the floods of the river Saale, with fires in the forests of Thuringia, and the sulphur in its wines.

The Satanic theory of the origin of evil has the advantage of great simplicity: it offers, if one could accept it, an easy and sufficient explanation of all existing and all possible evil, and absolves the divine rule of all complicity with it. But it does not relieve the theological difficulty involved in the incompatibility of evil with the supposition of infinite power and wisdom in the God of our worship. On the contrary, it bounds and circumscribes that infinity; and while it absolves the divine rule of the charge of willingly grieving or afflicting, it also limits that rule by the empire, larger or smaller, as we may figure it, of a border-power and an outlying hostile State. It disturbs and degrades our idea of God by circumscribing his sway. It is no longer Omnipotence that rules, but Omnipotence qualified by the Devil. Moreover, although it explains the existence of evil, it presents another problem of equally difficult solution. The hypothesis is convenient till we look behind it, and then we fall upon a new entanglement greater than the first. The Devil explains every thing, but who shall explain the Devil? A fallen angel, shall we say? — then explain to us that fall.

And here we come upon another proposed solution of the problem of evil, of wide acceptation in the Christian Church, — the fall, whether of angels in heaven or of man on the earth; more commonly understood of the latter; or let us say, sin, the necessary antecedent of the fall, and also its consequent. Sin, it is contended by Christian theologians of a school which still very widely prevails, is the cause of all the evils that afflict mankind. All physical infirmities, ails, and plagues, nay, all cosmic disturbances, the war of the elements, all calamities that befall, are traceable and rightly attributable to man's transgression. The world was what it should be, a garden of delights, the Eden of the Bible, the golden age of Gentile tradition, — no noxious plants, no venomous reptiles, no beasts of prey, no briers or thorns, no tempests and no sterility, no need of heavy and exhausting toil, no burdensome cares, no aches or pains, — till man transgressed. Then, suddenly, nature was put out of joint, the universe was dislocated: all these plagues and woes rushed in; and the enemies of human happiness hastened to their prey as vultures and vermin flock to the banquet of corruption. This theory, which throws on the free-will of man the responsibility of natural as well as moral evil, seems at first to honor God in affirming a creation originally free from the imperfections and disorders, the discomforts and disasters, which now attend it, and which only opposition to God's will could engender. But rightly considered, critically weighed, it furnishes no satisfactory vindication of the fact and agency of evil in the scheme of things. What is gained by it for one of the divine attributes is lost to others. It presents a God whose plans are traversed, his agency thwarted, his purposes of mercy defeated, by his creature. The divine Artificer constructs a world "of absolute perfection," exempt from all harm, fruitful of blessing, and only blessing: his creature disobeys, and constrains him to undo his work, to remodel the universe on a baser scale, adjusting it to man's unworthiness. So Milton's great verse, the highest expression which Christian literature has given to this hypothesis, represents the origin of evil in the natural world. The Creator, he says, after Adam's transgression—

> "Calling forth by name
> His mighty angels, gave them several charge
> As sorted best with present things. The sun
> Had first his precept so to move, so shine,
> As might affect the earth with cold and heat
> Scarce tolerable; and from the North to call
> Decrepit Winter, from the South to bring
> Solstitial Summer's heat.
> To the winds they set
> Their corners, when with bluster to confound
> Sea, air, and shore, the thunder when to roll
> With terror through the dark, aerial hall.
> Some say he bid his angels turn askance
> The poles of earth twice ten degrees and more
> From the sun's axle. They with labor pushed
> Oblique the eccentric globe, . . .
> . . . To bring in change
> Of seasons to each clime; else had the Spring
> Perpetual smiled on earth with verdant flowers.
> . . . .
> These changes in the heavens, though slow, produced
> Like change on sea and land; sidereal blast,
> Vapor and mist and exhalation hot,
> Corrupt, and pestilent . . .
> . . . Thus began
> Outrage from lifeless things . .
> Beast now with beast 'gan war, and fowl with fowl,
> And fish with fish; to graze the herb all leaving,
> Devoured each other."

Such, poetically set forth, is the theory of physical evil by moral delinquency. Making all needful allowance for the uses and laws of poetic representation, and granting, as we needs must, that a large proportion of the troubles and disasters that afflict mankind—some bodily infirmities and most civil disorders — are the fruit of sin, I cannot persuade myself that man's transgression has affected the poise of the planet and changed the angle of the earth's axis with the plane of the ecliptic from a right to an oblique one; or that disobedience to the moral law accumulated the ice of the poles and the sands of the desert, giving rise to the tempests which desolate sea and land; nor yet that vicious indulgence is the cause of all the earthquakes and all the malaria, and the blight and the famine, that distress the world. In fact, there is no pretence of any natural connection in these matters: it is not pretended that sin, by natural and necessary sequence, entails these disorders; but that God, by a special act of penal legislation, avenges sin by deranging the spheres and depraving the globe. However it may flatter the poetic imagination, this theory of the origin of evil fails to satisfy universal reason, and would scarcely merit a moment's attention, were it not still stoutly defended by writers of our time.

Another solution of this problem, or rather a way of disposing of it, is what may be termed the heroic method, as taught and professed, and to some extent practised, by the Stoics. It consists in denying the existence of evil, in indifference to all the vicissitudes of life; esteeming as equally vain what men call good and ill; serenely accepting, or rather ignoring, pain, privation, loss, and want, as things external and foreign to the soul, which therefore ought not to disturb its tranquillity, nor discompose the supreme content, which, based on the soul itself, is complete and impregnable. Here is no attempt to answer the question, "Whence and why the evil of this world?" but only a sublime irrecognition of any such question to be propounded. *There is nò evil*, the Stoics said: no evil and no good to the wise, in things external; no pleasure and no pain derivable from them. Of this doctrine a critic justly remarks: "It may be sublime, but is none the less absurd." It is worthy of note, that the Stoic philosophy flourished most in the darkest period of the world's history. These Stoics, says the critic, were optimists indeed, "optimists at the table of Nero and in the gardens of Tiberius. It was the enormity of evil which made them Sophists. They denied it in order not to curse it: they denied it in order to conceal it from their own eyes. By force of pride or of meanness, they acted an impossible part. Wounded on all sides, wounded unto death, they declared themselves invulnerable. O inanity of wisdom! . . . They wished to appear erect when already prostrate. . . . They sought to extract happiness from the bitterest rinds of pain, and to make us believe in felicity in the midst of that bath of blood and crime known as the despotism of the emperors." It is needless to enlarge on the theory of the Stoics. Whatever value it may have as a practical philosophy, as a theory the mere statement is its own refutation.

One other solution of the question in debate I can only glance at, although, in my judgment, the most defensible that has ever been propounded. It is that already alluded to in the word "optimism." This view supposes that God's creation is a perfect work, and the world in which we live the best possible world on the whole; not the best possible to the individual at any given moment, but the best possible on the whole: all creatures considered, and all the ages of man taken into the account. It supposes evil to be, in the first place, a necessary accompaniment of finite being; a condition inherent in the act of creation; a consequence resulting from the very limitations which bound individual existence. And, secondly, it supposes evil to be a necessary condition of development and growth. And this development and growth — not present supreme satisfaction — it justly assumes to be the true ideal of human life. There are some things of which it is no disparagement of infinite Power and Wisdom to say, that they are impossible even with God. God could not make an infinite, and therefore not a perfect being, — much less a universe of such beings. He could not make an imperfect being perfectly happy. The limit of nature is the limit of enjoyment; the end of power, the beginning of discontent. And yet a world of such beings may be a perfect world; that is, the best possible world to the sum of the beings contained in it, affording the greatest possible happiness to the greatest number. And that is all that reason needs, to vindicate divine perfection. Again: it was possible for God to create a world in which there should be no suffering. But the absence of suffering, so far from assuring the greatest conceivable amount of happiness, may be easily shown to be incompatible with that amount of happiness which actually exists, of which the two most essential ingredients are progress and hope.

On these two fundamental conditions, — imperfection, a necessity of finite existence on the one hand; and progress, the highest good, on the other, — optimism constructs its solution of the problem of evil, and bases the proposition of a best possible world. I am far from maintaining that this theory furnishes a full and sufficient answer to the question we are considering, and all the questions connected with it. I only contend, that, so far as it reaches, it is the most satisfactory answer that has yet been given; most truly reverent toward God, because most trustful in divine wisdom and goodness; most ennobling, because replete with encouragement and hope for man.

But after all is said that philosophy has to say on this subject, however satisfactory and incontrovertible in theory, the ills of life present an inexplicable mystery still to the heart. We may talk about the best possible world, and may think we believe in it: but a great sorrow makes us forget all that; and we feel in the marrow of our bones how insufficient for the heart is every solution which philosophy can offer of this terrible enigma. The enigma is not solved by philosophy, but solved, if at all, by an act of faith. Faith has its own optimism, very different from that of the understanding, or very differently put. It is perfectly expressed in that homely phrase, which contains, I think, the sum of all wisdom in relation to this matter: "It is all for the best." Not Seneca nor Leibnitz has said any thing which hits the heart of the matter like this.

"It is all for the best." All plagues and harms that lacerate the soul, the war of the elements, the wrath of man, "the slings and arrows of outrageous fortune," all wounds of the heart, all losses and deaths, are ministers of good: a divine purpose works in all. With these stones in our path, the unchangeable Love is laying the courses of the house of life, strong against all the accidents of earth and all the wear of time. As part and product of this earthly world, we belong to the system of subject-nature, we are tossed in its storms and mixed up with its wrecks. "We that are in this tabernacle do groan, being burthened." Subject-nature travails in us; but the travail is the birth-pang out of which is the life, secure within, tempest-proof, unracked by mortal throes.

All that reason teaches of God is expressed in the saying, "God is Law." All that religion teaches is expressed in the saying, "God is Love." Each of these aspects is the other's complement.

1. God is Law. That law embraces all that is or can be in the universe of things, — the wildest freaks of chance, the most exorbitant anomalies in nature, the toughest spasms, the slightest incidents of matter or mind, storm, earthquake, fire, the shoot of an avalanche, the dropping of a leaf, the eccentricities of a comet, the vagaries of a dream, the birth of a monster, the suggestion of a thought, every stroke of good fortune, every mishap that befalls. There is no accident in the scheme of God. What is casual and exceptional is as much determined as what is stated and constant; the earthquake which swallows up a city, as much as the motion of the earth on its axis; the lightning which shatters the human frame, as much as the electric currents which traverse the globe; the tempest which dashes the ship upon the rocks, as much as the earth's atmosphere; the disease which lays waste, as much as the physical economy it invades. Life would be intol-

erable on any other terms. More grievous than any actual calamity would be the thought, that calamity is unwilled and undesigned; that man is at the mercy of a lawless power. We are compassed about with perils and pains; but inviolable law encompasses them. And evil is not the fatal misstep of groping, reeling accident, but the conscious, measured tread of providential and paternal Power, — a part of that Providence which is co-extensive with the uttermost range of being, and co-present to every movement within its bounds; to which the farthest star beyond the dream of astronomy is not too remote, nor the smallest animalcule within the surmise of zoölogy too minute.

Why evil exists is a problem which no philosophy will ever solve with entire satisfaction of all the questions involved in it and all the minds perplexed by it. Pursue it, and it brings you at last to the previous question, Why God created a universe at all? Why went he forth of himself in creative action? Why, rather, did he not abide in himself, sufficient to himself? Whatever is created is finite; and a finite world implies evil, because it implies limitation, imperfection. The imperfect striving after perfection, — this is Reason's account of the origin of evil.

2. God is Love. And, because he is Love, he must will the best. This is Faith's theodicy. Faith does not reason about the limits and possibilities of things: it judges that God might make men happy in uninterrupted enjoyment, if enjoyment were the supreme good. But life has something better than enjoyment. The best of life is the work which it brings, and growth by work. Prolonged enjoyment hinders growth by

making us content without it. Suffering furthers growth by the stimulus of unrest.

Faith teaches that evil is good undeveloped, — a part of the process of which good is the end. It is the bitter, biting oil which makes the flavor of the orange and the peach.

View life as discipline, and you have the solution of all its enigmas, and a justification of all its ills. Use it as discipline, and you can never be quite overcome by its sorrows. It is because we do not so view it and use it that we quarrel with our lot. Believe that your lot, however crossed, is the best possible lot for you, the only one by which the ends of life for you can be attained. Believe, in all tribulation and trial, that God has considered your particular case, and adjusted the course of nature to it, as if nature existed for your behoof; not to gratify your selfish appetite, not to pamper your sense with sweets, or your pride with pomps, but to draw from you the uttermost that is in you of worth and of work.

The contradiction between the real and the ideal is the standing tragedy of human life, in which all tragedies and griefs are comprised. The order of events contradicts the standard in our minds, contradicts the wish in our hearts. All our jeremiads are variations of this theme. Man's business is to reduce this contradiction by conforming his ideal, in things fixed, to the scheme of God, and by compelling the actual, in things not fixed, to take the form of his ideal. There is in him a power transcending all material agents, greater than all the forces of this world, and able to bend them to his own behoof. As fast and as far as our knowledge extends, we push our conquests over nature, and become the Providence of this lower world. The refractory elements, rude Titans of the realms of matter, are brought under. One by one, the genius of humanity encounters these enemies, grapples with them, subdues them, makes them servants of his need. Forests are levelled, mountains scaled, gulfs bridged; fire, vapor, and all deeps acknowledge the sovereignty of man; heat, cold, lightning, space and time confess his might. "Thou madest him to have dominion over all the works of thy hands." Could he but learn to subdue himself as well; could he but achieve a dominion as complete in the moral world as in the natural; could he but chain the rebellious Titans of the breast; —what an empire were his! How vast his realm, how sure his sway! No contradiction, then, between the real and the ideal, when every wish and purpose of man's heart obeys the divine law, and the steadfast Order reigns in his will as in his destiny.

VII.

THE OLD DISCORD.

VII.

THE OLD DISCORD.

AMONG the traits which distinguish man from other known orders of being, we find that peculiarity of moral self-contradiction which we term "sin." Man, so far as we know, is the only being who sins: that is, the only moral being, the only one who sits in judgment on himself, the only one capable of conscious guilt.

For herein consists the essence of sin.* It is not the wrong act, but the wronged consciousness, the offended genius, defection from the inner, holy self. Sin does not exist until it is perceived; in other words, there is no sin but conscious sin. "If a man," says Novalis, "could suddenly believe in sincerity that he was moral, he would be so." It follows that sin ceases when the consciousness thereof ceases, whether the cessation result from atonement or consummate depravity. "Sin, when it is finished, bringeth forth death," — the death of the moral nature to which alone sin can be ascribed. Devils (if such beings exist) are sinless. Possessing no higher self, they experience no internal

* From the German Sünde: the root is found in the word *sühnen*, to expiate. It means that which requires to be expiated, the unatoned self-alienation, which is alienation from God.

discord, no self-alienation, but accept and rejoice in evil as their normal state.

Within the known world, the sense of guilt is a purely and peculiarly human experience. No creature but man is conscious of wrong in the moral sense of that term. Other creatures appear to transgress; but transgression in them is obedience to a law more binding at the moment than that which they violate. Where they deviate from the given track, their very deviations are justified by imperious necessity: they may seem to go astray, but they are never morally wrong. Amenable only to the law of instinct, their aberrations are all lawful, as the irregularities in the heavenly bodies, once supposed to be imperfections of the solar system and to threaten eventual dissolution, are proved by science to have their own law to which they yield punctual obedience; a limit which they never exceed, and a compensation which adjusts and corrects the threatened disturbance. There are acts of brute animals, especially of such as man has impressed and trained to his service, which seem on the surface to be morally wrong because we impute to them our own associations, because we ascribe to them liberty of choice, and moral perceptions. But the liberty of choice is only apparent, or does not exist to such an extent as to constitute accountableness: moral perceptions are altogether wanting. The sense of wrong is not in their experience: what has that appearance in the looks and motions of domestic animals is due to fear, and possibly to shame, but never, I suppose, to conscious guilt.

The sense of guilt is a thing unknown beyond the

sphere of self-consciousness, i.e. of humanity. Nature bears not this stain on her brow, feels not this sting in her breast. There is no self-questioning in nature, no scruple, no repentance. Stars, plants, and beasts rejoice in eternal innocence. They obey without a struggle the law prescribed for them. Impulse is their religion, instinct their duty: they experience no conflict with opposing passions in what they do, and no compunction when it is done. They know no law but the moment's choice or the moment's necessity. The law in their members is also the law of their mind. Man alone is capable of guilt, the only being whose nature contradicts itself, the only being who feels remorse; who does that which he would not, and repents what he does. Man alone "perceives another law" in his mind; the law of duty, which he feels to be the paramount law of his nature, — a moral statute, whose claim he feels to be more imperative than any instinct or impulse beside, and whose precepts he cannot transgress without crime.

This, then, is the peculiarity of the moral law, distinguishing it from every other, and distinguishing man, as sole subject of that law, from the brute creation, — that the violation of it carries a sting essentially different from all other suffering, — the sting of conscious guilt. Whence this anomaly of human experience? What is the import of this sensation? Other laws may be transgressed with impunity, so far as the mind is affected by transgression. The penalty affects the body only. If the State should enact a law requiring me to be a spy upon my neighbor, or to aid in enslaving a brother-man, I should feel no compunction in refusing obedience. But, when I have consciously wronged another, my soul is troubled by the thought of that wrong; and the pain I incur by it exceeds, if my conscience is tender, the pain I inflict. What is the import of that sensation? what means the sense of guilt?

It means that I ought to have done differently. And the *ought* apparently implies the *could*; the sense of obligation pre-supposes the power to act in accordance with my moral perception, or pre-supposes, at least, a belief in that power. And yet, if I go back in my recollection of such a case, and recall its circumstances, and the motive power accruing therefrom, I find an overpowering impulse constraining me, — an impulse which, placed as I was, with the moral power which I then possessed, I could not resist. The *ought* does not always secure the *can*. Moral strength is not always commensurate with moral perception. But the judgment of conscience is none the less true; the pang of conscious guilt is no illusion. The moral obligation implies the moral power, but does not, of itself, secure for any given exigency the requisite degree of moral strength. It implies the moral power as a possible and needful acquirement, not as a present, fixed possession; it implies it as something to be developed and perfected in us, not as something already conferred in full perfection.

The pang of conscious guilt is no illusion. It is a reasonable sorrow, and the import of it is not exhausted in that first interpretation. It means not merely that we ought to have done differently in that particular case which awakened this consciousness, and in which perhaps, being such as we were, we could not do other than we did. It means a good deal more than this. It signifies a general deficiency of the moral nature; a want of that moral soundness, which, if possessed, would save us from that and all similar transgressions. It signifies the need of repentance; not of that one transgression only, but of all the transgressions with which we offend, of that unsoundness and defect of our nature whence all transgressions flow, of that general sin of which all particular sins are but the symptoms; as coughs and catarrhs, and pains of the head, and pains of the chest, are symptoms of disease, which is nothing more than absence of health, want of bodily soundness.

I indicate here the answer to the question concerning the nature of sin, — a question which the Church, or which theologians have needlessly mystified. Christian dogmatists have represented sin as a positive element in human nature. In addition to all other principles and propensities, they suppose a distinct ingredient in man which they call sin, — a positive something seated in the soul, the root and source of all the iniquities of human life. This view I believe to be essentially erroneous. The writers of the New Testament sometimes speak of sin as if it were a positive, antagonist power in man, which arrays itself against God and his righteousness. It must be remembered, however, that the Scriptures present these things not analytically, but popularly, — in language derived from the popular conceptions of the time. The popular conception of sin was based on the supposition of a personal evil Power in the world; a conscious, malevolent, almost omnipotent agent, a Prince of Devils, to whom all the sin and all the evil that is in the world was ascribed. But, independently of this hypothesis, it was natural enough, and is still natural, looking at the consequences, not at the essence of the thing, to speak of a negative power in terms which describe a positive one. We speak of darkness and cold, and even death, as positive agents: although the former is simply the absence of light; the second, of heat; the third, of life. Take the last instance, — death, — and see how all languages and literatures agree in representing it as a positive, aggressive, even conscious and voluntary power. Death reigns, Death works and walks about, and lurks and lies in wait, and shoots arrows, and has plans and propensities and predilections, and acts the part of a voluntary, intelligent being. And yet, if we ask ourselves who or what it is that does all this? what is death? the answer is, — nothing. Death is no *thing*, but the absence or cessation of a thing; it is pure negation. It is the name we give to the stoppage of the breath and the other vital functions. What wonder, then, that sin, the absence or cessation or limitation of the moral life, should be described in positive terms, — in terms expressive of positive agency and power?

The evil of sin, the deadly mischief and misery of of it, are nowise abated or disguised by this view, which regards it as negation. The results of this negation, the effects of sin, are damnably positive; and, naturally enough, they induce the conception of a positive power as their source and cause. And this notion of a positive element of sin in the soul may seem to derive some color of truth from certain phenomena of human consciousness. The resistance we sometimes encounter in obeying the moral law, the opposition we experience in our efforts to perform what we find it in our conscience to do, but not in our inclination, might seem to imply a contrary element, an antagonist quality in our moral composition, beside and distinct from all the other elements and powers of the soul, to which we give the name of sin. But, if we analyze the facts of this experience, we shall find that the conflict in such cases is not with sin as a separate force and distinct constituent of our nature, but a conflict of principles equally good in their place, and equally essential to man's well-being, when working in due order and right proportion, — a contest between the moral sense and some affection or propensity, innocent in itself but unduly active in this particular case, misdirected, and intent on some gratification forbidden by the moral law. When that propensity triumphs in the conflict, transgression ensues.

Sin is the transgression of the law; not a distinct principle within us which breeds transgression, but the act of transgression. What causes transgression is not a positive but a negative condition; it is not any one affection of the soul, in itself considered, but the absence of that restraining principle and power without which any affection of the soul may lead to sin. All human propensities, powers, and affections are good in their origin; sinful only in their perversion. All sin, when traced to its source, will be found to consist in the misdirection of principles innocent in themselves, and not only so, but essential to human well-being. What one of the normal affections or propensities of human nature is there which man could spare without loss to society? What one of our passions so ill-favored and hard-named, but careful scrutiny shall detect in it some virtue in disguise? Impartial analysis will discover self-respect in pride, respect for others in vanity, prudence in avarice, justice in revenge, in mad ambition some breathing after excellence, in lust some color of love. All our vices are perversions of some good. Sensuality, intemperance, selfishness, — what are they but perversions of the instinct of self-preservation? Dishonesty is perverted love of acquisition; mendacity, excess of caution, or perverted self-defence; even indolence, which of all the vices it is hardest to connect with any good principle in our nature, and which Lavater affirmed to be the original sin, is perhaps resolvable into love of freedom.

Sin is nothing special within the soul, but one of its states. Our virtues and our vices are products of one nature. Vice is the growth of the wild or neglected soil, and virtue the fruit of right culture and right use. The same affection which grows to virtue in one man may turn to vice in another. The reason of the difference is a want of something in the one case which exists in the other, — the want of that controlling power which limits the fleshly and selfish propensities, keeps the passions in due subjection, prescribes to the untamed forces of the breast their mete and bound within which they may act with beneficent effect, and impresses on the native bullion of the soul the form and stamp of righteousness. The want of that power and that righteousness is sin, or the cause of sin; which, accordingly, is shown to be a negative, not a positive state.

If we investigate the nature of that controlling power which is active in some men and wanting in others, we shall see that it cannot, from the nature of the case, be any thing foreign from the soul itself, however quickened by impulses from without, and aid from above. To suppose this would be to make righteousness external and accidental. This power is nothing imported into us from abroad, but something inherent, implanted in all men; patent in some, and latent in others; here born into active virtue, a beneficent agent, possessing the will and shaping the act; there, unquickened, a torpid germ without motion or life. In its active state, on the human side, it is the will self-determined to good; on the superhuman or objective side, it is God's determining grace in the soul.

The good principle in man, the power which subjects the appetites and passions, and turns them into virtues, the fountain of the moral and spiritual life, is none other than the Spirit of God in the soul, uplifting and consecrating its affections, directing and blessing its deeds. And this spirit is nothing imported, but native in man. For our spirits are God's spirit, one light in many lamps, one power in many agents, one treasure in many vessels. The dawn of that spirit in human life is a moral genesis resembling the material of Mosaic tradition. The natural man is a chaos of wild, waste powers and unorganized capacities; a world without form, and void. The Spirit of God broods over this deep; piercing its discord, resolving its confusion, binding its wild forces, commanding light to shine out of darkness, adjusting, reconciling, assigning to each element its proper place and function, until the waste chaos becomes a peaceful and happy world. In this process there is nothing added, and nothing taken away; the process but substitutes organization for disorder, peace for discord, measure for excess.

This view of sin, as negative not positive, not a principle but the want of one, is charged with an import in which the whole scheme of religion is concerned. If sin were something positive, lodged in the soul, born with us at our birth, an original endowment, part and parcel of our nature, then would God be the author of sin, not indirectly, in the sense of permitting, but directly and solely. This doctrine either charges infinite Goodness with what is wholly and purely evil, or else it changes the nature of sin; which, being in that case the creature of God, must be right and good, not a transgression of the law, but the law itself, divinely written on the heart. The existence of moral evil is, in any view, a perplexing problem. That view of it is most rational and welcome which is most consistent with the moral attributes of God; and that is the view, that God has implanted no propensity in man which is evil in itself, and which needs to be extinguished before man can accomplish his moral destination; but that every property with which he has endowed us is good in itself, and only by perversion and excess, in the absence of a moral and controlling power, productive of evil.

The view is practically important as indicating the method and source of moral regeneration. If sin is not a property but a want, not a positive power but the absence of good, it follows that the way to deal with it is to educate the latent good until it gains the ascendency in us, and becomes the dominant power in our life. The problem of reform consists not so much in struggling with an inward, secret foe, as in cultivating and establishing an inward counsellor, protector, friend. Struggles there will be: no character was ever matured without them. But they are consequences, not means; they are the wreck and breaking-up of the past, not the source of the future; as the pangs of birth and of death belong to the old life which is passing, and not to the new that is coming. Observe how nature heals and corrects the evil in her kinds by evolving some opposite good. The diseases of the body are cured by the energy of the principle of life,—the increased action of the sound parts overcoming the unsound. And moral diseases are cured by evolving and establishing a principle of life, which shall purge away the excesses of passion, and harmonize the forces of the soul.

The main principle of life to the moral nature is faith: religion is the complement of all morality. Without a God, there can be no righteousness, because no supreme Right,—no standard and guaranty of moral truth. And if God is, then worship is the supreme ethic, and virtue true worship. Are we seeking deliverance from the yoke of the ever-besetting sin? The way is not to chafe against it with frantic effort, wasting time and wasting heart in a vain and endless conflict; but to turn to the infinite Good, whose holy idea is never far, but greets the mind the moment it looks up, and turns away from self and sense. Rally your faith in all the ideals; "rally the good in the depths of thyself." Will to believe in what is highest and best; choose to walk in the light of those ideas which the wisest of men have proved with their lives, and the best have sealed with their blood. Let the soul receive freely into her dark mansion the sunshine of the Spirit; and sin, which is nothingness and shadow, shall flee away.

Theologians would have us dwell in the consciousness of sin: they measure piety by self-reproach. They would make the impulsive utterance of St. Paul a rule of conscience for all men, and have each one think himself the chief of sinners. This is one of the enormities of false religion, and involves a principle as fatal to the health of the soul as the opposite extreme of moral indifference. The sense of sin is a necessary crisis in the moral education of most men; but, the perpetuation of that crisis is a state of arrested development which plainly contradicts the divine order. It makes religion, instead of a stimulus and an inspiration, a burden and a curse. It is a cruel act of religionists to endeavor to force the consciousness of sin on healthy, unoffending natures; that is, in effect, to make them sinners. No soul so pure but may find flaws in its consciousness, if put upon the search. The ingenuity of self-torture, when conscience is stretched on the rack, will always elicit a confession of guilt. One's very virtues are arrayed against him; what was fair and pure is turned to deformity and hideousness by this cruel exposure in this concave mirror of a morbid self-consciousness. St. Elizabeth, the sweetest spirit of her time, was spiritually murdered by her confessor; and how many saints have committed spiritual suicide, — by a misdirected piety turning the sword of the Spirit against themselves!

No sin which this process detects is so damning as the process itself; and no scepticism can be more fatal than the doubt of salvation in conscientious and religious men. No soul can heartily rejoice in God, that abides in this sickly contemplation of self. The office of religion is, not to drive us back upon ourselves with anxious self-criticism, but to take us out of ourselves and unite us to the Whole, in loving self-abandonment. A man must take himself for better or worse, and forget himself, if possible: so shall he soonest arrive at the beatific vision.

VIII.

THE OLD FEAR.

VIII.

THE OLD FEAR.

"Tolle istam pompam sub qua lates et stultos territas: Mors es, quam nuper servus meus, quam ancilla contempsit." — SENECA.

IN every life there are two points of paramount interest, — its beginning, and its close. No life so barren, so insignificant, but some importance will attach to it at these extremities. "Twice in the course of his earthly career," says Jean Paul, "the humblest mortal becomes an object of supreme moment to those about him, — once, when he arrives on this earth; and, again, when he quits it."

Birth and death! the rising and the setting of a human soul, — alike in this, that, of all the events of man's life, they alone are universal, how unlike in the feelings with which they are regarded! The one a festival, a gospel of glad tidings; the other a message of grief and gloom in the circles in which they occur. Why this contrast? Why have we only smiles for the new-born, and only tears for the dying? Why must joy and welcome auspicate our coming, and only tragedy celebrate our exit? If either is fit subject of congratulation, by all the affirmations of religion and experience it is the departing. Setting aside the belief in a life to come, when we think of uncertainties which hang over this, the certain disappointments, cares, and griefs which await the most favored, the anxiety which rocks the cradle of childhood, the far deeper anxiety which tracks the trial-steps of youth, the sore conflicts which heave the bosom of manhood, the infirmities and impotence of age, — when we think of these, it should seem that solemn forebodings must gather round the entrance of life, and a shade of sadness mingle with the welcome which ushers in the new-born on this earthly shore; and that congratulations belong more fitly to those who are about to lay down the burden of life and to be delivered from the evil that is in the world. It was some such feeling as this which suggested the bitter saying, "It is better to walk than to run; it is better to lie down than to walk, better to sleep than to lie down, better to die than to sleep." It was this that suggested to the dreamy Hindoo his doctrine of despair, which makes annihilation the supreme good.

As a practical principle, we feel the falsity of this view of life, since the true philosophy of life finds its use to consist, not in profit to ourselves, but in service to others; not in comforts enjoyed, but in work performed. But, viewed as a question of selfish advantage, one would say, with Pliny, that the best gift of fortune is an early death! And if to all this we add the belief in immortality; if we think that the soul which sets on this world is rising at the same moment on some other sphere; if we think that its life is progressive, that new conditions will supply new forces, and open new and richer fountains of being and of action, — then, certainly, death, in itself considered, is a more legitimate cause for rejoicing than birth; a happier event to the individual who goes hence; a worthier occasion for congratulation to those who remain.

But the instinct of life is deeper than all our philosophy, and stronger than most men's faith. Argue as we will, our nature clings to this familiar world, to earth and man, to the cheerful day, and shrinks from the private pass, and the nameless future to which it leads. Death is reckoned an enemy still, after so many ages of mental discipline. It is the last enemy that will be put under. The ancient Egyptians are said to have placed a larva, by way of *memento mori*, at their banquets. A larva still, at the feast of life, is, to most mortals, the thought of death. "The heaviest stone which melancholy can throw at a man," says Sir Thomas Browne, "is to tell him that he must die." No religion has yet been able to eradicate this traditional dread. Nay, religion itself has enhanced the terror by representing death as the fruit of sin. Milton, who embodies the popular conception in his immortal epic, finds its origin in Hell. There the word was first uttered, which when uttered,

> "Hell trembled at the hideous name, and sighed
> From all her caves, and back resounded Death."

And not only is death, in the popular conception, the penalty of sin, but it introduces the sinner to new and direr penalties and woes. To the "natural man," before religion had made him a coward, to die was to sleep, —

> "No more, and by a sleep to . . . end
> The heart-ache."

But religion suggested that "to sleep" was "perchance to dream," and scared him with thinking "in that sleep of death what dreams may come."

Paul boasted, in the beginning of the Christian era, that Christ had given his followers the victory over the grave. The victory is not so apparent as it might be. It is doubtful if Christians have made any great advance on the ancients in their feeling about death. It is doubtful if they manifest even so much of equanimity in this respect as the stoics of Greece and Rome.* The larva still frowns at the feast; an image of terror and gloom is the thought of death to most mortals.

The terror and the gloom exist only in our imagination: we shut out the light, and see spectres in the dark. A fixed look dispels apparitions: let us look steadfastly in the face of this larva, holding up to it the lights of reason and of faith, till we see it to be a phantom of the brain.

Think of death not as inevitable merely, but as something divine; a process of the universal Love, a moment in the universal life. Here is nothing monstrous or out of the way; no frightful anomaly, no dispensation of wrath; but something of a piece with the setting sun and the waning moon and the falling leaf, — a part of the great order, a necessary link in the universal chain which binds all being to the throne of God. A true religion will adjust itself with it, — will look upon

---

* The Romans celebrated the death-day of their heroes as we dc their birth-day; and they called the death-day the *dies natalis*.

it as we do upon the parting day and the dying year, with minds sobered and thoughtful indeed; for all changes and all endings are sad, but not with horror and dread. St. Francis of Assisi, who embraced all nature, brute and plant as well as man, with affectionate sympathy, included death also, as a part of nature, in his infinite good-will. "Welcome, sister Death," he said, as he felt his end draw near.

Death is natural: let us hold by that. The nearer we are to nature, the more fitting and beautiful and welcome it will seem. In a primitive state, it has not, so far as we can judge, the terrible aspect which it wears in an artificial one. The notion that death is the penalty of sin could not have originated, I think, in a primitive age. The patriarchs knew nothing of it. Death to them was natural and right. The terms in which they speak of it express their entire consent. They call it a falling asleep,—the being gathered to one's fathers.

What is it that makes death terrible? The pain of parting with goods and satisfactions; with all that we have learned to love and enjoy in this mortal world; with the dear familiar uses of life. "O death! how bitter is the thought of thee to him that liveth at ease in his possessions, to him that hath prosperity in all things!" Death has no terrors for the wretched and forlorn; for those who have already died to all that makes life a blessing. "Death," says Lord Bacon, "arrives graciously to such as sit in darkness, or lie heavily burdened with grief and irons; to despairful widows, pensive prisoners, and deposed kings; to those whose fortune runs back, whose spirits mutiny.

Unto such death is a redeemer, and the grave a place of retiredness and rest. These wait upon the shore of death, and waft unto him to draw near, wishing above all others to see his star."

If, then, the delights of the world throw so dense a shadow on the grave; if goods and pleasures make death appalling; what remedy for such engorgement but renunciation? Not disuse of the thing enjoyed, if innocent, but moderation of the pleasure we take in it; the habit of regarding it as foreign, extrinsic, transient; not as the substance and life of our life. Medical art has invented a way to mitigate the worst diseases of flesh, by forestalling their action, by adopting them in the flesh, by inoculation. Let religion apply the same therapeutic. The cure for death is to inoculate ourselves with it, — to accept it in our meditations. When life is too sweet to be resigned without a pang, when we feel its satisfactions to be all-sufficing, then it is time to die to the world in thought and purpose and affection; to disengage the fond heart from the warm embraces of fortune; to untwist the golden links of pleasure, and teach the weaned spirit to stand alone.

Parting with beloved friends is another bitter drop in the cup of death. Bitter and sad are earthly partings; but those of death are not the saddest. We lose our beloved none the less, though death spare them. The friend whom we grapple to our hearts to-day will not be the same when a few years have passed over him and us, and we shall not be the same to him. We think we have him when another occupying his predicaments comes to our side, and converses with us as he was wont. The dear illusion satisfies us, until som reflective hour or some accident discovers our loss. In this age of photography, we are easily overtaken with such disenchantments, as we place side by side the impression of ten years since and that of to-day, and, looking on that picture and on this, perceive that time is more destructive of identity than death. The departed friend had left undisturbed an image which the living displaces.

When the mother closes the eyes of her little one, and sees the turf laid upon its coffin lid, her heart is torn with anguish; she thinks it the crowning grief of her life. But what if the death-angel had spared her darling; can she retain him? Impossible! The inevitable years will steal away her child as surely as any mortal disease. It is our living children that we lose, not the dead. Do you doat on the infant beauty which you fold in your arms? Say farewell! you will never see it again. "Eyes, look your last; lips, take your last embrace!" it is going; it is gone. Let the portrait of your boy be taken at the height of childish bloom, and, if you and he shall live so long, look at it thirty years hence, compare it with what he shall then have become, and you will see that you have lost your child as truly, as irrecoverably, as if those fair locks and that guiltless smile had been consigned to the ground. It is strange to think, that the most bronzed and hardened face that meets us in our daily walks, — the face on which the world and sin have set their coarsest and most forbidding stamp, — was once the face of a little child, over which fond parents doated, and dreamed their dreams. There are bitterer partings than death, and more heartrending farewells than those which we breathe over the grave.

And what is death? For those who reach maturity, what is it? Is it any thing more than the consummation of a process which begins with infancy, and continues and proceeds from day to day, every day of our lives? We die daily. That is something more than a figure of speech: it is literal fact. We call it death when the breath fails and the heart stops. But that is only the last in a series of acts, each one of which is fatal. Our life from the beginning is a constant descent into death. Why should we concentrate our regrets on the last step, when all our years have been travelling the same way? Are the last sands that run through the glass so much more precious than all the rest? Are these all diamond sparks, and the rest all flint? How many golden days, more fruitful and blest than we are likely ever to know again, have gone by, and no obsequies were celebrated, and no requiem sung! The death of our youth is so much sadder and more appalling than any other death; but no tear was shed, and no funeral prayer offered, and our step never faltered, and our heart never quailed, when we crossed that fatal bourne. And why? Because the passage was gradual? It is then merely a question of time, of slow or sudden, of early or late. If the youth of eighteen were to be changed by a stroke into an elder of eighty, human nature could not endure the metamorphosis. How much more appalling it would seem than sudden death! But we see nothing terrible in it when the change proceeds in the ordinary way, step by step, day by day. We are not sensible of death when our youth dies in us, although that death in reality is so much harder and sadder than the dissolution of the earthly frame.

We die daily: with each new section of our mortal history we give up something that belonged to the section preceding. We are losing continually a portion of our being; we suffer ceaseless dissolutions. Let the mature man compare himself with the budding boy, and see how much of death he has already experienced. How much of what he was has perished in him and from him, never to be restored! Where now is the careless mirth that lit up the boyish eye? where the sunny peace or gushing joy of the boyish breast? Where the boundless expectation, the implicit faith, the indomitable hope, the buoyant nature, the unshadowed soul, the exuberant life? Is not the loss of these as truly death as the putting-off of the fleshly tabernacle? Is it not as much dying to lose the splendor and joy of our young years, as it is to be divested of our mortality? The veteran, however blest with "that which should accompany old age," looks back upon his youth as a Paradise lost, never in this world to be regained.

> "O man! that from thy fair and shining youth
> Age might but take the things youth needed not!"

This ceaseless death would make existence intolerable, were it not balanced and compensated by ceaseless new births. The true soul gains as fast, or faster than it loses. Life is constant acquisition as well as constant waste; a series of resurrections as well as deaths. If we die daily, we are also renewed day by day. If we lose in buoyancy, we gain in earnestness; if we lose in imagination, we gain in experience; if we lose in freshness, we gain in weight; if we lose in fervor, we gain in wisdom; if we lose in enjoyment, it is to be hoped we gain in patience. If we gradually die to the world, it is to be hoped that we more and more live unto God.

Now, applying this principle to the final event which we call death in the usual and literal sense; if our life has been what it should be, — a constant effort for good and constant progress; — it will be found at last that we have accumulated more than we have spent; that, though flesh and heart fail us, the spiritual assets exceed the temporal failures. There is a feeling, that, however the body may perish, life preponderates over death in our system; that the bursting of the mortal hull will be the disengaging of a force which must still persist in its irrepressible career.

There is a dread of death independent of any views of the future destiny, — a dread of it as something unknown, and differing in kind from all that is known; a leap in the dark, a plunge into a new element, a sudden transition into something wide of all past experience. If death were this, — a transition from one state to an entirely different state, — it would destroy our identity, and would therefore be something with which, as conscious beings, we could have no concern. There can be no such leap, no abrupt transition in our mental life. Our mental life is a linked succession, a continuous series of consecutive states, each one of which is necessarily connected with the one which preceded it. Every moment of our being is the product of the previous moment, and the parent of the next. Death, like every other experience, must run along this line of successive moments; that is, it must be gradual.

However sudden to the senses, as a mental experience it must be gradual; else it would be annihilation. As a mental process, it is probably so gradual that the subject of it can never know at what precise moment he ceases to exist for this world and enters on another. We experience daily something of this sort, something which is probably the same as death to individual consciousness, when we lay ourselves down to our nightly rest. No man can tell the precise moment when his slumbers begin; when he passes from a conscious to an unconscious state. Neither can any man determine the precise moment of his waking. And death is a waking too, as well as a falling asleep, — a waking, it may be, after some brief moments of self-forgetting; it may be after countless millions of years. But of this we may be sure, that whether the interval of slumber be long or short, — whether it be for seconds or for æons, the waking, as a mental experience, will be gradual. By degrees we lose our conscious self; by degrees we find it again.

I brought together, at the beginning of this chapter, the two extremes of birth and death. These are but different aspects of one fact. Death is birth. The birth into this life was the death of the embryo life which preceded, and the death of this will be birth into some new mode of being. And as at our birth into this world we came slowly and gradually into conscious existence and the knowledge of our condition; so, in the life into which we next pass, our knowledge of that life, it may be presumed, will be a thing of gradual growth. Little by little, we shall find ourselves, and our new position in the universe. And as in this life we woke into consciousness in the arms of loving friends, so, we may venture to hope, our next waking will be bosomed by that eternal Love which provided this shelter for us here.

SUPPLEMENT.

CONVERSE WITH THE DYING.

WHO would not wish, if possible, to smooth their passage through the Valley, who are passing before our eyes? — to shed that comfort on their dying bed which we covet for our own?

An easy death depends in part on physical conditions which we cannot control, but in part also on mental conditions which we may control, or at least assist. It depends on the conduct, the converse, the very tones of surrounding friends. If these are sad and despondent, their sadness and gloom will tell on the dying, in that enfeebled state of mind when the feelings and opinions of others exert a disproportionate influence, and when it takes so little to bring a shadow upon the soul. Let the wants and necessities of the death-bed — I mean its mental wants and necessities — be studied by the living; for who knows how soon he may be called to minister to those requirements in person? On their careful study will depend the success of our ministry. This is a case in which reflection is a better guide than instinct, though it be the instinct of affection.

Shall those who are wasting away with a lingering death, be informed of their condition, — of the nature and impending issue of their disease, when recovery is seen to be hopeless? Assuredly, let them be informed of it, if their own consciousness has not anticipated such communication, while yet in full possession of their senses. For why will we deal deceitfully with a brother or sister in that solemn season when the false shows of this world are rapidly passing away, and the kingdom of eternal verities impends? Let there be that perfect understanding between the dying and their friends on this point, and all points, without which they are estranged, and can have no frank and hearty communion. But, when this understanding is established, let every thing about the chamber of death wear a cheerful aspect. Let the fading eye encounter nothing sad or harrowing. Let there be smiles and cheerful converse, if nature will permit; and let those tears and pangs which cannot be controlled be concealed. Let the tones which fall upon the ear be firm and calm. Let no heart-rending sights or sounds disturb the tranquillity of the closing scene, no agonizing demonstrations embitter the last farewell. In the place of that stillness which the spirit craves when about to commit itself to rest, let no lamentations make harsh discord in the ear, nor the final struggle be aggravated by the struggles of surrounding friends. What the dying want is quiet, — that quiet you so willingly accord to them, are so anxious to secure to them, when they close their eyes for temporary slumber.

As to offices of religion, and the character those offices should assume in the case of incurable disease, it seems to me that the only legitimate function of religion in such cases is to soothe and cheer, to meet such wants as are expressed or well understood, and not to force the consideration of questions, which, unless they have been already considered, can hardly be considered with profit then. It sometimes happens, that well-intentioned but misjudging friends of a different faith seek the presence of the dying, in order to draw their attention to points of sectarian theology, and to bring about a state of mind which they suppose to be an essential condition of future blessedness. Let such visitations and ministrations by all means be excluded, as tending only to perplex and agitate a mind too enfeebled for discussion or resistance, with no likelihood of future and final gain. For, of all the absurdities engendered by false views of God and man, there is none which exceeds the absurdity of supposing that the everlasting welfare of a human soul can depend on the presence of a certain idea in the mind a few moments before the pulsations of the animal frame have ceased. The future well-being, so far as it depends on moral conditions, must be the fruit of a life. Where the life has not produced this fruit, it is not likely to spring forth ripe and complete, from the pressure exerted on the mind in the dying hour. No doubt the character may be permanently benefited by the experiences of the death-bed; but they must be natural experiences wrought into the soul by the Spirit of God through the proper discipline of that season, and not forced experiences, produced by efforts from without, and the importunity of dogmatic presentations. Let religion offer to the dying such consolations and hopes as it can, consistently with its own convictions. There can hardly be a case in which religion has not some consolation to offer to the mind that desires it. It may be said there is danger of deceiving with a false hope. This one would not willingly do. Deception is bad, and self-deception is bad, at all times, in all things. It is better that the soul should have sight of the truth, the exact truth, whether bitter or sweet. But who has the truth? Who can be so sure of it as to know with certainty that the view he presents will exactly convey it? Our duty to the dying is to give them all the solace and cheer we can, consistently with our own expectations and beliefs, by every argument that does not belie our established convictions: and more still, by our deportment and looks and tones, to make death easy to the dying; to save them from all distress which it lies in our power to avert; to give them a staff and comfort, and words of cheer, through the way of mystery, that they may tread it with victorious step, and a joyful presage of light, and a freer horizon beyond.

IX.

THE OLD HOPE.

IX.

THE OLD HOPE.

> "Oh joy that in our embers
> Is something that doth live!" — WORDSWORTH.

> "At nihilo minus sentimus experimurque nos æternos esse." — SPINOZA.

MAN is a yonder-minded being, an embodied hereafter. There are faculties, purposes, aspirations in him for which this life affords no adequate scope, which therefore presage a life to come. Their import, it is true, may relate to the species, not to the individual. They may be but intimations of the higher capabilities of human life, and a better future for man on this earth; as certain rudimental organs in the lower orders of animated nature seem to be prophecies of a higher organism, which find their fulfilment in man. Yet, even so, they have a savor of immortality. The strongest proof of individual immortality is the fact that men believe in it. The ancient and wide-spread faith may be regarded as a pledge from the Power that made us, not indeed that each individual soul shall, without exception, perpetuate a conscious identity, but that immortality is within the possibilities and scope of the human constitution.

IX.

THE OLD HOPE.

"Oh joy that in our embers
Is something that doth live!" — WORDSWORTH.

"At nihilo minus sentimus experimurque nos æternos esse." — SPINOZA.

MAN is a yonder-minded being, an embodied hereafter. There are faculties, purposes, aspirations in him for which this life affords no adequate scope, which therefore presage a life to come. Their import, it is true, may relate to the species, not to the individual. They may be but intimations of the higher capabilities of human life, and a better future for man on this earth; as certain rudimental organs in the lower orders of animated nature seem to be prophecies of a higher organism, which find their fulfilment in man. Yet, even so, they have a savor of immortality. The strongest proof of individual immortality is the fact that men believe in it. The ancient and wide-spread faith may be regarded as a pledge from the Power that made us, not indeed that each individual soul shall, without exception, perpetuate a conscious identity, but that immortality is within the possibilities and scope of the human constitution.

The analogies of nature, so often insisted on in this connection, appear to me not to possess much weight. The old and ever-repeated illustration of the caterpillar and the butterfly fails in one or two essential particulars. First, The caterpillar, before developing into the butterfly, does *not die*, in any such sense as that which we intend when we speak of the death of man. Secondly, If the caterpillar does die by some fatal injury, or if such injury be inflicted on the grub, no butterfly succeeds. And, thirdly, The butterfly is not immortal, but, as if by way of compensation for her double life, perishes before the birth of her offspring. Nature, so far as we can see, is not concerned to perpetuate the individual, but only the species. I am not aware of any fact in nature which favors the belief in individual immortality. The affirmative voices on this question are not to be collected from the world of facts, but from that of ideas.

Moreover, the question of the immortality of the soul must not be confounded with that of the immortality of the conscious self. Most of the reasoning on the subject applies only to the former; but it seems to assume the identity of the two. The immortality of the soul being granted, it would still be a question whether the soul is the continent and carrier of the conscious self,* in such wise that the perpetuation of the one

* Perhaps we exaggerate the importance of this one aspect of the general question. There may be as much of egoism as of reason in the interest felt in the continuity of the conscious self. I cannot agree with those who would place the whole emphasis of immortality here, and who think that not to remember the I of the present life is not to live at all hereafter; since, then, it is not I that live, but another. It is still I in the sense most

necessarily involves the continuity of the other, — involves the recollection of the present life. Whether I — that is, this soul of mine — shall live again, and live for ever, is one question; whether I shall hereafter remember my present self is another, and, it seems to me, a quite secondary one. If any object, that not to remember the present self is not to remember the past at all; that, consequently, it is annihilation of the past, consequently, destruction of identity, consequently, not so much immortality, as new creation, — I reply, that memory has two parts, — retention and association. I can suppose that the ideas, and all essential knowledge acquired in the present life may be retained, while the association with the present perishes. Experience is not necessarily lost when the past is no longer recalled. Its substance may still exist without the form of memory. What is now memory, or remembered knowledge, may hereafter be intuition.

Leaving, then, the uncertain analogies of nature, and taking our stand in the world of ideas, I find there the idea of immortality; not a recent speculation, nor a private conceit, but ancient and universal as civilized man. What account can be given of it? Whence its origin? Shall we say that the wish is father to the thought? But how many things there are which we desire, which all men desire, with no accompanying belief in their possibility. I find no explanation of the

---

important to the whole, if not in the sense most important to self-love. It is still the same soul with all that earthly discipline has made it; and, by that discipline, fitted and endowed for its new career. This is all that concerns the city of God. The question of conscious identification ("Ille ego qui quondam") is a private affair, important only to self-love.

fact of this belief so satisfactory as the supposition of a truth on which it rests, and an understanding between the human and divine spirit, by which that truth is assured.

And I find in this idea the best solution of the moral problems and contradictions of human life. Of these contradictions, the most glaring, perhaps, is the incompatibility of the claims of the moral law with the instincts of nature. The moral law announces itself in our consciousness as the highest law of our being, as that to which we owe supreme allegiance, — the "categorical imperative." Deep in the universal soul is laid the conviction of moral obligation, of the binding necessity of right. The law of duty is unconditional: it demands unconditional obedience. It requires the sacrifice, not only of present ease, but of life itself, whenever they stand in the way of its sacred claims. It requires that we encounter all hazards, and count not our life dear, in any service to which the providence of God has called us.* We blame the man who abandons the post of duty from a cowardly love of life; the physician who deserts his patients attacked with infectious disease; the soldier who perils his country's cause through fear. But why do we blame them? Is not life the supreme end to which every thing else must be sacrificed? So says the instinct of self-preservation. But no! conscience protests against this view. There is something higher than self-preservation: duty is more sacred than life. Then what a contradiction is man! What opposite laws prevail in his constitution?

* The illustration which follows is from Bretschneider.

What means this sense of obligation which contradicts the instincts of nature? How can his self require him to expose his self to destruction? Here is a problem which requires immortality for its solution. Grant an hereafter, and the contradiction becomes intelligible. It is not our very and whole being that we are to sacrifice, but only the earth-life, brief and imperfect at best. The law of duty is not calculated for earthly limitations. Its scheme is irrespective of the bounds of time. The obedience it requires supposes an immortal nature.

For not only must that obedience be unconditional: it must also be complete and entire. A voice in man, speaking with divine authority, bids him make the law of duty the sole and uniform law of his life. This he can never succeed in doing; for he carries within him, beside the law of right, another law, — the law of selfish appetite. "The flesh lusteth against the spirit." He who is most intent on the right does not always perform what the spirit wills, and what the law demands. This conflict between flesh and spirit ends never while flesh endures. No man becomes in this world what he is capable of being, in moral purity and strength. The virtue that is in him is not brought out in mortal action. Will it never appear? Will it never become fact? Then the supreme Wisdom would seem to contradict itself. The order of God is to accomplish great ends with small means; but here the ends are little, and the means great. What wealth of faculty! What paltry attainments! The only solution of this inconsistency is the supposition of another term and a longer date for the moral life, and perhaps a better temperature of the spirit, that shall perfect the fruit which would not ripen in the climate of this world.

Great powers and small performance; vast schemes and petty results; "thoughts that wander through eternity," and a life that

> "can little more supply
> Than just to look about us and to die"!

Will any philosophy that denies immortality satisfy us with its reading of this riddle? It is true, these aspirations in man which transcend the scale of earthly life are not in themselves a sufficient proof of a life beyond. Still, the consciousness of an unfulfilled destiny, which afflicts alike the strongest and the weakest, in view of their attainments as compared with their designs, is hardly reconcilable with earthly limitations, if those limitations represent "the be-all and the end-all" of the soul. "Life's short sum," the poet warns us, "forbids the undertaking of a long hope." But who was ever persuaded to abridge his hope in accommodation to the narrow span? "Life is short and art is long," said the wise physician. Who was ever deterred from art by the known disproportion? And who ever lived to accomplish his uttermost aim? What career so complete as to comprehend all that is wanted of this world? We retire with an imperfect victory from the battle of life. The campaign is not finished when we strike tents. We have devised schemes of gain or ambition which are still in full operation. The scholar has unsolved problems at which he is laboring. The philosopher is summoned in the midst of experiments he cannot stay to complete. The philanthropist is overtaken in projects of reform that are to add new value to human life. We all stop short of the goal which entertained our livelong hope.

In this abrupt termination of the present existence, there lies an intimation of another state and a further existence for the scheming soul, whose schemes the present has failed to realize. I do not say proof; for it does not amount to that. The proof of immortality is faith in it. Alas for man, if his faith is at the mercy of his wit! Yet it is well to listen to these intimations: they help to illustrate what they cannot establish. It is a well-known fact of familiar experience, that no dream is ever finished. They all break off in the midst; they stop short on the eve of some further development. The reason is, that the law by which the dream proceeds and unfolds itself does not reside in the dream itself, but in a life behind the dream-life, and including that as one of its states or phenomena. If the dream subsisted by itself, and unfolded itself by a law of its own, it would continue to unfold until it reached its natural termination; and every dream would then be complete in itself, — a perfect whole. But being what it is, — a mere dependency of the waking life, and attached by a thread to the actual world, — the slightest disturbance in that is sufficient to break it up. So we may suppose, so indeed we know, that the law of our waking life — the law by which we live in the actual world — has its root in a life behind that. Our scheming and our action are projected on a scale of the soul; our existence as children of earth is projected on a scale of physical laws. The two scales do not coincide. The scale of earthly existence is a small frame applied to a larger plan. It bounds that plan for this world: does it bound it for ever? Does it bound the planning and producing soul? I see no reason to suppose that it does. What our dreams are to our waking existence, that our waking existence may be to an inner and larger life of the soul; and what we call the actual world — that is, our experience of it — may be but a dream of this inner life projected on a scale of physical laws, and bounded by them, as our nightly dream is bounded by them in its narrower limits; and what we call death may be but the breaking up of this more protracted dream, at the point where the scale of physical laws intersects the inner life; consequently a waking-up of the soul to a more intense and expanded consciousness, — a consciousness which shall bear the same proportion to this present state that the present does to the nightly dream.

What a miracle it is, for all our familiarity with it, when we wake in the morning, new-born, into the great, wide world of day, after being shut up for some hours in the narrow confinement of the world of sleep! How little and nugatory seems to us then our dream, if remembered at all! Only when, in that dream which we had, some fierce passion was called into play, or some terrible calamity pursued us, do we dwell upon it still, for a while, in the growing dawn, until the importunate realities of waking existence chase its image from the soul. I can imagine a waking consequent on death, or coincident with it, which shall give us a consciousness by so much the more vivid, a morning by so much the more resplendent, a world by so much the larger and more glorious, as our conceptions and the possibilities of being transcend the actual experience of life. And perhaps every future life of the soul may be as a dream to that which succeeds it, and the only waking life in the universe be that of God.

I assert nothing. On this subject all dogmatizing is ridiculous. All positive assertion is rebuked by the consciousness of ignorance and limitation. I stand with profound submission and with reverent expectation before the veiled future which bounds this mortal span. It is not the light of revelation, but the candle of conjecture, which I hold out into the uncertain dark.

Thus much we may affirm; and the more we meditate the matter, the more the conviction grows, that this interior force which we call the soul, this scheming and productive power which works in us and through us, shaping our life in the world, and, in some small measure, the world by our life, contriving and producing, — that this power, I say, does not exhaust itself in these productions. The capacity remains in man's consciousness, of further production. The scale of mortality which bounds and measures the product is not the measure of the power. It is not the measure of the soul. We die in the midst of our schemes. The fault is not in the schemes that they break off and stop short of their fulfilment. Nor is it the incapacity of the soul that fails to fulfil them; but another law coming in, another force breaking through, a physical necessity, cuts them short. Does that force destroy the producing power, or only arrest its action for a season, as the winter stops the flowering of the plant, leaving the root unimpaired for further production?

The organism in and by which we performed our tasks is broken up. Are we that organism? Is what we call the soul the product of organization? If so, then death puts an end to us and our work for ever. The particles which composed the machine may work again in other forms of which they shall become part; but of us and our work there is an end for ever. But we are not that organism. No man identifies himself with his bodily organs, but regards these as something external to himself, something which clothes him, something which he inhabits. We are not the hand surely, nor the foot, nor the trunk. We separate in our consciousness between self and each particular part, between self and the totality of parts. There is a feeling of something distinct, detachable, something which is not part, but whole and indivisible, transcending organization, surviving it.

We lived before we saw the light. Our embryo life may have been a conscious life: if so, what dreams and associations were interrupted and broken up when the new-born emerged from his narrow, dark world, —

> "Like a shipwrecked sailor tost
> By rough waves on a perilous coast,
> Flung by laboring nature forth
> Upon the mercies of the earth"!

The present life may be embryonic with relation to some future life of the soul, and the discipline of this world a process of gestation, in which the great Mother travails with her children until they burst the matrix of mortality, and put on new life. The embryo state ceases: the life it enclosed survives.

But how survives? In what form? with what surroundings? with what human or superhuman conditions? Is it here, on this earth, that we resume and pursue our calling? Do we re-appear again and again in new forms of humanity? Or do we migrate to some other sphere? Or does the dissolution of the mortal body disengage an ethereal form, invisible to the eye of flesh, which, without any grosser embodiment, contains and perpetuates the conscious life? These are questions for which reason and religion have no legitimate answer, other than a candid confession of utter and helpless ignorance. Every theory we may frame of the future of the soul is a baseless speculation. No conclusion which philosophy has drawn from nature or consciousness can lay any claim to scientific credibility. All our inquiries and soundings of this matter bring us no nearer the truth. We want the first and most essential condition of a rational theory on the subject. We do not even know what the soul or self of the individual, as distinguished from the visible person, is. The most intelligible theory that has ever been propounded is that of a succession of human births; the soul, at death, investing itself with a new body, and living a new life on the earth. The early Christians also believed in a new life on the earth for the saints, but one invested with the same body, which they supposed would be raised and re-animated * for

* Science protests against the doctrine of the resurrection of the body as a physical impossibility, on the ground that the same particles have, at different times, been constituents of different human bodies. I attach no great importance to this reasoning, and rather suppose, that, if the resurrection of this identical body were desirable, the divine chemistry is competent to that result. Besides, the doctrine does not contemplate the restoration of every ounce of flesh, but conceives that the resurrection-body will recover so much of the present as to constitute essential identity of the outward man. But there are other weighty objections to the doctrine, which survives only in the creeds of Christendom, not in its thought.

the purpose, and for whose millennial abode the earth itself would be renewed.

There are moods and moments when the wish to renew our relations with this earth, or to know, at least, of its on-goings, predominates over every other feeling in our contemplation of the hereafter. The founder of the Hebrew Commonwealth is represented, in the Pentateuch, as dying within sight of the promised land which had been the object of his lifelong endeavor. When I think of him looking from the summit of the border-mountain into that fair Canaan into which it was whispered to his soul that he should not live to enter and take possession in person, it seems to me that an irrepressible longing must have seized the heart of the prophet to visit, in the day of their prosperity, the people he had guided in weakness and want, and to witness the maturity and power of the State of which he had laid the foundations, at the foot of Horeb and on the banks of the Nile. We, too, from the height of our own time, from the height of modern civilization, discern a future of rich promise, — a Canaan of social progress and prosperity, into which our descendants shall enter, but of which the distant vision only is granted to us. Who so cold or so indifferent to human weal as not to desire, in the future of the soul which lies for us beyond the Jordan of death, to see with our own eyes the realization of this great hope? Who would not wish to know the condition of society as it will be after the lapse of another century, when the tendencies which are now at work in human affairs shall have consummated their legitimate fruit? An astronomer, speaking of Halley's comet, which returns to that point in its orbit from whence it is visible to our earth after an interval of — I forget how many years, remarks, that, "while we gaze on this mysterious visitant, not without a feeling of sadness, knowing that its larger year outspans the cycle of one of earth's fleeting generations, and that, when it once more returns, it will tell of the victories of science, not to us, but to those who are fast forgetting us, the thought clutches by the heart, that man must be immortal." From the same feeling it might be argued, that man does not quit this earth; that the life of the individual must be co-present to all the generations that come after him; that he must realize, in his individual experience, all that collective humanity, in all time, is destined to know, to produce, and to be.

This, however, is reasoning on the assumption, that the interest of this present must be the interest also of the life to come; that "quæ cura fuit vivis eadem sequitur tellure repostos." It is quite possible that we may exaggerate the importance of the future of this planet and of human society, in relation to the whole to which they and we belong; that, however momentous all this may seem to us now, its importance will dwindle into nothing when we wake from the dream of mortality, and take up our new position in the universe of God. This world and its belongings may then be no more to us than last night's dream, whose intense interest we scarce recall in the morning, and whose history we soon dismiss from the mind.

Besides, the future of this earth, — is it not in ourselves? All that collective humanity is capable of, all that the ages to come of human existence shall unfold in long procession, — the whole scope and theme of mortal years, — is it not folded up in the individual soul? All that man can be is in us; and, wherever our being may lodge in the great hereafter, fast as that being unfolds we shall read the history of advancing man in our own progressive life.

The more prevailing doctrine concerning the form and method of the future life is that of the "spiritual body," so called, — a finer frame, supposed to be contained within this visible, to be disengaged from it by death, and to constitute thenceforth the vehicle and dwelling of the soul. The "spiritual body," if I rightly apprehend it, is a more ethereal body, differing from this present mainly in the matter of weight, and exemption from animal functions. The future state is supposed to be a realm inhabited by these ethereal bodies, and is called "the spiritual world." Whatever may be thought of the ontology of this view, its claim of spirituality is founded on mere difference of mass and bulk. But the essence of spirit consists not in levity. When we talk of spirituality, it is not a question of specific gravity, of thick or thin, of solid or fluid. A cubic foot of oxygen is no more spiritual than a cubic foot of lead. Light and electricity are just as material as density and gravitation; and a body of a hundred pound weight is just as likely a vehicle of spirit, and just as much entitled to be called a spiritual body, as any imponderable substance.

We speculate into thick darkness when we try conclusions with the region beyond the grave. Impervious night baffles all intellectual adventure in that direction. We shall have to be content with the simple fact of immortality, suggested by the longing heart, and confirmed by the general faith of mankind. Enough to know that the bounded horizon of this mortal is not "the butt and seamark of my utmost sail;" that the tickings of the fleshly heart are not the measure of the soul's unending day. More than this is not revealed; and, however curiosity may burn to penetrate the secret, our riper reason must needs bless the veil of inscrutable mystery which a kind God has thrown around our passage hence, and the deep, unanswering silence, which baffles science but fosters hope.

The only thing that can, with any degree of certainty, be predicated concerning the life to come, is, that its character, so far as our own consciousness for good or evil is concerned in it, will mainly depend on ourselves. Whatever may be the mode of existence hereafter, whatever the embodiment, the locality, that which to us is most essential in it is that which we bring to it of our own. Our life is from within; and he who would know what his state and pursuits and sensations will be, when this mortal is put off, must look into his own heart, and see what he finds there: what aptitudes, what tendencies, what inclinations and desires. To suppose that Omnipotence — if such a thing be possible — will take a soul out from all its past habits and belongings, and set it down in some new state entirely foreign from its bent and wont, is a vain imagination. But this we may hope, that the God to whom all souls are dear will compensate past defects of circumstance and means, and provide such guidance and such drawing as, not resisted, shall bring the wanderer to blessedness at last.

X.

FREEDOM IN BONDS.

X.

FREEDOM IN BONDS.

THE beginning of conscious existence to finite beings is the sense of limitation. The first experience which consciousness reports is one which separates us from all other being, and draws the boundary-line of our personal estate. The first thing which the infant learns from its contact with the world is the fact of bounds. Its sensations are crossed by a foreign existence; its efforts are thwarted by a foreign power. Every subsequent age repeats and confirms this first experience. We are not free, as "the natural man" interprets and postulates freedom. Our freedom, in that sense, is narrowly circumscribed. On all sides, we are straitened and cramped, — walled in by adamantine necessity.

Every wish we breathe confesses limitation. Every wish is a feeling of restraint, a conflict between soul and circumstance. And wishes multiply as fast as the means of gratifying them. You are straitened in your affairs; you desire a competent support. Imagine that competence obtained, and desire is as active as before. Your property must be so vested as to give absolute immunity from loss or care. Health you must have to enjoy your fortune; social position, to command the respect of your fellow-men. You must be happy in your family, happy in all your connections. You must live to a good old age without the infirmities of age. And, when every thing is fixed according to your desire, the end of all things stares you in the face; and you find, in your finite nature, a limit which bounds the uttermost good that fortune can bestow.

Every lot in life has its limits, and the limits are equally oppressive in all. From whatever point we set out, the goal of perfection is equally remote. Happiness is not the end of a line, along which our fortunes are ranged in different degrees of proximity: it is the centre of a circle; and all human conditions lie in the same circumference, at equal distances around it. The feeling of limitation depends, not on circumstance, but on ourselves. With a happy temper, the law is easy, and the limits large; with a discontented, fretful spirit, the limits are close, and the law is hard. But none are so happy as never to feel the restrictions which limit and shut in our mortal life. We may not rebel against our lot; and yet the universal conditions to which humanity is subject shall sometimes pain us with their sharp restraints. Time and space, climate, weather, sickness, death, everywhere oppose our desires. We feel our incapacity to be and to do what our better instincts prompt; we can never quite come up with our conscience; we can never quite burst the meshes of weakness and sense. Then, too, the inevitable course of events rushes on, regardless of our wishes; and all our sighs and prayers cannot extort the least dispensation from nature or time. When heaviness weighs on our spirits, we cannot take wings and fly away; we cannot escape the weary sameness and wearier changes of life. We cannot prevent the loss of friends and the bitter disappointments of fate. We witness suffering which we cannot relieve, changes we cannot avert, vice we cannot reform. Who so hard or who so wise as to care for none of these things, — as never to wish that the everlasting law might for once relent in his behalf?

We find a limit in the strict compensation which pervades all departments of life, and qualifies all the gifts and advantages allotted to man. One thing is set off against another. You can have no good, without incurring the risk of some proportionate evil. You can have no pleasure, but some pain goes with it. Nothing is given for nothing; every thing must be bought with its proper price. Our very existence is not *given:* we must pay for it with ceaseless care and toil, and the moral obligations it imposes. The higher the condition into which you are born, the greater the struggle to maintain that condition, and the greater the cares and obligations which it brings. The savage needs little to maintain his meagre existence. His rude weapons and strong limbs will procure him the food and raiment which his fathers enjoyed. His means are as ample as the forest and the flood; but his wants are cheap, his gratifications few. The civilized man has greater needs, and greater pains to satisfy them. He asks more of the world, and the world demands more of him. The more we multiply the means of enjoyment, the more we multiply the sources of pain. If you build an expensive house, and surround yourself with splendid furnitures and costly decorations, you have the trouble of keeping these things in order, and the fear that they may pass out of your hands. You must burden yourself with domestic cares: for every convenience which you introduce into your establishment, you must take some inconvenience in its train. If you live simply and at little cost, you forego some of the gratifications of taste; but you avoid also the cares which they involve. If you indulge your affections, form friendships, gather a family around you, and enter into near relations with your fellow-men, you gratify your social nature, and enjoy the precious satisfactions of love: at the same time, you lay yourself open to painful anxieties and poignant griefs unknown to him who leads a solitary life. If you lead a solitary life, you escape a world of care, and lose a world of enjoyment. Whatever is gained in one way is lost in another; whatever good you pursue, you must pay its price. If you seek wealth, you must pay the price of ceaseless drudgery and livelong care; if you seek knowledge and intellectual culture, you must pay the price of long devotion, rigid self-denial, late watchings, early risings, and a resolute renunciation of other good, which may or may not be added unto you. If you seek ease and present comfort, you must pay the price of obscurity and insignificance. If you seek the kingdom of God, you must renounce the world; if you love the world, you must forego the kingdom of God.

Life itself, and every circumstance of life, is amenable to the law of compensation. It is the first statute, — the regulative principle in all human things. It pervades, like gravitation, the whole economy of nature. Disturb it in one place, and it rights itself in another. If the tide rises here, it ebbs there. If the ocean loses by evaporation, the air gains. It always takes so much to effect so much. Eternal Justice holds in opposite scales the good and ill of life: whatever is added to one scale is rectified by its just equivalent in the other. There may be occasional oscillations; an unwonted pressure, a momentary success, may cause one side or the other to preponderate for a while: but the re-action is always equal to the action; the equilibrium is never long disturbed.

We find a limit in the law of retribution which avenges every unlawful advantage, and punishes every sinful act. Since the beginning of the world, no man ever wronged another without wronging himself. No man ever consulted his private advantage at the expense of his neighbor, or the gratification of his senses at the expense of his morals, without incurring the penalty annexed to such acts. It is the underside of that evil deed of which the advantage sought is the upperside. Cut never so fine, shave never so close, you cannot divide the benefit from the wrong. The penalty is a part of the thing. Sin is a poisoned fruit. No art has yet been able to separate the sweet from the noxious, the taste in the mouth from the mischief in the soul. Every little dishonesty in worldly dealings, every falsehood of speech, every spiteful word or act, every sensual excess, judges itself more surely, more adequately, than any court can judge it. Men do not see the judgment, because it is not an object of sense; but to deny it is not to believe in the soul. Every temptation to which I yield is so much lost to the soul's growth. Every sin is a misstep which has got to be rectified. By just so much as honesty is better than fraud, by just so much as kindness is better than injury, by just so much as self-command is better than indulgence, by just so much am I punished for every transgression. The gratification sought by unlawful means is never realized: it slips through the fingers; and, in all the annals of crime, there was never a transgressor who would say that he had bettered his condition by any wrong act which he did.

So, then, in every direction I find a limit which bounds my will and defines my life. I am fenced with stern conditions, compassed about with everlasting denials. My freedom is an island of small extent in an ocean of necessity which opposes, on every side, an inexorable bar to my finite power. In vain do we chafe against these bonds; in vain do we strive with the limits which contain our little life. There is nothing for it but to take the conditions we cannot annul, and accommodate ourselves as we may to our narrow orbit. Is it an evil that we are thus limited, — that our freedom, our capacity, is not absolute, but circumscribed? Behold here the method of the highest good!

For what *is* the highest good? Every creature has its proper destination; and, in the fulfilment of that destination, the highest good for that creature consists. But no creature can fulfil its destination, except it abide within the limits prescribed for it. The inanimate substances of nature are useful only when restricted and confined. Gold would be useless, if less rare than it is. Iron is useful only when reduced to suitable forms; and all form is limitation. The burning gas is useless while it flickers and flares in unrestrained freedom; but reduce and control its issue, and it radiates a serviceable light. What more useless than the vapor which escapes from boiling water, in its free and diffuse state? It wastes itself in air; it mingles with the clouds, and returns to the earth again according to its circuit. But confine it within the iron chambers of a steam-engine, and it becomes a mighty and beneficent power; it gives wings to motion, extends the spirit's conquest over matter, and is made subservient to all the arts of life.

Look next at organized beings. Consider the plant. That blade of wheat is destined to bear so many kernels, according to its kind. But not one kernel could ever come to perfection, were not the plant confined within certain limits which it cannot transgress. Nature must bound herself in one way, that she may glorify herself in another. If the growth of that stalk were not arrested when it reached a certain prescribed stature and bulk, if it continued to grow beyond its proper dimensions, the vegetative power allotted to it would be exhausted in disproportionate expansion of volume, and the stalk would absorb what was meant for the fruit. The plant would fall short of its destination in striving to exceed it. In like manner, the animal economy is a system of forces and limitations, working together for a common end. Every muscle is balanced by some antagonist muscle, every organ is qualified by some associate organ, every instinct is limited by some counter instinct; and so the whole is kept within the type, and made to fill up the type, in which and for which it was formed. The bird has wings which lift it above the earth; but, lest it should lose itself in endless space, it has instincts and gravitation which draw it to earth again. Beasts of prey have instincts which prompt them to devour; but, to keep the peace of nature, they have also a love of repose which prompts them to rest when their hunger is stilled.

So man, the head and crown of creation, has *his* type and design, within which his perfection and happiness lies, and out of which there is no perfection or happiness for him. If he transgresses this type in any direction, he sacrifices more than he gains. If he goes too far in one way, he loses something in another. If he attempts to be more than man, he becomes less than man. The chief and only good is to be man, — simply man; to unfold, in its just proportions, our human nature, taking heed that no part or function or faculty shall trespass on any other, but that all conspire to fulfil the perfect image of God in which our being is cast. This type of ours is constituted and maintained by those very laws, physical and moral, which we find in our experience, and to which we must needs submit, seeing that obedience to them is sure and only good.

Imagine these limitations removed, suppose these laws abolished, paint to yourself that unbounded capacity or that unbridled license which your fancy may have craved when hampered and confined by the close conditions of life; you will see that nothing would be gained, that every thing would be sacrificed by the abolition of those laws against which you chafe. The imagination can picture no condition more appalling than that of a creature absolved from law. Suppose an instance of such emancipation. Suppose the All-ruler to take off the restraints of law from matter. Or suppose but one law — the law of gravitation — suspended, and suppose that suspension to take effect in a single planet only, of the solar system. Imagine one lawless planet. Loose the centripetal bond and set it adrift. See it wander madly from its native sphere, aimless, pathless, into infinite space. It entangles itself with foreign firmaments, amazing, with its lawless presence, the loyal orbs that move obedient in their steady rounds; perplexing their path with incalculable nodes, and missing the sweet influences of its kindred sky, — an intruder in orderly places, the vagabond of creation, unblessing and unblest. Suppose that body endowed with consciousness, how would it long for its old beat! how gladly submit itself to saving law, and return, after fruitless and joyless roving, to its safe perihelion and its brother stars! Carry this idea into the moral world. Suppose mankind absolved from their allegiance to right and duty; suppose that no one finds in himself, or out of himself, any law restraining his inclinations; that each one does what passion urges or impulse suggests; — would that be a comfortable state of society? No hell within the compass of human imagination could exceed the possibilities of such a state.

But aside from those possibilities, and aside from the harm to others, consider only the loss to himself which man must suffer in the absence of law and restraint. Pushing his propensity in one direction without limit, as each should incline, none would fulfil the design of his being; none would be man, but something else and less than man. Pursuing one object and excluding others, he would sacrifice his entireness to that one. This man would give himself to sensual indulgence, and become an organ of sense. That one would give himself up to repose, and become a stone. One would be all intellect, another all feeling; none would be man. To be an entire man, to fulfil his type, is the highest to which man can aspire. To this end, as the vessel is conformed to its mould, we are placed in a framework of laws which prescribe the dimensions and the plan we are to fill, that no propensity may exceed its due, but each be developed in harmony with all the rest, until we reach the perfect man. We are limited on every side, and bound in each particular, that we may be glorified in the whole. Our nature, to be perfect, must be restrained. Let us not chafe, but glory in these bonds, and welcome every law which we find in our condition and in ourselves as the finger of God in the uncertainties of life, pointing out the path which alone can bring us the satisfaction we seek.

I have spoken of law as a limitation of freedom; but law is also a condition of freedom. A nearer view will show that law and liberty are co-ordinate. We find, as we ascend in the scale of life, each order of beings more free than the one beneath it. The plant is rooted in the ground: it has no freedom of locomotion; its only liberty consists in turning its leaves to the sun, and opening its pores to the atmospheric influences which supply it nurture. The shellfish clings to its native rock, and has no liberty but to open its valves and receive the nourishment conveyed to it by the element it inhabits. The quadruped has the freedom of the field and the forest: it procures its food by its own effort, and exercises volition. Man has the range of the planet, and not only freedom of locomotion, but freedom of thought and action: he can choose his path and mode of life; he can choose between good and evil. Man is freer than planet or brute; but is man less subject to law than they? On the contrary, the laws which govern him are more numerous and complex than those which govern the inferior orders. The plant obeys no law but that of vegetable life; the brute obeys no law but those of animal nature: but man, in addition to the physical laws which comprehend him with the rest of creation, is amenable also to civil, social, moral and spiritual laws, which claim his allegiance.

Law is a restriction of liberty to those only who resist its control. The way to surmount this restraint is by perfect obedience; by accepting the law so entirely, by so identifying our wills with the supreme Will which ordained it, that we become ourselves a party to the law. Then it ceases to be restraint, and becomes our own volition. We say that the plant grows freely when it grows as nature designed, without artificial restraint, according to the law of its organization. We call the bird free when it moves in obedience to the law in its members. If tree and bird were conscious, they would feel that they were following their own inclinations, although the direction of every twig in the one, and the motion of every muscle in the other, is determined by strict necessity. Man is free when he freely obeys the law in his mind. There is no freedom if we look for it outside of ourselves, if we seek it in circumstance. The inner world alone is free or capable of freedom. We are all thrown upon circumstances which do not answer to our ideal; the universe about us has its laws and methods against which human passions beat in vain, and gain nothing but their own foam flung back upon them from the adamantine negations which God opposes to their hungry tide. The world is inexorably conditioned, and conditions us; and we sometimes weary of our estate, and pine as in bondage. The homesick soul demands its release. Oh that we had wings to lift us above the confining tasks and drudgery of life! The only way to escape this bondage is to give ourselves to it with mind and heart; to find our life in our task, our freedom in our obligations; to make our good-will as broad as our necessity. Resist the law of duty, and it galls you with an iron grip; seek to evade it, it pursues you with a merciless lash; accept it, and it becomes a law of liberty. The skin which bounds this mortal body we do not feel to be a confinement, because it is a part of ourselves, a secretion of kindred matter, a fabric of our own blood. So, when we have come into perfect harmony with God by willing obedience, the law which had seemed to us imposed by a foreign power shall be seen to proceed from ourselves, to be a part of our nature, — the spontaneous expression of our wills; and therefore no longer a bond, but a graceful and transparent covering with which the soul arrays and protects its sacred life. We shall see the absurdity then of wishing that any thing in this world were other than it is. Every regret will be seen to be injustice to ourselves and impiety toward God. Then shall cease the feeling of obligation. The language of command shall be heard no more. "Thou shalt" and "thou shalt not," "must" and "ought," those stern sentinels of the soul that keep such jealous watch of our actions, shall be discharged from their superfluous posts. Choice shall then be our only obligation; "I may" and "I will," our ten commandments.

BOOK SECOND.

Rational Christianity.

PRELIMINARY.

THE CAUSE OF REASON THE CAUSE OF FAITH.

BOOK SECOND.

Rational Christianity.

THE CAUSE OF REASON THE CAUSE OF FAITH.

THE earliest controversy in the Christian Church, though concerning a matter of purely practical import, involved a theory of the rights of reason which marked the new era then dawning on the world. It was virtually a conflict of reason with authority, — a revolt of the emancipated intellect against ecclesiastical rule. Antioch, representative of rationalism and liberty, was arrayed against Jerusalem, jealous custodian of old tradition. The remarkable thing in this controversy is, that the rationalistic side was the side of faith. Although, in relation to Judaism and Jewish Christianity, the rationalism of Paul and his party assumed a negative and destructive character, its real import was divinely positive. Opposition to authority was only deeper fidelity to Christ. The cause of reason was, in this case, the cause of faith; and the term "Faith" became the technical designation of rationalistic or Pauline, as distinguished from Jewish, Christianity.

In many of the later controversies of the Church, and especially in those of the eleventh and twelfth centuries, we note the same coalition of reason with faith in the war against authority. The men of faith were the infidels of the Church. Such were Abelard, and Arnold of Brescia, Henry of Cluny, and Gerhard of Parma.

And the great controversy of all, the central controversy of modern history, — that which severed the German churches from the Latin, — exhibits pre-eminently this relation and antagonism of faith and reason with authority. Luther, the arch-rationalist of the old Church, is the hero and type of faith to all succeeding generations of the new. In every clear conflict between reason and authority, the genius of Christianity inclines to the rational side. The cause of reason is ever the cause of faith.

Yet no delusion is more current than that which identifies faith with implicit submission to ecclesiastical authority, and confounds rationalism with unbelief.

The Protestant Church, while practically basing itself on the rights of reason, in its abnegation of irrational dogma, has never duly appreciated, or even theoretically acknowledged, that position, — has never heartily accepted the legitimate construction of that position, and its obvious consequences. The term Rationalism, which truly expresses that position, is, with Liberal Christians as well as with the exclusive sects, a term of reproach, conveying an idea of some impious and unholy license. In the mind of the liberal as well as of the exclusive, faith is associated only with authority, and dissociated from reason. Rationalism is regarded as in principle unbelief, in practice sacrilege. This abuse of the term, and consequent disgust to the thing, is partly due to the old association of the word with a class of theologians now extinct, and whose methods and conclusions rational criticism itself disavows. But the misapplication of a principle does not invalidate the principle itself, nor ought the mistakes of a Paulus or a Strauss to discourage the application of reason to religion. Rationalism means that, and nothing more. Reason may err in some of its conclusions; but reason is none the less the supreme arbiter in theology. Its errors can be consistently refuted by Protestants, only on rationalistic grounds. Only the Romanist can with consistency speak of rationalism in the way of reproach. Protestantism assumes the application of reason to religion as the basis of its ecclesiastical life. Whoever calls that principle in question, whoever finds or intends reproach in the word Rationalism, abandons the Protestant ground, and confesses himself in spirit and temper a Romanist. Whoever allows that principle at all, and allows it in himself, must allow it in others, and allow it without stint, while even rejecting the conclusions of those who adopt it. Reason or Rome,—there is no middle ground.

If the Protestant principle is false, then the Church of Rome is infallibly true in all its policy and all its doctrine; and we are all heretics and doomed who are out of that communion, having the understanding irremediably darkened, for ever alienated from the life of God through the blindness of our hearts. If, on the other hand, the Protestant principle is true,—if we believe in it and profess it,—then in Christ's name let us stand by it manfully, and follow it boldly, and confide in it frankly, and not be scared by a name, nor wish to scare others. When a fellow-Protestant advances opinions which seem to us false, irreligious, dangerous, let us try those opinions by their own merits or demerits, and judge them by their own evidence or want of evidence, and not assail them with the anile cry of Rationalism, as if that trait were itself a sufficient condemnation, whereas in fact it is their only title to be so much as criticised. As Protestants, we are all rationalists in the fundamental principle of our ecclesiastical position: we may repudiate this or that rationalistic conclusion; but we may not repudiate, or repudiating cannot escape, the principle itself. If rationalism be a sin, that sin have we incurred, and are now —

> "Stepped in so far that, should we wade no more,
> Returning were as tedious as go o'er."

There is nothing for it but to hold on, — if we admit the principle at all, to stand by it manfully, to acquiesce in all its legitimate applications, to let full daylight in on our beliefs, to follow trustingly where reason leads, to accept the results of competent, honest criticism, and whatever unbiassed and conscientious investigation shall approve. We must seek some other term to express that negative position and tendency in religion which piety deplores. If criticism in any case exhibits an unmistakable spirit of hostility to religion, call it irreligion, infidelity; — give it some name expressive of that hostility, and not one which, so used, casts reproach on criticism and on reason itself.

Protestantism is, historically and theoretically, a contest of reason against ecclesiastical authority. In prosecuting this contest, the Reformation summoned to its aid another authority by which to offset the authority of Rome, — the Bible. The consequence was, that the Bible came, in the Protestant world, to occupy the place which the Church had occupied in the Roman Catholic. Not only authority, but infallibility, was claimed for it, — an infallibility extending to every jot and tittle of the text. An infallible book replaced the infallible Church. The letter of Scripture was now the immediate voice of God, and must countervail the clearest perceptions of reason and the strongest testimony of the heart. A more developed and instructed Protestantism perceives the monstrousness of this assumption, and steadfastly protests, and will continue to protest, against it. I call it an assumption because it is wholly destitute of either external or internal evidence; and, in spite of the rooted impression of most Protestant communions, and hard as the assertion may sound, I have no hesitation in saying that this assumption of the infallibility of Scripture in every topic and word of its contents is more indefensible and wide of the truth than that of the infallibility of the Church of Rome, or the claim of her primate to be the vicegerent of Christ on earth. Authority is not infallibility; neither is inspiration infallibility. The authority of Scripture is incomplete without the assent of reason; and, in things doubtful and insusceptible of demonstration, authority can mean nothing more than the strong presumption in favor of a view or a fact from the providential position and inspiration of the writer. For, not to insist on the previous question, whether in the nature of things a writing can be, not only a permanent depositary, but a lasting and everlasting and exact exponent of the truth, our evidence that any particular writing is from God can never be stronger than the evidence of reason for or against the matter contained in it.

This momentous principle — the very kernel of Protestantism — was clearly seen and distinctly stated by Locke. "Revelation," he says, "where God has been pleased to give it, must carry it against the probable conjectures of reason. . . . But yet it still belongs to reason to judge of the truth of its being a revelation, and of the signification of the words wherein it is delivered. Indeed, if any thing shall be thought revelation which is contrary to the plain principles of reason and the evident knowledge the mind has of its own clear and distinct ideas, there reason must be hearkened to as to a matter within its province, since a man can never have so certain a knowledge that a proposition which contradicts the clear principles and evidence of his own knowledge was divinely revealed, or that he understands the words rightly, . . . as he has that the contrary is true, and so is bound to consider and judge of it as a matter of reason, and not to swallow it without examination as a matter of faith."* And again, "Faith can never convince us of any thing that contradicts our knowledge." Locke did not apply this proposition to the Bible. The revelations he had in his mind were pretended revelations claimed by enthusiasts

* Essay on Human Understanding, book iv. chap. 18.

independent of the Church. In those days, when criticism was yet in its infancy, and discrepancies undetected which are now familiar, the Bible was either received as a whole or rejected as a whole, and Locke was of those who received it. But the application of this great principle to Scripture is obvious, and the bibliolatry which refuses so to apply it — which refuses to discriminate between different degrees of authority and authenticity, between genuine and spurious, between poetry and history — is not of the nature of faith, but of fetichism.

This sluggish acquiescence in something external, this slavish reliance on a letter, an institution, on the "says so" of an individual, is precisely the state of mind to which the name and credit of faith are commonly assigned. This is the kind of faith which the Church of Rome demands and fosters. The entire surrender of the understanding to a symbol, of the will to a priest, is the highest virtue in that communion. The noblest saint in the feminine calendar, the holy and beautiful Elizabeth of Thüringen, though clothed with every virtue which could merit a seat among the saints in any age or Church, was chiefly lauded by her judges for unqualified submission to her confessor, even to the extent of renouncing, at his dictation, her works of love. Her only weakness was esteemed her supreme merit. An intelligent female convert to Romanism in our own land was asked how her disciplined mind could reconcile itself with certain dogmas of her new confession. The answer was, "I do not exercise my mind upon them; I *suspend my reason* on all questions on which the Church has pronounced its decision." Romanizing Christians may see in this suspense of reason the crowning triumph of consummate faith. I can see in it only the dying confession of faith *in articulo mortis*, the religion of despair, — despair of the inner light, despair of divine guidance, and the Holy Ghost. Such confessions throw a ghastly light on the true nature of such conversions, — on all conversions from the light of reason and rational faith to obsolete dogma and ancient night. Suspense of reason! the history of Christendom for twelve centuries is expressed by that phrase. "And the times of that ignorance God winked at, but now commandeth all men everywhere to repent." Whatever merit blind acquiescence in blind authority might once have had, it has none now, and will find no longer a conniving God in the providential eclipse of the gospel. The light is there: if any prefer the darkness to the light, the darkness they have chosen is their doom. "For it is impossible for those who were once enlightened, and have tasted the heavenly gift, and were made partakers of the Holy Ghost, and have tasted the good word of God and the powers of the world to come, if they shall fall away, to renew them again, seeing they crucify to themselves the Son of God afresh and put him to an open shame."

It is not a healthy and robust faith that seeks refuge in authority, and flies for shelter to an antiquated creed. In the beginning of the Anglican Tractarian movement, one of its leaders complained that the "Church had too much light." Following this hint, the more consistent Tractarians turned their backs on such light as they had, and, retreating beneath the shadow of the Church of Rome, escaped the annoyance altogether. It is the only safe course for men who do not wish to see what they believe. Let the blind follow the blind into congenial darkness, and let the seeing gratefully accept the light. It is not complete illumination as yet; it is not co-extensive with all our belief. There are many dark passages in life and religion, where we must walk by faith, not by sight. We must walk by faith in a vast number of cases, whatever church we walk in, and though we walk in no church at all. Man is a poor creature if he does not believe a great deal more than he sees. Nevertheless, we will walk by sight, even in religion, where we have sight to walk by. We will not shut our eyes for the mere pleasure of groping in the dark. We will thankfully accept the light we have, and strive for more.

And is there, then, no infallible authority in religion? You take from us first the infallible Church, and now the infallible Book. To what oracle then shall we flee for safe conduct in the controverted questions of theology, — for safe deliverance from the agonies of doubt and the endless mazes of the mind? To the question, What is Truth? — the supreme question of the soul, on which hang the issues of everlasting life, — is there no expressed and unmistakable answer of God, on which the soul may repose with the certainty of infallible truth, and there end the bewildering quest? No infallible oracle out of the breast. The oracle within, the answer of the Holy Ghost which the listening, waiting soul receives in the innermost recesses of her own consciousness, is for each individual the high tribunal of last appeal. However desirable it may seem that infallible guidance from without should have been vouchsafed to our perplexity, however we may covet it and sigh for it, it has not been so ordained. We have not been so constituted as to see infallibly or to act infallibly. And perhaps, if we duly consider the uses of the world and the needs of the soul, we shall cease to think it desirable, shall see it to be incompatible with moral discipline and moral growth. For what, after all, would be the difference between infallible guidance and mechanical guidance? The theory of infallibility is at variance with all the known methods of divine Providence. God does not act on the mind mechanically, but morally. He does not compel belief by absolute certitude, but persuades belief by fair probability; the individual mind, with its idiosyncrasies, being one of the factors by which that probability is constituted. It is very essential to our growth, as individuals and as society, that we should not have certainty, — that faith should be elective, and not the inevitable result of evidence acting with mechanical compulsion on the mind. It is the liability to error and the experience of error that make us human, that furnish to human nature the topics of discipline and the means of growth. The better part of truth is the search after truth. Lessing was right in his preference when he said, "If God should offer me the absolute truth in the right hand, and the love and pursuit of truth in the left, I should choose the left." The absolute is not for man.

The cause of reason is the cause of faith. In affirming this, I but re-affirm what the wisest and devoutest of the Church have always maintained. But indeed the proposition is a necessary inference from the nature of man; it lies in the very constitution of the human mind. Reason and faith have one interest, — Truth. They differ only in their mode of apprehension. Reason has the clearer discernment; faith, the stronger hold. Faith has the ampler discourse; reason, the more accurate survey. Faith, conversant with matters beyond the scope of reason, "is the evidence of things not seen." But reason, so far as it reaches, is sight. Reason, therefore, so far as it reaches, is the necessary corrective of faith. Faith is determined by accidental causes; it has no necessary relation to the truth. A strong persuasion, but no objective certitude. It embraces error as well as truth, and embraces it with equal affection. But reason, in its proper nature, is identical with the actual truth of things, that is, their relation in the mind of God; and human reason, on any intelligible theory of God's government, must be a continual approximation to absolute truth. The faith of the Brahmin in the ten incarnations of Vishnu, or that of the Catholic in the Transubstantiation of the "elements," or the Tri-personality, is as strong as that of the Protestant Christian in the unity and providence of God. But the relation of reason to these different dogmas is very different. The former demand a suspense of reason; the latter, if not an original perception of reason, is at least an invitation to reason to follow and find.

An original perception of reason, it is not. Nor are any of the primary and fundamental truths of religion original perceptions of the mind. And here let me say, that, in advocating the cause of reason in religion,

I am far from maintaining the sufficiency of reason as a substitute for faith in spiritual things. On the contrary, it is my belief that reason in its own original capacity and function has no knowledge of spiritual truth, not even of the first and fundamental truth of religion, the being of God. "Natural theology" supposes that this and kindred truths are reasoned out, or may be reasoned out, by a process of induction, in the same way that the truths of astronomy were reasoned out by Kepler and Newton and Laplace; that the being of God is as much an inference from the facts and processes of nature, as the earth's motion is an inference from the oscillations of the pendulum and the changes in the sky; that the inference is inevitable, and would have been reached by competent logicians without the light of revelation and without *the idea of God pre-existing in the mind.* I do not believe in any such induction. I deny the logical sequence in that argument. I deny the logical soundness of that conclusion. I deny the ability of the human intellect to construct that ladder, whose foot being grounded in irrefragable axiom, and its steps all laid in dialectic continuity, the topmost round thereof shall lift the climbing intellect into vision of the Godhead. Between the last truth which the human intellect can reach by legitimate induction and the being of God there will ever lie —

"Deserts of vast eternity."

Not by that process did any soul yet arrive at that transcendent truth; not from beneath, but from above, — not by intellectual escalade, but by heavenly condescension, — comes the idea of God, even by the condescending Word, "of the Eternal co-eternal beam," the fountain of all our ideas of spiritual things, the well from which reason draws, but not to be confounded with it. What is true of the being of God is true of all kindred verities. All our perceptions of the primary truths of religion are products of divine illumination. All religion that is true is revealed religion. But revelation is education, — education of the reason as well as of the heart. What reason in its own original capacity could not discover, it may come by divine education to apprehend, and even, in a negative way, to substantiate, by removing objections and showing the absurdity of a contrary supposition. The office of reason in religion is not discovery, but verification and purification. Its function is to make and keep religion true and pure, by eliminating from the code of elemental beliefs the human additions and corruptions that have gathered around it. This, faith cannot do: faith can only embrace, not discriminate, and, for want of discrimination, may soon degenerate and turn to monstrous superstition, as in all historical dispensations of religion it has done. Faith is no critic. In its own nature and proper function, it chooses nothing and refuses nothing. Impartial and impolitic, it befriends itself with every enormity of the human mind. Nothing is too absurd for it, — nothing too hateful or too cruel. The wildest idolatries, the most brutal fetichism, the direst self-torture, the most ferocious persecution, Phœnician lust-offerings, Aztec blood-offerings, Egyptian magic, Hindu suttees and gymnosophism, Christian inquisitions and immolations, demonology and witchcraft, — these things are as natural to faith as belief in the Holy Ghost, and, but for the veto of educated reason, as near to it now and here as in any land or time. It lies in all of us so to believe and so to act: thanks to our rationalism, we think and act otherwise.

I say, then, that the cause of reason is the cause of faith, because the corrective of faith. Each is the other's complement. Reason requires the nutriment and impulse furnished by faith. Faith requires the discreet elaboration of reason. The one has the substance; the other, the form. Reason alone would give us a world without a God, bodies without spirits, earth without heaven, a day without a morrow, a way without a goal. Faith alone would give us a pantheon of questionable divinities, a pandemonium of unquestionable fiends, an overshadowing theocracy for civil rule, a dispensation of dark ages without end.

From the genius of the gospel, no less than the constitution of the human mind, I infer the right of reason in religion. Christianity is professedly a revelation of reason. The first systematic statement of it by a competent witness affirms this, and justifies rationalism in one word. And that word is the Word, — in the original tongue a synonyme for Reason. "In the beginning was the Word (or Reason), and God was the Word," and in Christ was the Word "made flesh." The eternal Reason revealed in the human; not different from the human in kind, for it comes to "his own," and is "the light that lighteth all who come into the world." St. Paul, though disclaiming, as "carnal wisdom" and "the wisdom of this world," the philosophic prepossessions of his time, is himself the subtlest of reasoners, — an inveterate rationalist, never more thoroughly in his element than when arguing the claims of Christianity on psychological grounds, or boldly rationalizing the Old Testament to rebut the scruples of his countrymen. The authorities at Jerusalem — Bishop James and Peter and the rest — stood aghast, and no wonder, at this "terrible child" of their communion; they spoke doubtfully of "our beloved brother Paul" and the "hard things" in his Epistles; they could not quote him without a caution; but who at this day doubts that Paul's idea was nearer the mind of Christ than the views of his Judaizing critics? Providence adopted it; it carried the age; Jewish Christianity decreased, Liberal Christianity increased, — and will increase.

The history of a religion, like that of a nation or an individual, is its verdict, the test of its proper quality, a revelation of its innermost idea, a public confession of the meaning which lay in its germ and constitution. Try Christianity by this test; compare it with the elder religions, or its younger sister, Islam. What is the characteristic fruit of Christian history? One fruit is humanity; another, equally generic, is rationalism. Not intellectual life as such, for Hinduism has developed that, and developed it more abundantly; but that form of intellectual life in which reason is the dominant element, — the application of reason to nature and society, to art and literature and life. For proofs of this assertion we have but to look around us. This Protestant Christendom, with its schools and its arts, its traffic and its liberties, comprising whatever is progressive and humane in the present, and containing —

who can doubt it? — the future of humanity, the moral destinies of this planet, — this embodied, practical, beneficent rationalism I claim as the genuine fruit of the gospel, — humanity's late but how significant answer to the condescending Word for whose communication in old Judæa the heavens were opened.

The prominent feature of Christian civilization is science, that new estate of the social realm which never before, since the world began, attained the consequence and moment it now has in the scale of the forces that govern society. Science is sometimes found in opposition to the Church, which accordingly rages against it, — the old with bull and ban, the new with the cry of "infidelity," and both with the same result. As I view it, the denial of God's light and truth in human reason implies a far deeper infidelity than any questioning of the truth of a letter.

It is a losing contest which theology wages against reason and fact. In striking at science, the Church but dashes her ineffectual arm against the thick bosses of the Almighty's shield. For what is science? It is simply the truth of things, i.e. the truth of God, and as surely a revelation of God as the gospel, — a revelation to reason of things mundane, as the gospel is a revelation to faith of things supermundane. The two revelations from one God can never really conflict. Whatever of seeming conflict there may be is the fault of the Church, which vainly opposes tradition to demonstration, and confounds the gospel with the Bible, which is only a witness of the gospel. If the demonstrated facts of science shall be found to contradict the text, the text must give way, and no harm is done to religion except in the fond conceit which identifies the cause of Christianity with the infallibility of a letter, and stakes that cause on that infallibility.

Moreover, in contending against science, the church denies and rejects her own. For science, after all, is the offspring of the Church. Born in monkish cells, the foundling of religious houses vowed to Christ and the saints, nursed by cowled friars, cradled among crucifixes and breviaries, with men like Raymond Lully and Roger Bacon and Albert the Great for its sponsors, the child was baptized with the Holy Ghost; and though in her maturity electing another path than that anticipated by her spiritual fathers, though adopting lay methods and associations, she has never belied the divine anointing, nor betrayed her sacred trust. For science, too, is a minister of God, — an evangelist whose mission is to "show us the Father" and regenerate the world. With no conscious God in her perceptions, she yet refreshes and expands the idea of God by new revelations of the heights and deeps and infinite riches of the wondrous All. With no moral sensibility of her own, she yet deepens the sense of obligation in man, and solemnizes human life by showing how most exact is nature's frame in which that life is set, where the severe and geometrizing God suffers no transgression and no defect that is not compensated by its just equivalent, — where every law is self-executing, and the wildest excesses — the meteor's path, the earthquake's brief spasm, the comet's long but measured furlough — are all minutely prescribed and timed. With no human sympathy in those eyes that look creation through, she yet strengthens the bonds of love by a wiser adjustment of human relations, by multiplying means of beneficence and extending opportunities of good. With no charity in her aim, she yet evangelizes the world by closer commerce of man with man, by furnishing wings to missionary zeal, and implements to charity, by dissolving the rocky barriers of prescription, by developing the vast resources of nature for the comfort and relief of the suffering, and the edification of human kind.

Does theology understand, does the Church suspect, what a reign this is which is now establishing its throne among us, and stretching its sceptre alike over priest and people? A veritable kingdom of God, because a kingdom of light and truth. Who hath eyes to see, let him see how old things are passing away, and all things are becoming new. Let the clergy lift up their eyes, and welcome the prophet whom nature vouches, the fellow-laborer who also cometh in the name of the Lord. Let the Church make haste to acknowledge the credentials which bear the seal of sovereign and puissant fact, — the plenipotentiary of Him "who layeth the beams of his chambers in the waters and walketh upon the wings of the wind." And let the Church understand that she must either accommodate herself to the new dispensation, or else go down before it, as the temples of heathendom went down when the waters of Christian baptism prevailed on the earth.

Let there be no strife between theology and science: there need be none. The gospel of Christ and the gospel of science have essentially one mission. The methods differ; the end is the same. "Glory to God in the highest, and on earth peace and good-will toward men," was the mission divinely proclaimed for the one:

to minister to "the glory of God and the relief of man's estate" was the calling which England's great Chancellor, its own high prophet, prescribed for the other.

If the cause of reason is the cause of faith, then it is also the cause of the Church, and then theology may not dispense with its aid in constructing the doctrinal fabrics in which the faith of the Church is to dwell. For want of the counsel and concurrence of reason in time past, theology hath builded her house in vain. Showy and imposing structures they were, which housed the faith of the fathers, the Gothic style of theology,—those groined and carved and turreted systems of divinity,—but without internal coherence, having no sure principle of support in themselves, requiring stays and props from without, and needing constant repair. They resemble the material edifices, their counterparts, the churches of the Middle Age,—that much-vaunted but unsubstantial Gothic architecture, as characterized by Michelet, and by him contrasted with the scientific building of Florentine art. "The Gothic architecture," he says, "made great pretensions; it was ostentatious of calculation and numbers. The sacred number three, the mysterious number seven, were carefully reproduced, either in themselves or their multiples, in every part of these churches. . . . Build by three and by seven, and your church will be solid."—"But why," then, continues he, "this army of buttresses surrounding it, these enormous stays, this everlasting scaffolding, which the mason seems to have forgotten to take away?" The very ornamentation conceals iron clamps which deoxidate continually, and have to be replaced. "A really robust edifice would cover and enclose its own supports, the guaranties of its perpetuity. But the Gothic, which leaves these essential members to chance, is constitutionally sickly, necessitating the maintenance of a population of doctors; for so I call those little hamlets of masons which I see established at the foot of these edifices, — the hereditary repairers of the fragile creation which is mended so constantly, piece by piece, that, after two or three hundred years, not a stone perhaps of the original structure remains."

Brunelleschi, "the sceptic, the denier of Gothic architecture," first Protestant in art, when intrusted with the completion of the cathedral at Florence, proceeded on a different plan. He went scientifically to work: he studied the strength of materials, the principles of form, the proportion of part to part, and so built the Maria del Fiore. "Without carpentry, without prop or buttress, without the succor of any exterior support, the colossal church rose simply, naturally, as a strong man rises in the morning from his bed, without staff or crutch; and with terror the people saw the hardy calculator place upon its head a ponderous marble hat, — the lantern. He laughed at their fears, assuring them that this new weight would only add to its solidity."

And thus, says the historian, "was laid the corner-stone of the new era, — the permanent protest against the halting art of the Middle Age, the first but triumphant essay of a serious structure self-sustained, being based on calculation and on the authority of reason. Art and reason reconciled, that is the new era, the marriage of the beautiful with the true. . . . 'Where will you be buried?' they asked Michel Angelo, who himself had just completed St. Peter's at Rome. 'Where I may for ever contemplate the immortal work of Brunelleschi.'"

What the *Duomo* at Florence, what a really scientific building, is to a crumbling Gothic edifice, such is a rational theology to the rotten systems of the past. As that, in the language just quoted, is the marriage of the beautiful with the true, so this is the marriage of the holy with the true, — the marriage of Faith and Reason.

It will be understood, that in arguing this cause, in contending for the faithful and fearless application of reason to religion, I am advocating a principle, not a particular view or result. I have wished to contribute something to do away the false association of rationalism with unbelief, as if the sole function of reason were to deny, and negation of existing beliefs, its legitimate fruit. The rationalist is not necessarily one who rejects the miraculous element in the gospel history, and denies the exceptionally divine in Christ. For my own part, I believe both, and claim to do so on rationalistic grounds. I claim to have reached these conclusions by no bias of authority or ecclesiastical tradition, but by rational criticism applied to the facts in the case. It may be a limitation in me to believe thus; then it is a limitation of my faculty, and not an intentional limitation of the principle I am advocating. I demand an unlimited application of that principle; and I firmly believe that the full and conscientious and persistent use of reason in religion will restore and confirm much that the partial use has discredited and disturbed. It is not, as I judge, the maturity and strength of reason that repudiates those truths, but its rawness and weakness, — its enslavement to negative experience, and inability to construe the arc of which the seemingly straight line of our experience constitutes so small a segment. That is not a pleasing view of divine operations, or of human things, which supposes the Universe and Providence bound to an everlasting mechanical sequence of events; it is not one which will permanently satisfy human reason. The virtual atheism of such a view no formal acknowledgment of a great First Cause can redeem. Reason demands, and true theism supposes, a present as well as a former God, — a God co-ordinate with and exceeding creation, — a God untrammelled by custom, or what we call law, which is merely a human form of thought, and not an objective reality. This regular sequence of events, which seems so necessary, so absolute to our mundane experience, may be in the infinite consciousness of God a free and incalculable spontaneity. If miracles, as I believe, are not to be eliminated from the canon of historical facts, then science, I doubt not, will come to know them, and reason will rationalize them without impairing their miraculous character.

I am far from maintaining that Christianity must stand or fall with the belief in miracles; but I do maintain that Christian churches, as organized bodies of believers, must stand or fall with the Christian confession, — that is, the confession of Christ as divinely human Master and Head. Men of wit and spirit, earnest and able speakers, outside of that confession, will not want hearers, and may gather congregations around them which shall wait on their stated ministry. But such congregations, so far from being Christian churches, may even come to assume an attitude of open and avowed hostility to Christian doctrine and life. Things exist in this world by distinction one from another. Enlarge as you will the idea and scope of a church, there must be somewhere, whether stated or not in any formal symbol, a line which defines it, and separates those who are in it from those who are without. The scope of the Liberal Church is large; but every thing and everybody cannot be embraced in it. The Christian confession is its boundary-line, within which alone it can do the work which Providence has given it to do. This boundary-line I have all along assumed. The distinction involved in the Christian confession is organic and vital; its abolition would be the dissolution of the ecclesiastical world and the end of Christendom.

One thing more. In pleading the cause of rationalism, I am supposing the use of reason in religion to be a conscientious use, and the critical investigation to be conducted in a spirit of Christian reverence and love. The most searching investigation, actuated by ill-will to the Christian cause, is no more secure of the truth than blind acquiescence or blind infidelity. A negative and destructive spirit will find many things doubtful and many things false which a pious and affirmative spirit, exercising an equal measure of critical acumen, would approve and confirm. Criticism is not all negative; nor does Biblical criticism in Germany, as many suppose, pursue an arbitrary, wilful course, minded only to destroy, and never to rest till the last support be removed from the New Testament, and every vestige of documentary evidence for the truth of the Gospel done away. On the contrary, destructive criticism, not arbitrary but scientific in its method, and generally unbiassed in its motive, has already reached its limit. The work of negation — an honest and necessary work — has been accomplished. Little more, I conceive, remains to be discovered or propounded in that direction. Criticism has done its uttermost with the New Testament. What is now left standing is likely to stand. What the microscopic eye and remorseless knife of Strauss and Baur have spared, may be presumed invulnerable. And what is it that is thus secured to us? Enough in those Epistles of Paul, whose genuineness remains unquestioned, to establish the great facts of the doctrine of Christ and the gospel story. Enough to substantiate, to fair and rational criticism, the crowning fact of the Resurrection. I do not say to demonstrate beyond doubt or cavil, but to make it reasonably certain to reasonable minds. In spite of all cavil and evasive interpretation, this fact must stand, and with it the miraculous gospel, — a divine interpolation of the Spirit in the secular text of history.

Destructive criticism has done its work: henceforth we may expect that the work of criticism will be mainly constructive and restorative. Who can say how much may be accomplished in that line? Already signs of agreement are perceptible among competent critics of different schools. Some approximation has been made to settlement of controverted questions, that is, to certainty in Biblical theology. This agreement among theologians cannot fail to exercise a reconciling influence on Christian sects, and will tend to abolish the boundary-lines which now divide the Christian world. One need not despair of a Catholic Church in that sense in which alone Catholicism is possible or desirable. We do not expect or desire complete uniformity of administration and rite, or even of doctrinal type. There must always be differences of administration, of worship, and of doctrine. Catholicism does not consist in uniformity of articles, but in unity of spirit, — not in a common exposition, but a common confession and mutual good-will. Where the catholic spirit is, there is the Catholic Church. We may hope for so much of that spirit as shall serve to secure a full recognition of the Christian name for all who honestly claim it, and a friendly co-operation of Christians of every type for practical Christian ends.

The time is prophetic of new modifications of the ecclesiastical world and a better life for the Church. In our own land, the unlimited freedom of opinion accorded by law, and encouraged by the absence of a national Church, has ceased to develop new sects, and is drawing the old into nearer communion. It is widely felt that existing lines do not rightly define the parties they divide; theological distinctions are becoming more and more indistinct; the separative tendency has exhausted its force; a unitive tendency has begun. In England, writers in the Established Church are taking the lead in liberal views and critical inquiry. In Germany, criticism, once prevailingly negative, assumes more and more an affirmative tone. In Italy, where many of the best ideas of modern society had their rise, and where commenced the revival of the Unitarian faith, the eldest faith of Christendom, — in Italy the temporal power of the Pope — that public offence of the Christian world — is melting away. A Catholic Church without a hierarchy may become a progressive Church, and meanwhile furnishes the surest guaranty for the unity of Christendom.

Throughout the Christian world the prevailing influences favor liberty; the auspices look toward an era of spiritual life untrammelled by priestly rule and dogmatic conditions, carrying its own authority in its own triumphant and beneficent sway.

A celebrated mystic of the twelfth century * predicted a third age and dispensation of God, corresponding with the third Person in the Trinity. The first age, representing God the Father, was the dispensation of the Law, the age of the Old Testament, — an age of bondage and fear. The second, representing the Son, was the age of the New Testament, — an age of instruction and discipline, a dispensation of doctrine. The third, representing the Holy Ghost, is to be an age of knowledge and spiritual emancipation, a dispensation of liberty and love. The first he characterizes as an age of bondsmen; the second, an age of freedmen; the third, of friends; — the first, an age of old men; the second, of the middle-aged; the third, of children. Six hundred years have rolled by since that Calabrian monk delivered this sublime burden of the Lord: so far

* Abbot Joachim of Floris.

does the vision of holy and loving spirits outstrip the tardy-footed ages charged with the execution of "the pattern in the mount."

Six hundred years! and the Christian world still waits this consummation of its destiny.

I.

CULMINATION OF PERSONALITY IN THE CHRIST OF THE CHURCH.

I.

CULMINATION OF PERSONALITY IN THE CHRIST OF THE CHURCH.

"Die Persönlichkeit der Hebel der Weltgeschichte." — BUNSEN.

IN the various attempts which during the last half-century have been made to construe the veritable image of Jesus * from the ill-digested and often conflicting accounts of the four Evangelists, no result is so conspicuous as the impossibility of any valid and final solution of that problem. The historical and legendary are so confused in these narratives, the genuine sayings of Jesus are often so undistinguishably blended with the comments and interpolations of his reporters, that criticism, incompetent to the work of elimination, can do no more than furnish an approximate and conjectural reconstruction, liable to be set aside by each succeeding critic who brings to the subject a different precon-

* Of these attempts the charming work of Dr. Furness ("Jesus and his Biographers") may be characterized as written in the interest of faith and in a spirit of enthusiastic affirmation; that of Strauss as written in the interest of scepticism; that of Neander, in the interest of conservatism; that of Schleiermacher (posthumous work just edited), in the interest of impartial criticism; that of Renan, of historic speculation; that of Schenkel, of historic probability.

ception, or adjusts his conclusions by a different light. It comes to this at last, that every reader must construct his own Christ from the fourfold record, according to his own impression of the verisimilitudes of the case. And, on the whole, the impression derived immediately from the record by a thoughtful reader, with no theory to support and no case to make out, is quite as likely to be correct as any obtained through a foreign medium.

Were it possible to reproduce, with exactitude beyond dispute, the portrait of the true historical Jesus, the image, I suppose, would be found to differ widely from the Christ of the Church, or the Christ received by the great majority of Christians. Yet there is one point in this personality, in which, it seems to me, all candid inquiry must agree, — one fact which no criticism professing to treat these narratives as in any sense historical can set aside; — this, namely, that Jesus felt himself "sent" and ordained by God in a quite peculiar and exceptional sense, divinely commissioned to establish a heavenly kingdom on the earth; that he looked upon himself as distinguished from other men by virtue of this calling. Whether differing from them, or not, in any metaphysical or ontological sense, he felt himself officially, politically, discriminated from them in this respect.

If any thing in the New Testament is historical, it is this, — that Jesus called himself "the Son of Man." Whatever may be the precise meaning of that phrase, there can be no doubt that he meant to designate by it a distinguishing peculiarity. It is equally certain, that he appropriated to himself the Messianic prophecies of his countrymen; that he assumed to be the Christ, —

not indeed as the Jewish people figured their Messiah at that time, or at any time, — but as he himself interpreted the import of the national hope.

This seems to me beyond legitimate question. It is not more certain that such a being as Jesus existed, than it is that he supposed and represented himself a being apart from other men, in the sense now explained. M. Renan declares, that the consciousness of God in Jesus exceeded that of all other men.* To this we must add, that he was aware of the peculiarity of this consciousness. He nowhere assumes to be an incarnation of God. Such an idea, as M. Renan again very justly remarks, was entirely foreign to the Jewish-mind.† And when, in such sayings as those reported in the Fourth Gospel, "I and the Father are one," "He that hath seen me hath seen the Father," he identifies himself with the one Supreme, he does so in the sense of personation or representation, not of co-entity. To constitute, or at least to establish, the identity contemplated by the Monophysite doctrine, it would not be sufficient that Jesus should even say in so many words (what he never did say), "I am God." It would further be necessary that God should say, speaking by some other voice *of equal authority*, "I am Jesus," — a thing inconceivable and self-contradictory. At the same time, it is probable that the sayings referred to furnished one of the factors in that deification of Jesus by the Church which still prevails in Christian dogma-

* "La plus haute conscience de Dieu qui ait existe au sein de l'humanité, a été celle de Jésus." — *Vie de Jésus.*

† "Une telle idée était profondément étrangère à l'esprit Juif." —*Ib.*

tic. Alexandrian speculation supplied another; and a third may be found in that view of atonement which assumes the necessity of an actual contact of God with man, in order to any complete redemption of human nature.

All the varieties of opinion which have been entertained respecting the person of Christ may be comprehended under these four heads: 1. Christ is mere man, — the old Jewish (Ebionite, Nazaræan) and modern Humanitarian view. 2. Christ is mere God, — the old Docetic, Patripassian, Monophysite, and modern pseudo-orthodox view. 3. Christ is neither God nor man, but a being between both, — the Arian view. 4. Christ is both God and man, — the Catholic and genuine Orthodox view.

I have named these opinions in the order in which they make their appearance in the history of Christian doctrine. This order is by no means an accidental sequence or wilful determination, but represents the natural history of Church Christology, which is not to be conceived as a human invention, but a natural, spontaneous growth.

The prevailing doctrine of the first century concerning Christ was Unitarian. Jewish converts and Hebrew-Jewish ideas had then the ascendency in the Church; and Judaism, as such, was strictly and purely Unitarian. The Jews, at least the unlettered and unspeculative among them, were rigid Monotheists; the idea of division or multiplicity in the Godhead was utterly abhorrent to their conceptions, and outraged all their prejudices. Their God, their Jehovah, was not only one, but an individual, — a great and powerful individual, defined, discrete, and incommunicable; not sole, universal Being, but a single, particular Being, who created the world in the beginning, created it once for all and put it from him; not immanent but transient in creation, and now and for ever apart from his works; different in substance as well as in power and glory. This rigid Monotheism contained an error which gradually undermined it. It necessitated in philosophic minds the conception of an intermediate being between God and his works, which became, as we shall see, a middle term or point of transition between Hebrew Jehovism and Trinitarian theism.

Meanwhile, that class of Jews who for the most part embraced Christianity untinctured by such speculations, received it as fulfilment of their national prophecies. Christ to them was the Beloved in whom God was well pleased, the national Messiah, — Son of God, not in the sense of generation, but in the sense of election and divine favor. God was in heaven, and man on the earth: nothing could bridge the distance between them. The risen Christ was gone to God and would soon return to judge the world, and establish his throne on the earth. This was the earliest doctrine concerning Christ, the Jew-Christian doctrine, the Christology of the apostles. The doctrine was Unitarian; it distinguished broadly between God and Christ; — no hint, as yet, of an Athanasian Trinity. It was the doctrine of the first century. There is no Christian writing, whose date can be proved anterior to the close of that century, which recognizes a different doctrine, unless it be as a heresy to be repudiated. The Book of Revelation, which recent criticism assigns to the year 69, knows nothing of a God-Christ, but speaks of the Lamb as entirely distinct from God, — symbol of the mediatorial office.

But when, with the fall of Jerusalem, the Palestinian Jews lost their influence in the Church, and Gentile tendencies and Gentile conceptions gradually obtained the ascendency, a new phase of the doctrine concerning Christ, diametrically opposed to the foregoing, and representing the contrary extreme, developed itself; a view which, overlooking his Messianic character, denied the proper humanity of Jesus, and affirmed him to be "very God;" God in a human body, — that body his only human attribute. Some* even went the length of denying to that body material consistency: it was no true body, but an apparition; — the visible Christ an apparition with which, through the medium of their deluded senses, God acted on the thoughts and faith of mankind. Others, who allowed the fleshly body, denied the human soul, and all the other attributes of humanity. They knew no difference between Christ and God: these were only different names for one and the same person.

This view, known as Patripassian in relation to Christ, as Monarchian in relation to God, prevailed especially in the Western portion of the Church. Both West and East meanwhile united in the common confession of three sanctities, — Father, Son, and Holy Spirit. But in the West the Monarchian view of the divine nature regarded these three, not as separate persons, but only as different names for the one God.

---

* The Docetæ.

In the East, on the other hand, theological speculation inclined to hypostatize Son and Spirit, while at the same time it recognized a human nature in the Christ.

And now comes in that most important element in ecclesiastical Christology, as elaborated by eastern theologians, the idea of the *Logos*, — a kind of secondary Deity, — whose origin requires a word of explanation.

We observe in the animal kingdom a regular gradation of being, in descending series from man through the simiæ and other mammals and vertebrates; through serpents, mollusks, medusæ, down to the rhizopod, or whatever may be the lowest term and extreme limit of animal nature. Analogy suggests a similar gradation in the spiritual world, — an ascending series reaching up from man to God. But the supposition of such a series is contradicted by the very idea of an Infinite Being. We may push our scale up through the heavenly principalities, from angel to archangel, from cherub to seraph; but the highest finite is still a creature, — it had a beginning, an origin in time; between it and the uncreated there is still a gulf, which creation (as the Jews understood creation, and as most Christians understand it) cannot bridge. So long as the Infinite is conceived as a separate Being, the topmost round of your ascending scale, the highest finite is logically no nearer the Infinite than the lowest.

To bridge this gulf, to bring the Godhead into such connection and communication with the worlds, — especially the human world, — as religion craved, Jewish philosophy had recourse to the supposition of an intermediate agent; a power intervening between God and creature, and connecting the two, — Wisdom, or the Word (*Logos*). This conception, not yet hypostatized, is shown to have originated in the Jewish mind * before the Christian era, and independent of Platonism, to which it has usually been referred.

Christian theology applied this conception to the Messiah, using the term "Son" as convertible with "Word." The Christ was the incarnate "Word." But now, though the reason of this conception seemed to imply the eternity of the Word, a question arose: Was the Son, supposed to be incarnate in Jesus, created or uncreated? The Arian controversy concerned precisely this point. Arius, considering the matter from the ground of the understanding, maintained that the Son was a creature. Otherwise, he said, you must either suppose two original divine essences (ditheism), or else, if you substitute "generation" for "creation," you suppose with the Gnostics a partition of the divine essence. Accordingly, the Christ of the Arian view is neither God nor man, but a being intermediate between the two. And this is the third of the four hypotheses concerning the nature of Christ.

But Arianism leaves the chasm unatoned. If the Son is a creature, then (it was urged) there is still the infinite distance between God and man. But, in order that man may be redeemed, Divinity must be in immediate contact with humanity. God and man must unite in one person. To meet this difficulty, the Orthodox claimed that the Son was not created, but generated, and

* See an excellent dissertation on this subject by Michel Nicolas: "Des Doctrines Religieuses des Juifs."

that from all eternity. Consequently, the Son is of the substance of the Father (*homousion*), and there never was a time when the Son was not. Both parties held that the Logos was incarnate in Jesus. According to one, it was the incarnation of a creature, leaving a void between God and man. According to the other, it was the incarnation of an uncreated, eternal and divine Power, whereby the void is filled; man being, in Christ, in immediate contact with God.*

Arian Christology triumphed for a time; but Athanasius, the bulwark of philosophic Christianity, the hope of the Church, was inflexible. His single indomitable will decided the destinies of Christian theosophy. The Homousian doctrine, already approved by the Council of Nicæa in 325, was re-affirmed and applied to the Spirit as well as the Son at the second œcumenical Council, assembled at Constantinople in 381, when the Trinitarian creed, as we now have it, was adopted and established.

Another question remained to be considered, and another half-century was spent in discussing it. Granting the complete Deity of the Son or Divine Word, how

---

* The fallacy of this conclusion is very transparent. Allowing that God is exceptionally present, in the coarse, materialistic sense supposed, with the man Jesus; still, Jesus was an individual, and being thus excepted, and abnormally possessed, there is a gulf between him and other individuals, which the Trinitarian theory leaves unfilled, and which only the dogma of Transubstantiation, affirming the actual, material participation of Christ (that is, in the Trinitarian view, of God) by believers in the Eucharist, can bridge. Transubstantiation is the logical complement of that materialistic view of atonement by substantial contact of God, conceived as individual, with a certain human individual.

is that Deity united to humanity in Jesus Christ? How do God and man in Christ consist together? On this point, two parties were opposed to each other in mutual mad strife. One party would merge the human in the divine, and know no Christ but unmixed God. The other demanded the human nature undivided and unimpaired. The controversy was, in some sort and in some of its stages, a feud between the intelligent, refined, and conscientious ecclesiastics on one side, and the ignorant, rude mob, led on by the turbulent and unprincipled Cyril, bishop of Alexandria, on the other. Thoughtful men, like Nestorius, while admitting the deity of Christ in the sense of the creed of Nicæa, stumbled at such conceptions as that expressed by the phrase "Mother of God," applied to Mary. They protested that "a child of two years old" was no God. But the mob of ecclesiastics rejoiced in such views, and, headed by Cyril, who brought a band of ruffians to the Council of Ephesus for that purpose, with intimidation and intrigue enforced their adoption by that Council, A.D. 431, together with the doctrine of the one undivided person of Christ.

But wisdom and order finally prevailed. The attempt to force on the reluctant Church the Monophysite doctrine — the doctrine of one nature in Christ, and that nature the divine — was foiled at every turn; and, at last, the Council of Chalcedon, in 451, decided that two natures, a human and divine, subsist together in Christ, without conflict or confusion, each doing its own work, each preserving its own property, and both combining in one appearance and one effect. In vain the Monophysite party struggled a century longer, under differen pretexts, with various devices, to overthrow the decision of this Council: it continued to be the Orthodox faith. As such it was re-affirmed by another Council at Constantinople (fifth œcumenical, 553), a century later; and when, in the seventh century, the question came up in another form, — the question of one or two wills in Christ, — a sixth Council (sixth œcumenical, Constantinople, 680) decided, in perfect agreement with that of Chalcedon, that two wills were united in Christ, without schism and without confusion, — "the human invariably subject to the divine."

That final decision of the Council of Chalcedon has never been set aside, it remains to this day the Orthodox doctrine. Very different, indeed, from the would-be Orthodoxy which overlooks or postpones the humanity of Christ. The true significance of that decision is not generally understood. It is the most comprehensive view that has ever been propounded respecting the person of Jesus. While it acknowledges the divine origin and authority of the Christian dispensation, and gives assurance that this mighty agent in the education of the human race is no accident or human invention, — not born, as the Scripture says, "of the will of the flesh, or the will of man, but of God;" that God himself conducts the education of man, and is spiritually, as well as providentially, immanent in this human world, — it also declares, that man is the medium, as well as the object, of this dispensation, — of this system of divine education; that the highest revelation and expression of the Godhead is man; that human nature, in its purity and truth, embodies the divine. The creed of Nicæa, the first authoritative step in the formation of the doctrine concerning Christ, declares that the Word made flesh in Jesus is of one substance with the Father. This statement is one which concerns human nature as well as the divine. If, on the one hand, it represents God as self-communicating, as passing out of self in action and revelation, contrary to the Hebrew idea which made God an isolated, incommunicable individuality; on the other hand, it represents man as partaker of the divine nature, as the vehicle and manifestation of Godhead. For the Son of Man is humanity's type; "the Lord from heaven" is human nature in its heavenly image. "Christ," said Irenæus, "became what we are, that we might become what he is." We cannot be too thankful, that the Athanasian view in this Council prevailed against the Arian, which recognizes no divinity in man.

The same view was more fully developed and more adequately expressed, although unconsciously perhaps to those who framed them, in the formulas of the Council of Chalcedon; the substance of which is, that God and man are one in Christ, and the deep interior sense of which is, that God and man are one, — that human nature is in real communion with the divine. What was true of Christ historically is potentially true of all men. There is nothing between God and man but man's self-alienation through waywardness and sin. The most liberal and radical of modern theologians, the late Dr. Baur of Tübingen, does but re-affirm the decisions of the Councils and the Orthodoxy of the Church, when he declares that "the most essential and distinctive doctrine of Christianity is, that God became man in Christ;" and when he states, as the sense of the dogma of the Trinity, that "God and man are one in the self-consciousness of the Spirit."

It must not, however, be supposed, that this interpretation of the doctrine of Chalcedon was popularly received and understood, or even that the doctrine itself of the two natures in Christ, though established by Council, was the commonly received view, and the one which practically prevailed in the middle age. The interior sense of that decision was far in advance of the consciousness of the Church, in that and subsequent times. The humanity of Christ was sunk in oblivion; the two natures were merged in one, — that one the superhuman and divine. Christ was God, and only God, in the popular conception of that and the following ages of the Church. There was no wilfulness in this, and no mishap. There were good and weighty reasons for it in the nature of man and the circumstances of the time. We may call it a corruption of Christian doctrine: only let us understand that this corruption was not designed, but providential, — a providential phase of Christian development, a necessary stage in the history of religion; necessary in the counsels of the Spirit, necessary in human experience. No doubt it satisfied a real want of the soul. Whether it was that the Christian religion obtained thereby an authority and sanction, which its moral superiority alone would not have secured to it; or whether the human mind required and still requires in the God of its worship a more definite and appreciable object than it finds in the proposition, "God is spirit," — an historical and human God, — whatever the occasion and cause, no doubt the general prevalence of this conception of Christ as God is justified by the moral and spiritual needs of mankind. I must suppose a providential order, a divine method and reason, in it. But observe, that, when Christ is declared to be God, that declaration is, properly considered, a definition, not of Christ, but of God. The rule is to define the less known by means of the more known. Of Christ we have some definite knowledge from the record of the New Testament. Of God we know nothing except by hypothesis or faith, and can apprehend nothing except by illustration. The unknown God may be made more intelligible by identifying him with the known historical character of the evangelical record; but the known historical character is made no clearer by identifying him with the unknown God. If a chemist should define electricity by saying, "It is the principle of life in the world of spirits," he would give me no clearer idea of electricity, whatever he might of the life-principle of the spirit-world. To say that Christ is God may bring God nearer to my apprehension: but, as to Christ, this saying but puts him further from me; and, instead of a genuine human life, a life of struggle and of suffering, — the life of one "who was tempted in all points as we are,"— it gives us a spectral illusion, at best a dramatic exhibition, a part enacted by Omnipotence in the scenes of time.

In point of fact, I suppose no man, whatever creed he may adopt, really believes, or can believe, that Christ is God in the sense which is sometimes claimed, — which was claimed by the old Monophysites, — in the sense that the Jesus who was born in Bethlehem, and died on Calvary, was identical with the Infinite Father, and co-ordinate with absolute Being. It is hardly possible to state the doctrine so as not to leave some loop-hole of escape from such a paradox. When the "Athanasian Creed," the highest Trinitarian standard, affirms the Father unbegotten and the Son begotten, it affirms an infinite difference between them.

The question concerning the nature of Christ was the first opened, and will probably be the last closed in Christian dogmatics. Scarcely can two individuals be found who think precisely alike in this matter; and yet all who rightly claim the name of Christian are agreed in this, that there is a divine and also a human element in the gospel and life of Christ. In what manner and proportion these elements unite, who can ascertain with perfect assurance for himself?—who will undertake to determine for others? Councils and creeds may decide the question for ecclesiastical use; but no council can determine and no creed can state it with such authority and such precision as to satisfy all the demands of the understanding and the heart. It is a question of philosophy, not of religion, and one whose theoretical solution is not essential to spiritual growth. The heart that seeks will find a practical solution of it suited to its own need; but all will not find the same. Some are born to one way of thinking, some to another. Some prefer to contemplate the divine in Christianity; some, the human. Some require a human God for their Saviour, and some require a mortal example for their standard and guide in action and suffering.

To me it seems, that the truest form of Christian faith unites both elements, the divine and the human; and that none can know the full power of the gospel, and experience all its height and depth and breadth, where either is wanting.

I. We want the divine; we want to see in Christianity the power of God and the wisdom of God made manifest for the moral welfare of man; we want to see the Spirit of God entering into human nature to revive and redeem it. We want a teacher conscious of God's inpresence, claiming attention as a voice out of the heavens. We want a doctrine which shall announce itself with divine authority; not a system of moral philosophy, but the word and kingdom of God. Without this stamp of divine legitimacy, without the witness and signature of the Eternal, Christianity would want that which alone gives it weight with the mass of mankind, and the place it now holds in human things. This it is which constitutes the specific difference between philosophy and religion; between the abstractions of the intellect addressed to the intellect, and truth incarnate, addressing heart and will.

II. We need in Christianity the human also. We need the Son of Man; we need the human example as model and motive. We need, for our Saviour, a nature to which no human experience is strange, — a nature that images but completes our own. If I saw in Jesus only God assuming human nature, enacting a human part for the inculcation of moral truth, I should see an illustration of the fair and good, but without flesh and bones; a hollow apparition. I need no gospel to show me that God is without sin, that God can act wisely, that God can bless. What I want to know is, that man can resist; that man can endure; that man can be holy, and live a sinless life on the earth. This is the lesson of the life of Jesus, and this its chief value for us. The gospel is given as a revelation of God, but is given also as a revelation of man; as a type of human nature, a pledge of human destiny; as encouragement to human frailty, as incentive to action; a call from the Son of Man to the sons of men, — a call to glory and immortality; a pledge of divine communications according to the measure of faith; a witness to all generations that the communications of Godhead, and the wonder-working power of the Spirit, are always equal to man's receptivity, and that the measure of man's receptivity is his obedience.

II.

LIMITATION OF PERSONALITY IN THE CHRIST OF REASON.

II.

LIMITATION OF PERSONALITY IN THE CHRIST OF REASON.

"Then shall also the Son himself be subject unto him that put all things under him, that God may be all in all." — St. Paul.

It is the tendency of intellectual progress to displace personalities with ideas and laws. This is strikingly manifest in the change which the progress of science effects in man's conception of material nature. The savage sees in nature an aggregation of innumerable personalities. Mountain, lake, and forest are alive with conscious, invisible agents. Earth and sky are peopled with friendly or malignant beings; every natural process is the voluntary act of some good or evil spirit, designed for the benefit or injury of human kind.

The early religions incorporated this view of nature in their systems of divinity and the objects of their worship. They adored every natural agency, almost every natural object, as embodying or (in the case of Fetichism) as *being* a divine person. Every tree and every river had its god; the ocean swarmed with divinities; the very winds were sacred personages, — all natural agents conscious individuals, objects of religious worship. Not only the Greek and Roman polytheisms, with whose fanciful impersonations we are more familiar, but most of the religions of antiquity, like most Gentile religions of our own time, personified and deified natural objects and agencies. The devout Egyptian, beset before and behind with his copious mythology, could scarcely steer his daily course amid the sanctities which environed him, without profaning some god by unritual contact and secular use. The Persian derived from his two supreme Principles of Good and Evil an infinity of good and evil spirits. The Hebrew, even, believer as he was, by calling and profession, in one only God, adopted from his neighbors, as objects of faith, if not of worship, a mythology of angels, good and bad, which formed no part of the law of Moses, but which a later superstition engrafted on the earlier creed.

The progress of science dispels these illusions, replaces the mythological view of nature with the scientific, puts natural forces for voluntary agents, dethrones the old divinities, disenchants the landscape, unpeoples earth and flood, and gives us a code of rational laws instead of a hierarchy of gods. The first effect of this change from mythology to science is to rob nature of half her charms. It seems to take from the landscape its best interest, — the interest of personality. The world, as interpreted by science, seems cold and desolate and dead, compared with the populous and teeming nature of old poetic tradition, — the world of sylphs and dryads and nereids and gnomes, — a world in which the whispers of the poplar and the pine could seem intelligent and articulate voices; the sparkle of the wave, half seen through the bushes, the smile of some inhabiting spirit, — a world where the deepest solitude promised the richest communion; not internal, spiritual, but visible, audible communion with angel or sprite. The most Christian of the poets of this century, smitten with the recollection of those old beliefs, now become pleasant fables merely, could exclaim in a moment of impatient protest against the sordid utilities of modern life, —

> "Great God! I'd rather be
> A pagan suckled in a creed outworn,
> So might I, standing on this pleasant lea,
> Have glimpses that would make me less forlorn, —
> Have sight of Proteus coming from the sea,
> Or hear old Triton blow his wreathèd horn."

But a better experience succeeds. It is true, the charm of the old world, born of mystery and ignorance, vanishes with the dawn of science; but a new interest, born of light and knowledge, springs in its place. Pleasant was the old belief in personal powers pervading nature with conscious effort, — spirits of earth and air: but a nobler satisfaction attends the revelations of that science which presents the authentic marvels of creation, and enlarges indefinitely the sphere of our perception; which rolls back the curtains of time and space, and discloses a universe immeasurably wider, grander, richer than the wildest imaginings of the men of old, — revealing, in the boundless empyrean, worlds so remote that all the ages of human history would not suffice for the swift-footed light to accomplish the distance between them and us; which finds past eternities chronicled in the earth's crust, — foregone creations pressed, like a botanist's herbal, between the leaves of the rocks; which encounters microscopic nations in a handful of dust, and sees continents reclaimed by successive generations of insect architects, converting sea into dry land; which discovers, in all the realms of organism and in all the processes of chemic and mechanic nature, such marks of pervading mind, such vestiges of all-present Deity, as abundantly compensate the absence of the fauns and dryads of Greek superstition, or the elfs and gnomes of the Gothic creed. The poet whom I have quoted is glad, in a happier mood, to acknowledge this holier Presence which replaces to the modern, instructed, thoughtful observer the trivial beings of the old mythology, —

> "A presence far more deeply interfused,
> Whose dwelling is the light of setting suns,
> And the round ocean and the living air,
> And the blue sky, and in the mind of man, —
> A motion and a spirit that impels
> All thinking things, all objects of all thought,
> And rolls through all things."

What science has done for nature, Christianity, when first promulgated, did for religion: it discharged the mind of its former reverences, while, at the same time, it instilled a far profounder reverence for new and sublimer ideas in the soul. The preaching of the gospel scared the old sanctities from all their haunts, as the cockcrow scares the spirits of the night. It shook the gods, like withered leaves, from all the branches of mortal life; but new-hallowed the tree by deriving its sap direct from the one Supreme, and grafting on its stock the divine humanity from which, as a branch abiding in the vine, every faithful soul imbibes its portion of divine nature. It expelled from the field of faith and worship all lesser personalities, and claimed the whole ground for the one eternal Person above all and through all and in all. The birth of Christ emptied the pantheon, and disenchanted the landscape.

> "From haunted spring and dale,
> Edged with poplar pale,
> The parting genius is with sighing sent."

And piety resented the desecration. Nothing in primitive Christianity more shocked the Roman world than its want of divinities. It was not enough that Christians believed in One above all: intelligent Gentiles did the same. "We know," says Plutarch, "that, among the great company of gods which are generally believed, there is but one who is eternal and immutable: all the rest, having been born in time, shall end in death." But then the Gentiles *did* believe in those inferior divinities: the Christians did not, and were therefore accounted atheists by their fellow-citizens. In the persecution of the Christians instituted by the Emperor Diocletian, when the church at Nicomedia was destroyed by the imperial commissioners, the people ransacked the sacred precincts in vain for shrines and statues, representing Christian divinities, on which to wreak their spite. No statue, no idol, found they; no sacred thing which they could insult; nothing but a copy of the Scriptures, — the Church Bible, — which they brought out, and publicly burned in the market-place. The fact is symbolic: it illustrates the grand distinction between the Christian religion and most of the religions of antiquity. No idol but a book. Above all personalities, the Sacred Word; the best thoughts of the best minds; their holiest and deepest, purged of all personal infirmities and limitations; the purest utterance of the Spirit.

Christianity, we know, did not keep in this its first estate. The idols it expelled returned to confuse and corrupt the Church. Canonized saints succeeded to the seats of heroes and demigods; a Christian pantheon replaced the gentile; a new mythology filled its niches and shrines with a new code of sacred personalities, superior indeed to the old in its moral scope, but, like that, entangling devotion with secondary objects, and interposing inferior sanctities between the soul and the All-holy.

One principal effect, as it was one principal aim, of the Protestant reform, has been to purify Christian worship; to recall devotion from the adoration of all lesser names, and fix it on the true and only God. And if some who profess the Christian faith have gone further in this reform than others; if, not content with repudiating the worship of the Virgin and the saints, they also deny to the person of Christ the supreme homage which belongs to the Supreme God, they have been, whether right or wrong, impelled to this result by precisely the same feeling which actuated the early reformers in their renunciation of saint-worship and Mary-worship, — the desire to come into primary and direct relation and communion with the Father of spirits, and the consciousness that the fact of creation, as well as the calling in Christ, entitles and invites to such communion.

Another cause conducing to the same result is the preference given by this class of minds to the ethical above the dogmatic in religion. What they value most in Christianity is its clear revelation of moral truth; its sharp and emphatic enunciation of the law of love; and the aid it furnishes to purity of heart, and righteousness of life. In this consists, as they believe, the transcendent merit of the gospel, — that it tends above all other religions to this result. Nothing is so near to God, or brings man so to near him, as this. Every other approach, except it in some way ministers to this, is delusion. Every attempt to draw near to him by ecstasy or passion is a vain imagination; at best, a temporary spasm. There is no true union with God but loving and loyal obedience. And when religion is divorced from practical goodness; when this most Christian element is out of it; when the doctrinal interest or the ecclesiastical interest, or even the devotional interest, supersedes the moral,—it loses its practical significance; — Christianity, its distinctive value as a practical mediator between the human and divine. This is what believers of the class I am considering find and prize in the gospel of Christ. To them it is an ethical rather than a sacramental or dogmatic code, — a dispensation of grace and truth, and not an ecclesiastical rule.

It follows, that, in their conception, the person of Christ has not the same aspect and meaning which it has in most ecclesiastic and dogmatic systems. The denial of supreme worship implies the denial of deity to Jesus in the would-be orthodox and monophysite sense, and the limitation of that revered personality within the bounds of historic fact. Viewed historically, Christ to them is a sacred memory, the model man in whom was the fulness of the Godhead; who illustrated, as no other has done, the divine humanity which he affirmed; who alone could say from the fulness of his moral consciousness, "I and the Father are one;" and who therefore remains to all ages a standing witness of the height to which human nature has attained; the Providential type of spiritual sonship, of the adoption of the human into the divine. Viewed in the present, Christ to them is a holy aim; the ideal Head toward which the Church, or human society, is to grow, "till we all come unto a perfect man, unto the measure of the stature of the fulness of Christ," — the ideal Vine in which the body of believers is rooted and grafted, and by union with whose idea they are made fruitful of good: they abiding in his word and love, his word and love abiding in them. This is what Christ is to minds of this class; a method, a way, the approach to God; not a vicarious sanctity, an interposed secondary person, intercepting and superseding the Supreme.

To me there has always seemed, in the views and language of Christians claiming to be orthodox on this subject, a baleful and hopeless confusion. Their Christology and their common sense — the dogmatic and historical conscience — conflict. They would have their Christ to be "very God," and worship him as such, and still retain the mediatorial idea, and make the Christ serve in that capacity also. But the two uses are incompatible. In the region of dogmatic we may speak of two natures in one person, and invent philosophic formulas for that conception; we may say that Christ is "God-man," and this may be the truest word concerning him, the truest definition of the Christ ideally considered. But practical religion, and especially private devotion, craves more precise conceptions. If God is one, and the human individual is one, they cannot both be the same one, though both may unite in one appearance (*πρόσωπον*, person); that is, the visible, human individual may personate or represent the invisible God. But the appearance is but a transient, earthly phenomenon, though embodying an eternal idea; and if we are logically honest, and in the spirit of that honesty analyze this conception of the God-man, we shall see that the phrase denotes an idea, and a personal appearance in the scenes of time embodying that idea; a divine demonstration, not the individual through whom and in whom that demonstration was made. The Christ of the Gospel is that demonstration, — God in man. The image which Jesus has stamped of himself on the Church and the world stands for that. But when from the Christ of the Church we turn to the actual Jesus, as we figure him; when we think of him as a presently existing individual, we shall see that this individual must be one of three things: 1. The Supreme God; 2. Neither God nor man, but an intermediate being; or, 3. Pure man.

1. If we say that Christ is Supreme God, we not only deny a presently existing Jesus distinct from God, but we virtually deny that any such individual ever existed (unless we suppose him annihilated at death). We make the Christ of the Gospel history a mere apparition, that history an illusion, — a phantasmagoria with no human reality subtending it. They who hold this opinion have lost their Christ; not in the sense contemplated by Paul as the consummation of the Christian

ages, when Christ is to deliver up the kingdom to the Father; but in the sense that there is and was no Christ other than the Father. Instead of two they have only one; it is either Christ that they have lost, or else it is God. It follows further from this view, that all praying to God in the name of Christ is glaring contradiction, or an impious mockery of devotion; addressing Christ, and using him as a third person at the same time. There should be no confusion in prayer. Devotion requires for the being addressed a simple, however imperfect and inadequate, conception. Dogmatically, we may speak of two natures in one, or say that the Godhead is contained in two persons, or in three; but, practically, we cannot address one person as two, or as three, without confusion of mind; and we cannot address two persons, or three, as co-equal, without polytheism.

2. If we say, in accordance with the Arian view, that the Christ is neither God nor man, but a being distinct from both, we remove him so far from our sympathies, and all our associations and habits of thought; we make him so unreal, so chimerical, so abnormal a being, that we know not how to adjust ourselves with one whom we can neither adore as God nor sympathize with as man, and so must needs lose the best effect of his idea.

3. If, finally, we say that Jesus, as presently existing, is pure man, a glorified human spirit, we have a precise idea in our minds, and a definite object of contemplation; a being with whom the consciousness of Christians may find itself in true relations, but still a finite being, and therefore not one who can fully satisfy the craving soul, or take the supreme place in our devo-

tions; and though, theoretically, there would seem to be no reason why prayer should not be addressed to Christ, and though we readily conceive that a Christian soul may be moved so to pray, yet to one who rationally ponders the matter, it will probably occur, that the feeling which prompts one man to offer prayer to a glorified Jesus may prompt another to pray to a glorified St. Paul or St. Augustine; that the principle which justifies the one will justify the other, will cover the broad *hagiolatry* of the Church of Rome. Moreover, it might seem that Christ himself has forbidden prayer to himself, in those words of his: "In that day ye shall ask nothing of me." And when, above all, we recollect, and lay it to heart, that the one chief aim of the gospel is to reconcile and unite to God, — to bring the soul into conscious relation and immediate contact with the Father; then all dwelling in inferior sanctities, all pre-occupation of mind and heart with lesser names, will be seen to be a traversing of that intent, and contrary to the doctrine of Christ. If "the Son can do nothing of himself but what he seeth the Father do;" if the Son can give nothing but what he receives, — then why not go to the Father at once? why stop short of the infinite fulness? Why kneel at the pool, when through the pool the everlasting prime Fountain invites every soul to full participation of the underived, supernal grace?

The mystic words of St. Paul, prefixed to this chapter, seem to anticipate the view, here presented, of the personality of Christ. The language is obscure, its import somewhat uncertain. Criticism is not authorized to pronounce definitively concerning it. But I can suppose, that the rapt apostle, discoursing of the "resurrection" and immortality, and rising, in his argument on this sublime theme, to the height of prophetic vision, foresaw the approaching deification of the Son of Man; divined its reason and necessity in the counsels of God and the wants of the Church; and so announced, that Christ "must reign till he hath put all things under his feet." But, casting his inspired glance along the line of the Christian ages, he foresaw that this deification would be temporary, because no created or generated being can hold for ever the place of the Supreme, by whose will alone he can hold it at all; and so predicted "the end, when Christ shall deliver up the kingdom to God, even the Father," and when the Son himself should "be subject unto Him that put all things under him, that God may be all in all."

Assuming this to be the true interpretation, the first part of this saying has been signally verified. Its verification has been the chief topic of the doctrinal history of the Church. Christ did not reign as God when Paul wrote; he did so reign in the ages which followed. And we can see, in the retrospection of those ages, how needful it was, for the triumph and perfect dominion of the gospel, that Christ should be the God of the nations that renounced for his sake the gods of their inheritance, and deserted their country's altars. We can see that the abstract God of our theology — the God who is absolute being — would not suffice for the peoples just emerging from the darkness of polytheism, and used to succinct and concrete divinities. They needed a precise, historical God; one to lay hold of with their conceptions, one whose portrait could be painted in mortal colors, whose actuality was vouched by mortal witnesses; a God of whom you could tell anecdotes, and show the birthplace and earthly abode; a God whose being was not an inference, or fact of revelation, but a fact of history, a well-attested human experience. Such a God the Church supplied in the Son of Mary, as Christian tradition presented him; the divine mystery, "manifest in the flesh, justified in the spirit, seen of angels, preached unto the Gentiles, believed on earth, received up into glory;" the being who was cradled in prodigy, and moved in an element of perpetual marvel; whose manger angels heralded, whose sepulchre angels unsealed; whose birth into this world was heavenly condescension, whose going out of it was heavenly triumph. This august being the grateful adoration of the Church, and the will of the Father, lifted into Godhead, — the worthiest figure that had ever occupied that place. And there he reigned from age to age, and put all things under him. All the gods of the nations to whom his word came he put under his feet, — Olympian Jove, and his shining progeny, Phœbus Apollo, great Diana of the Ephesians, and her Tyrian counterpart, "Mooned Ashtaroth," "Peor and Baalim," and the stormy spirits of the Norse Walhalla. The devils quailed before his sovereignty. Satan as lightning fell from heaven, whole mythologies withered away, the forest and the sea and the lonely mountain-top gave up their divinities, Death and Hell were cast into the burning lake, the old heavens and the former earth passed away, and the new creation acknowledged with divine honors its author and Lord.

So truly and exceedingly has that saying of Paul hitherto been fulfilled.

As to what remains, — the predicted end when Christ shall deliver up the kingdom to the Father, and the Son himself be put under, — it is easy to speculate; and some may think to find the fulfilment of that prophecy in the blank denials and repudiations of a shallow iconoclasm. But fulfilment comes not by way of denial: it comes by complete development. It is easy to speculate and easy to deny; it requires little wit to spurn and reject an old belief which we cannot rationalize: but only time and the ever-progressive consciousness of Christendom can unfold, and only the fully unfolded fact can rightly interpret the folded truth of the prophet's word.

Meanwhile, this truth remains, and may serve as our guide in these inquiries, — that the function of the person is historical, and therefore transient. In the sphere of spiritual contemplation, no personality abides but the ever-becoming personality of God, conceived by faith, and born of faith, in the individual soul. Infinite and underived being alone can satisfy the freely inquiring, freely aspiring. Only that which bounds the uttermost thought, and tops the boldest imagination, can fulfil to reason and faith the idea of God. Whatever derived and secondary power by divine permission may hold that place is a temporary vicegerent, occupying a borrowed throne, and exercising a delegated sway, which he must finally deliver up to God, "even the Father." — "For when," says the brave apostle, "he saith, 'all things are put under,' it is manifest that He is excepted which did put all things under."

III.

MIRACLES.

III.

MIRACLES.

"Mais il faut remarquer que ces mots, de 'sur humain' et de 'surnaturel,' empruntés à notre théologie mesquine, n'avaient pas de sens dans la haute conscience religieuse de Jésus." — RENAN, *Vie de Jésus.*

THE earliest records of our religion — the books of the New Testament — contain accounts of certain transactions to which, as exceeding the ordinary experience of human kind, we give the name of miracles; that is, wonders.

These accounts, in time past, were received without question. But the prevalence, in our day, of the scientific mind, and the progress of critical inquiry, have brought such narratives into disrepute, as conflicting with those laws of nature which science claims to have established. The events in question, it is urged, cannot be explained by known laws: they have no parallel in our experience, and therefore are not to be received as historical.

The repugnance to miracles, so far as the Christian records are concerned, is due, in part, to the unwise use which modern theologians have made of them as proofs of divine authority, and therefore evidences of

Christian truth. The claim of the gospel to be a divine dispensation has been rested upon them. The uncertain evidence of human testimony, reported by uncertain tradition, has been preferred above the witness of the Spirit, which speaks for itself, and is always its own demonstration. This is all wrong, and is felt to be so by Christian thinkers at this day. Miracles are valueless as proofs of divine authority, because, with our views of such matters, it is easier to believe in the thing to be proved than it is to believe in the alleged proof. It is easier to believe that a teacher is divinely inspired, than it is to believe that he exhibits any prodigy which contradicts, or seems to contradict, the possibilities of nature.

In the age which produced the writings of the New Testament, when the laws and limits of nature were less generally understood, when belief was less critical, and marvels of all kinds more readily received, this difficulty, of course, did not exist in the same degree. Yet, even then, a mind that was sceptically inclined, or predetermined against the revelations of the gospel, would not have been likely to be convinced by the demonstration of a power which many in that day were supposed to possess, and a class of works which many, beside Jesus, assumed to perform. In fact, so common in the ancient world was the claim of miracle, that a statute of Moses expressly provides against receiving that as a test of prophetic truth.

Nor does it appear that Jesus aimed to force conviction in that way. Whatever may be the truth concerning the miracles ascribed to him in the New Testament, they are represented as works of love. To suppose them performed for any other purpose is to substitute an inferior motive in the place of that divine beneficence, which gives to these acts, if real, their highest value. No unprejudiced person can read the record, and say that Jesus ever sought to surprise men into belief; that he ever stormed the senses in order to carry the heart. Had such been the motive, the miracles would have been in accordance therewith: they would all have been of that portentous kind which he repudiated when urged to exhibit "a sign from heaven." Had it been his policy to work conviction by appeal to marvels, he would have multiplied marvels where incredulity was greatest. He would have hurled prodigy upon prodigy at the head of unbelief, until it should capitulate, and cry, "Lord, I believe." But such is not the nature of man, and such is not the nature of faith. The senses do not command the soul. No evidence of the senses will convince a man of that which all within him contradicts. The senses, in such cases, are suborned by the will, and refuse to testify truly. Or, if the senses say true, the understanding, like a tricksy advocate, has always an argument at hand to invalidate their testimony, — can always put a contrary interpretation upon it, or find some method of evading the conclusion to which it points. Two persons of different persuasion, and different tendencies of mind, shall witness the same phenomenon without seeing the same thing; they shall state it differently in their reports; they shall draw entirely different conclusions from it.

There is no such connection between supernatural power and spiritual truth, as would make a miracle a sufficient and infallible test of divine revelation. A man may work wonders before my eyes. I know not by what means he operates, nor whence he derives his wonder-working power. But, without other evidence, I shall not therefore consider him a divine person, or divinely commissioned prophet. I shall not receive his doctrine, if it contradicts the voice in my heart.

Let me fetch an illustration from our own time. We have heard of certain phenomena — perhaps have witnessed them — known as "spiritual manifestations;" such as moving of furniture by invisible agency, detonations syllabling words and names, involuntary writing, and the like. These phenomena are affirmed by those who pursue them to be the work of invisible personalities called "spirits." We have here a species of miracle as well attested as such things can be. It is not my purpose to discuss these phenomena. Suppose them real, not empty illusions, and suppose them to be the work of the agency to which they are ascribed: the question is, what evidence do they furnish of prophetic wisdom or spiritual truth? None whatever, that I can discern. I can see no connection between the prodigies in question and the truths of religion, or any other truths. Invisibility is to me no pledge of superior wisdom. The word of a wise and good man, speaking from the fulness of a sound mind and an honest heart, communicating by natural organs, unaccompanied by any extraordinary manifestations, would weigh with me more than the utterances of a hundred mediums, purporting to speak by dictation from the shades. And, if a doctrine were propounded to me, through such a medium, which contradicted my own conviction, I should certainly have no hesitation in rejecting it, though I might not be able to disprove the dictation, and though I should admit the marvels appealed to in defence of that origin. I should say, I know not what latent powers there may be in the air or the human organism, by which such wonders are effected; but the doctrine is all the more questionable which comes to me from such a source. I should say, that these invisibles — if spirits they are who dictate such stuff — were more in need of instruction themselves than able to impart it; and that if they are really, as is sometimes claimed, the great departed who deliver themselves thus, then to die, for them, has not been gain: they have lost the wit which they had in the body, and verify the melancholy saying, that "a living dog is better than a dead lion."

Had Jesus been disposed to act on the faith of men by means of marvels, he yet knew too well what was in man not to know that the senses do not lead, but follow, the convictions of the heart; that faith is not the offspring of miracles, but miracles, of faith. Had he been disposed to enforce belief by signs and wonders, he would have multiplied those wonders where unbelief was greatest. So far from this, an evangelist tells us, with great frankness, that Jesus "did not many mighty works" in his own country, "because of their unbelief." Do you wonder at such incredulity? The wonder is rather that so many believed on him. To one who regarded only the circumstances of the man, what was there to inspire trust? His fellow-citizens saw in him a townsman as lowly born, as poorly circumstanced, as themselves. The people of Judea saw in him a Galilean whose origin seemed a presumption against him. There wanted the prestige of the Pharisee, the learning of the scribe. There was a rumor of wonderful cures; but rumor is so apt to exaggerate! Did he cast out devils? It was by Beelzebub, the prince of devils. Do we wonder that Jesus was so judged by his age? Was there ever an age that would have judged otherwise? Was there ever an age that would have been more ready to receive such a prophet, to see the divine in him, than were his contemporaries? Regarding him from our point of view, it seems to us, that such purity, such devotion, such beneficence, would have won our belief, had we come within their sphere. It is easy to see these qualities in the past; but to see them in the present, to see them in one who offends our cherished convictions or pre-conceptions, is quite another thing. If we had lived in those days, we should have seen through our prejudices as those people did. We should have seen what our prejudices permitted, and nothing else. Miracles would not have convinced us, if otherwise indisposed to believe. It is folly to imagine that we could be made to believe against our wills by any material sign. Our unbelief would put its own construction on that sign. We should find an explanation of it congenial with our views. We should see it through the medium of our prepossessions. We should see it, not as it was, but as we are.

No one who rejects the divine origin of Christianity will ever be brought to believe in it on the ground of its miracles, for the obvious reason that they never can be proved to the satisfaction of unbelief. No amount of evidence is sufficient for that purpose. A miracle is insusceptible of historic proof, because, as a matter of external evidence to be weighed in the balance of probabilities, the *à priori* presumption against such facts outweighs any testimony that can be adduced in its support. The Princess Ulrica of Sweden wished to test the reality of Swedenborg's intercourse with the spiritual world. She asked him to report to her the substance of a conversation which she had had with her brother, a short time previous to his decease, of the nature of which she was sure that no living person could have any knowledge. A little while after, the seer, to her amazement,—so the story goes,—fulfilled her request. But she would not accept the conclusion which seemed to follow from that test. Her answer was, "How M. v. Swedenborg has possessed himself of this knowledge, I cannot guess; but I do not believe that he has conversed with my departed brother."

The presumption against the supernatural is not only stronger, with those who disincline to believe, than human testimony; it is even stronger than the evidence of our own senses, as is shown in many remarkable cases where individuals have been unable to see what others saw, or unable to believe that they had seen it. Shakespeare understood the human heart when he made Hamlet, after conversing with the ghost of his father, speak of "the undiscovered land from whose bourne no traveller returns." It is in vain to appeal to ocular demonstration, — to say that seeing is believing. Unbelief will see with the eyes of unbelief; for we can see only as we are.

Let us bring the case home to ourselves. Suppose a prophet sent to our time, and reported to work miracles among us. He is said to have raised the dead. Would the sceptically inclined give credit to such a report upon any conceivable testimony that might be adduced in its support? Nay, suppose them to have witnessed it with their own eyes, — to have stood by the graveside of some Lazarus when the inhumed came forth, would they even then believe that they had seen the dead arise? Would they not find some explanation of that or any similar phenomenon, which should strip it of its miraculous character, and range it with the uniform experience of mankind? Only when we had been brought into contact with the prophet himself, and had read divinity in the light of his eye, and imbibed its influence by coming within its sphere, and been all penetrated with reverence and love, — only then should we — I will not say believe in those miracles — but only then should we be in that moral condition in which belief in miracles is possible to disciplined and intelligent minds. We should then have gone behind the miracle, and conversed with its source. We should have stood at the power-fountain of miraculous goodness to which all things are possible. Happily, we are so constituted that we can believe in something higher than the senses and the understanding. We can believe in something which does not admit of demonstration. What would become of us, embosomed in this material, with no nurture but hard facts, and no light to guide us but our bounded experience; — with no mystic border to our existence in the flesh, and no horizon of celestial ether to our day?

The argument which Hume draws from the undemonstrableness of miracles is conclusive only against the use of them as evidence, not against the facts themselves. It does not follow, because a miracle is insusceptible of proof, that a miracle is impossible. The understanding tolerates nothing supernatural: and we do right to explain what can be explained, by known causes, — to suppose no miracle where other supposition will serve; as far and as fast as possible, to translate the supernatural into the natural.

But, on the other hand, we are poor creatures if nothing is dreamed of in our philosophy but square and compass, and mechanical laws; if our logic rejects every thing that cannot be measured by feet and inches, and weighed in market-scales; if there is no corner in our mind or heart where faith in miracles can lodge.

And now, a word concerning the objection to miracle, drawn from "the order of nature," so called, — the alleged inviolableness of natural laws. The argument amounts to no more than an *à priori* presumption against any event which contradicts the common experience. It is not conclusive, and cannot be accepted as proof, without absolute assurance that all the laws and possibilities of nature and spirit are known to us. But who will pretend to such assurance? Who will pretend, that his knowledge embraces all the possibilities of nature? Who will pretend, that all the possibilities of the human organism, much less of the human spirit, are known to him? A mathematician demonstrated by mechanical laws the impossibility of the leaps performed by athletes on the stage: they contradicted the order of nature. And they were repeated night after night. One law overrules and subordinates another in the daily experience of life. I contradict the law of gravitation whenever I jump from the ground. Whenever I will to hold my breath, I contradict the known laws of the human organism. What we call the order of nature is simply a convenient formula; safe enough in its ordinary applications, but a mere illusion when urged as alone conclusive against extraordinary events. What we call the order of nature is but the statement, in objective terms, of the limitation of our human experience. To one who had never seen or heard of an eclipse of the sun, the first experience of that phenomenon would be a violation of the order of nature. It would be just as correct to affirm that the method of nature is miracle, as it is to affirm with some that "the method of nature is not miracle, but law," if by miracle we understand the unprecedented, or a new creation. The new is as much the result of law as the old; the unprecedented, as much as our most familiar experience; a miracle, as much as the constancy of things. The experience of a few thousand years affords no warrant for pronouncing dogmatically what is or is not a violation of the "order of nature," — an order of which the catastrophes and cataclysms known to geology, and distanced by millions of years, are as much a constituent part as the rising and setting of the daily sun. In Babbage's calculating machine,* a law of increase which had operated, with unbroken uniformity, in a hundred million and one instances, is overruled in the hundred million and

* See "Vestiges of Creation," American edition, page 156.

second instance by another law coming in and changing the rate of increase from one to ten thousand at a single leap. That new term was as much a part of the constitution of the machine, as much in the order of its mechanism, as the uniform regularity of the hundred million and one instances which had preceded it. In the dateless mechanism of the universe, the rarest exception is just as legitimate as the rule; and in human life, for aught we know, there may be exceptional experiences, exceptional powers, exceptional *souls*, which are just as much a part of the divine order as the most familiar events. It ill becomes man, whose history bears no larger proportion to the age of the world than the life of the ephemera bears to recorded time, to speak too confidently of the order of nature.

"But is not a real miracle simply a violation of the laws of nature? ask several. Whom I answer," says Carlyle, "with this new question, What are the laws of nature? To me, perhaps the rising of one from the dead were no violation of these laws, but a confirmation, — were some far deeper law now first penetrated into, and by spiritual force, even as the rest have all been, brought to bear on us with its material force." "But is it not the deepest law of nature that she be constant? cries an illuminated class. Is not the machine of the universe fixed to move by unalterable rules? Probable enough, good friends. . . . And now of you, too, I make the old inquiry, what those same unalterable rules, forming the complete statute-book of nature, may possibly be. . . . Have any deepest scientific individuals dived down to the foundations of the universe, and gauged every thing there? Did the Maker take them into his counsel, that they read his ground-plan of the incomprehensible All, and can say, This stands marked therein, and no more than this? Alas! not in anywise. These scientific individuals have been nowhere but where we also are,—have seen some hand-breadths deeper than we see into the deep that is infinite, without bottom as without shore."—"The course of nature's phases on this little fraction of a planet is partially known to us; but who knows what deeper courses these depend on, — what infinitely larger cycle (of causes) our little epicycle revolves on? To the minnow, every cranny and pebble and quality and accident of its little creek may have become familiar; but does the minnow understand the ocean-tides and periodic currents, the trade-winds and monsoons, and moon's eclipses, by all which the condition of its little creek is regulated, and may, from time to time (unmiraculously enough), be quite overset and reversed? Such a minnow is man, — his ocean the immeasurable All; his monsoons and periodic currents the mysterious course of Providence through æons of æons."

The radical mistake in the scientific objection to miracles consists in defining a miracle to be a violation of the laws of nature. Such a definition must needs provoke the opposition of all whose function it is to ascertain and promulgate natural laws. Suppose we define it, an effect from an unknown cause, or the operation of an unknown law, subordinating or holding in abeyance a known one. So defined, its incredibility is made to consist in its unwontedness, which may furnish a presumption against the alleged fact, but cannot be considered a valid refutation. The unknown law may be conceived as a spiritual fact beyond the reach of natural science, — as belonging to that region of forces and experiences, which, in current phraseology, is termed "supernatural." That phrase "supernatural," however, must not be construed as unnatural or contranatural, but only as designating a higher plane of the universal Will, which comprehends in one omnipresent, omnipotent agency the seen and the unseen, the world of causes and the world of effects. The real final and efficient cause of every event is the will of God. All causes and laws which science knows, and all which science does not know, are but different phases of the one Supreme.

I am far from maintaining that belief in miracles is a necessary article of Christian faith. I only protest against the crudeness of that dogmatism which affirms *à priori* the impossibility of all that cannot be explained by known laws, or that does not agree with universal experience, and exalts its idol of the tribe, its misconceived "order of nature," above the incalculable power of the spirit.

I distinguish, moreover, in the so-called miracles of the New Testament, between the essential fact and the manner in which it is presented in the record. I conceive that a nucleus of historic truth, in a credulous age, may gather to itself a mythic embodiment which is questionable. Intelligent criticism must separate, if possible, the one from the other. For criticism has its legitimate function in relation to these as to other parts of the Sacred Writings, and to all writings. But legitimate criticism has also its limitations, and must not assume to rule out in the mass whatever conflicts with the critic's prepossessions, and only because of those prepossessions. It must not reject, on the ground of imperfect evidence, what does not admit, in the nature of things, of any other.

Not only is a miracle insusceptible of proof, but revelation itself is insusceptible of proof, — of any other proof than its own interior light. Revelation transcends, and must transcend, demonstration. This is its specific distinction, — without which it is not revelation, but philosophy, — that it speaks with self-evident authority. Christianity has been more injured than aided by the indiscreet attempts of its defenders to ground its authority on external proofs. The misstatements of unbelievers should be exposed, their false conclusions refuted; but, beyond this, all so-called "evidences of Christianity" are worthless and vain. That would be a very insufficient religion which could be proved by testimony exterior to itself. If it does not speak with authority above all others, it speaks in vain.

Attempts to prove the truth of Christianity are like attempts to prove the existence of light. The light shines, and proves itself by shining. It is its own demonstration, and no demonstration can make it clearer. So this moral light — the light of the gospel — which shines into every soul that is willing to receive it, and which makes our soul's day, — what can we say of it that shall be so convincing as itself? If we have any other argument more cogent than that, we have a higher revelation, and need not its light.

There may be errors respecting the nature of the light, and false theories there may be concerning its source; but what of that? Astronomy may be mistaken in some of its calculations: is the sun, on that account, less glorious or less dear? I need no astronomy to tell me what a blessing it is. And suppose we have not, in these biographies, unmixed historical truth; that some errors and misstatements have crept into the records; — is the character of Christ, on that account, less noble, or his word less divine? The question is not whether Jesus said precisely this, or did precisely that, in each particular case; but whether Christianity, on the whole, is divine, — whether this light, which for so many ages has irradiated the world, and given us such guidance as we have had in spiritual things, is God's truth, — a ray of heaven conducting to endless day, or a meteor born of the night, and misleading the blind. And this is not a question of logic, but a question of experience, which every soul must answer for itself. Christianity is not a matter of records and parchments, but a light and a life: which, if a man has it not, no logic can reason into him; and which, if a man has it, no logic can reason out of him. Nay, if you could prove that this record which we have of the sayings and doings of Jesus is a fable and a myth, even then you would not have destroyed Christianity. In that case, I should say, Whether fable or fact, the mind that could conceive and give to the world such a portrait as that of the Christ, is itself the Christ. The product of that mind would still be the wisdom and the power of God. Suppose you could prove that no such person as Michael Angelo ever existed; that the name is not historic, but mythic; the tradition we have of him a fable; — the Church of

St. Peter's would still be the wonder of the world, and the mind that planned it a master mind. However we may speculate concerning its origin, the Christian Church, — that stupendous fabric of which St. Peter's is a feeble type, — that august temple in which so many ages have knelt and prayed, — stands, and will stand, in spite of criticism. Christianity is: it is a fixed fact, — a part of the round world. And when I consider what it is, and what it has been; how many millions of believing souls have found peace in its doctrine, and freedom in its spirit; to how many it has been their guide in life, and their stay in death; and how it has changed the face of the world; — it seems to me a small thing, in view of all this power and glory, to quarrel about the record, and fight against miracles, with this miracle of all time staring us in the face.

Some of the miracles recorded in the New Testament I cannot receive in the sense of the narrative: but I believe in the possibility of miracles; i.e., of works transcending common experience. I believe in them because I believe that spiritual powers are superior to physical, and may hold them in subjection; because I believe that the soul is stronger than material nature, and may command it when it truly commands itself; because I see in the person of Jesus a greater miracle than any of the works recorded of him. When I think of the greater, I can easily believe the less. I contemplate the portrait of Jesus as presented in the gospel; and it seems to me so great and real, that material nature, with its uses and forces, looks shadowy beside it; so solid and commanding, that all things must needs be subject to it. And, after all, I find in miracles no difficulty greater than I encounter when I reject them. I know of no canon of criticism by which I can eliminate every thing miraculous from the record, and yet retain the rest. If I reject them, I must reject the whole; and, rejecting the whole, I do such violence to historical evidence as would undermine all history, and annihilate the past.

At the same time, I would not be bound to a rigorous construction of the letter of the narrative in every case in which a miraculous event is represented in the text. I will not suffer my judgment to be brought into bondage to a letter. We have not, in these writings, contemporary documents; but later productions, into which it is fair to suppose that some errors may have found their way. Whatever is written is open to criticism; for the soul is greater than any scripture, and nothing can be more foreign from the spirit of Christianity than a slavish interpretation of its records. The intelligent reader who brings to the New Testament a candid temper and an ordinary share of understanding will make such allowance as may be needful to reconcile the credit of the record with the credibility of the facts recorded. He will separate what is essential in the record from what is incidental; the central fact from the form in which it appears. He will not always see a miracle where the narrative has that look; and, where he acknowledges a miracle, he will not always accept the common interpretation. In a word, he will give due honor to this memorial of a heavenly life, without doing unnecessary violence to reason and common sense.

But be it remembered, that common sense and common experience are not the sufficient and only measure of spiritual truth; and that, unless by the power of faith and the power of the spirit we can raise ourselves to a plane of vision above the level of ordinary life, the divinest word that ever yet found utterance in human speech, or embodied itself in human life, will speak to us in vain.

IV.

THE REVELATION OF THE SPIRIT.

IV.

THE REVELATION OF THE SPIRIT.

THE New Testament speaks of "the Spirit" very much as the Old Testament speaks of Jehovah, or "the Lord." Where the Old Testament says, "The Lord spoke," or "The word of the Lord came," to this or that prophet, the New Testament substitutes Spirit. "Jesus was led by the Spirit into the wilderness." — "The Spirit said to Philip." — "The Spirit said to Peter," &c. &c. The same thing is meant in both cases, but the different phraseology marks a difference between the two dispensations. The same fact, the same power, is differently conceived. In one case, it is formal, concrete, — an individual. In the other, it is liberal and diffusive, — an influence. When the Jew thought of his Jehovah, it was somewhat as the Gentile thought of his Jove. He thought of him as a powerful individual, as a wise and strong man. When the evangelists thought of the Spirit, they thought of it as a breath, a vision, a whisper in the heart; a subtile influence informing the mind, inspiring the will, directing the life.

The personification of the Spirit in the New Testament is merely rhetorical; but the Church, not satisfied with a figure of speech, converted the rhetoric into dogma. They constituted the Spirit a distinct person in the Godhead. No harm in this, if by "person" is meant nothing more than a mode of manifestation. But with many the idea of person hardens into that of independent individuality. The Spirit is conceived as a being, distinct from the Father, instead of a character of, or in, God the Father. This was not the intent of the doctrine, as defined by the councils of the Church. It conflicts with the accompanying doctrine of the "procession," as it is called, "of the Holy Ghost." The Spirit is said to "proceed" from God. And this procession was not once for all, but still continues. It is not a past transaction, a fact accomplished, but a present and constant process. The language is not "proceeded," but "proceeds." The question arose in the ages which developed this doctrine, whether the spirit proceeds directly and solely from God, or from God through Christ. The Greek Church taught, and still teaches, that the Spirit is wholly and only from the Father. The Latin or Roman-Catholic Church maintained, and still maintains, that the Spirit proceeds from the Father and the Son. And the Latin Church is right: the interior meaning of that doctrine is, that the spiritual creation, like the material, is based on intelligence. There can be no holiness without insight.

The Holy Spirit is that particular agency of God, direct or indirect, which concerns itself with the moral and religious education of mankind. It is God acting in this particular way as distinguished from God in nature.

Self-manifestation — the revelation of himself in rational minds — must be supposed to be the end of all God's doing. The visible universe is one revelation, — intelligible only when viewed as such. "Day unto day uttereth speech, and night unto night showeth knowledge." Nature reflects to intelligent minds the divine Wisdom and Love. But Nature could never convey the most distant idea of moral good. The truth which we attempt to express, when we say that God is just, that God is holy; the fact of a moral law, duty, conscience, accountableness, — these have no prototype or symbol in Nature. This is something of which Nature is unconscious. The animal world exhibits something of instinctive love, something of blind attachment, but nothing like justice, holiness. This is "the way which no fowl knoweth," which "the vulture's eye hath not seen," and which "the lion's whelps have not trodden." "The abyss saith, It is not in me; and the sea saith, It is not with me." We should know God only as mighty, wise, and beneficent, never as holy and just, were there not another creation and revelation co-parallel with the material, — the moral creation, the revelation of the Spirit, in which God is revealed as Moral Law, and as Moral and Spiritual Good.

The element and medium of this moral creation is the moral nature which always accompanies conscious intelligence, here and wherever conscious intelligence is found. Its materials are rational souls. Of these "living stones" the divine Architect, the Holy Spirit, compiles the spiritual fabric which all good men are helping to build, and whose completion will be the consummation and crown of time. The Christian Church,

in the vision of the apostles, was identified with that fabric, "Christ himself being the chief corner-stone; in whom all the building, fitly framed together, groweth unto an holy temple in the Lord." The Christian Church, in their theory, is not only the product, but the earthly representative and embodiment, of the Holy Spirit. At once both agent and object, creator and creature, it sends forth the influences which convert the world, and grows and reproduces itself by the influences it sends forth.

If, now, from the theology of the Holy Spirit, we turn to its practical human side, we find in its action on human individuals a twofold influence. The Spirit acts on the reason and on the will. It inspires the knowledge of moral and spiritual truths, and it quickens the moral and spiritual life. We are influenced by it in our perceptions and in our practice.

First, our perceptions, — the knowledge of moral and spiritual truth. All knowledge partakes more or less of inspiration. Our mental faculties are not the sources of truth. In and of themselves, they see nothing and know nothing. They are but organs, — secondary agents. As the soundest eye conveys no image to the mind, until the light from without has touched its nerve; so the keenest intellect can never comprehend the simplest truth, until moved to action by some impulse from abroad. Not that any knowledge, strictly speaking, is imparted. We acquire nothing by passive reception alone. All truth is the product of our own minds. But the mind can produce only as it is quickened from abroad. If this is true in respect to secular knowledge, how much more in respect to spiritual!

If the truths which relate to the kingdoms of nature come by inspiration, how much more the truths which relate to the kingdom of heaven! Why was it that all the wisdom of antiquity failed to penetrate those mysteries which are now familiar to the dullest minds? Why is it that many an uneducated Christian possesses on these subjects a depth of insight which puts to shame the wisdom of the world? Why, but that truths of this order are apprehended by some other faculty than the sensuous understanding. The Holy Spirit is the teacher here. And the fact illustrates the equalizing power of the Spirit, which not only overrules the factitious distinctions of social rank, but sets at nought those intellectual disparities which separate more widely between man and man. More than any scheme of human polity, it levels society by raising the lowest to an equality with the highest in that which in all is highest and best. It preaches its gospel to the poor, and so maintains the equal rights of the mind, without which all other equality is futile and vain.

What, then, it may be asked, is the agency of the Spirit in the communication of truth? It is the agency of the sun in the natural world. The Spirit is to the mind what light is to the eye. Its office is not to impart truth, but to show it. To those who seek the truth in sincerity, the aid of the Spirit will not be wanting. Let the eye be open, the heart free, and the understanding will be full of light. Doubt and unbelief will vanish away: the Spirit will guide into all truth.

2. The Spirit is not only light to the understanding: it is also motive and guide to the will. Its agency affects not only the knowledge but the practice of the

truth. By it we are filled with holy aspirations, and moved to good deeds. All goodness is from God, just as all power is remotely or directly referrible to him. This divine influence is not incompatible with human freedom. Every act of goodness is still an act of the will. Omnipotence itself will not enforce obedience. Nevertheless, it is God who worketh in us, both to will and to do. From him we derive the capacity and the impulse. But capacity is not necessity, and impulse is not coercion. We are moved, and yet move freely; we accept the divine influence, yoke it with our destiny, and choose that the Spirit of God shall reign in our wills. Liberty is not absolute disengagement from all rule. It does not consist in lawless roving, but in free consent with legitimate sway, in free co-operation with the Supreme Will. Some rule we must obey; but we may or may not elect our ruler. Two opposite currents of influence traverse the world. The one leads Godward; the other, deathward. To move with the former is moral freedom; to be carried with the other is contradiction and bondage. To say that God is the author of our goodness, no more detracts from the power of the human will, than to say that God is the author of truth detracts from man's intellectual powers. He acts upon us, not as compulsory force, but as quickening influence.

The operation of the Spirit is not always a direct action on the individual mind. More frequently it acts through the instrumentality of other, subordinate agents, — through the lips and lives of men, by teachers and books, by instruction and example, by institutions and ordinances, by every influence which moves the soul to well-doing. When we read a good book, and are profited by it; when we listen to discourse that acts favorably on our moral nature, that awakens good impulses in the breast, — we are visited and moved by the Holy Ghost. The Church, and every institution established for moral and religious ends, so long as it fulfils its original design, is a medium of this influence. It is the Holy Spirit made concrete.

But, though this indirect operation is the more usual mode in which the divine influence is communicated, it acts also without the intervention of any visible agent: it acts as direct inspiration. There are motions of the Spirit in us which are not to be ascribed to any external influence: they are the Spirit of God acting on the instinct of goodness in the soul. There is this instinct in every soul. It is not the most patent, but the deepest, of all our instincts. Often neutralized by other propensities, it needs the quickening of the Spirit to give it life. Then it manifests itself in those moral aspirations by which the most thoughtless are sometimes roused to conscientious and beneficent action. If ever, at some moment of solitary musing, we have felt within ourselves a stronger conviction of moral and spiritual truth, a stronger determination to good; if ever we have seized with truer insight the meaning and purpose of our being, and have formed the resolution to live for duty and for God, — it was the Spirit breathing on the latent spark of spiritual life in the breast, which gave us that vision, and caused those fires to glow. And, if we analyze our experience at such seasons, we shall see how man's free agency may consist with divine impulsion. We shall see, that while the determination of the mind to moral ends is a free determination, calling into action the whole force of our own will, it is still a divine impulse that moves us, and a God that works in us to will as well as to do.

The agency of the Spirit, as now defined, is impartial, in itself considered; but its efficacy in each individual is limited by personal conditions. It is limited by the receptivity which we bring to it. And the receptivity which we bring to it will depend in a great degree on previous training. I do not deny original differences of moral endowment. Some men seem born to goodness as a natural heritage: it is their patrimony. Their way apparently is smooth and free. No obstacle seems to intervene between the purposes they form and the ends they contemplate. The intent and the act hang together by natural dependence, like the links of a chain. We admire the facility with which they appear to glide onward to perfection, while we are constantly thwarted, and pulled back by inward contradiction or external force. Something of this difference may be due to natural inequality of moral constitution; but more is due to self-discipline. If the Spirit of God has greater influence with some than with others, the reason is generally, that, by early obedience and long discipline, they have attained to higher degrees of spiritual life. Their previous habits have disposed the mind to be easily affected by such influences; the will has not been perverted and depraved; the first impulses of the Spirit in them were not resisted, but received into willing minds, and suffered to acquire a permanent control of the thoughts and desires. In nothing is the truth of the saying, that "to him who hath shall be given," more evident than it is in relation to the moral life. Therefore said an apostle, "Grieve not the Holy Spirit of God." By a figure derived from human affections, the divine agency is represented as a friend who wills our good, but may be vexed and alienated by our opposition or our indifference. Not that we can actually change the purpose of God, or avert his grace. Nothing that we can do can alienate his love, or render the Father of spirits less willing to aid and to bless. He is true to us, however we may turn from him. Nevertheless, we may destroy the efficacy of his gifts in us; and, by alienating our own minds, may virtually alienate his love. The effect for us is the same, whether he is turned from us or we from him.

There is a very remarkable coincidence between this apostolic precept and the doctrine of some of the ancient Gentile philosophers. Gentile philosophy taught, that a good spirit waits upon all who choose to accept its guidance. The great Athenian personified in this way the nobler instincts of his mind. He spoke of a dæmon (or, as we should say, a good genius) who informed and impelled him. And Seneca, the contemporary of Paul, says more explicitly, as if he had received the thought directly from him, "There dwells in us a holy spirit who watches all our good and all our evil deeds, and who treats us according to the treatment he receives."

Subjectively, then, the Holy Spirit is to be considered a divine instinct in man; a special faculty, differing from reason and understanding, and the other faculties of the mind, in this, that it always speaks with authority;

it addresses us, not as argument, but as command. So it appears in numerous instances in the history of the apostles, who are represented as urged and impelled by this divine instinct to do, or refrain from doing, sometimes contrary to their own judgment or their own will. Paul and Timothy, it is said, "assayed to go into Bithynia; but the Spirit would not suffer them." It was reserved for Protestantism, in harmony with its true, original tendency, to follow out these hints, and unfold this subjective side, as the elder Church had developed the positive theological view of the Holy Ghost. Honor to George Fox and the founders of the sect of Friends, who first did justice to the Christian idea of divine inspiration; who re-affirmed the spiritual instinct, and vindicated the inward light! What to the elder Church was a barren dogma, a scholastic abstraction, an hypothesis, the third person in Trinity, — to them was a spiritual fact. "When the Lord God and his Son Jesus Christ," says Fox, "sent me forth into the world to preach his everlasting gospel and kingdom, I was commanded to turn men to that inward light, spirit, and grace, by which all might know the way to God; even that divine Spirit which would lead into all truth, and would never deceive." His theory, and that of his followers, was and is, that man, if he will, may have the immediate guidance of the Spirit of God; that inspiration is not a past fact, but a present reality.

"Grieve not the Spirit!" Be true to your highest instincts! Often, in temporal matters, we are warned by a secret voice, which comes to us like a mandate from above, to do or forbear. It is always wise to accept such warnings. We cannot hope to prosper, if we sacrifice our own instinct to formal reasons and the judgment of others. People come to you, when you are hesitating between two courses of conduct, and say, Do thus and so. It is all very well, so long as no instinct of your own prompts otherwise; but if something within you says, Do no such thing, then be sure you do no such thing. If this is true doctrine in matters of temporal import, how much more in things pertaining to our spiritual well-being! Resist not this sacred force! Beware of alienating the divine influence! Whenever you feel yourself prompted to any good work, to any act of kindness or self-denial, to any course of discipline or holy living, accept the impulse, hasten to obey while the fire burns. It is God that speaks in these secret promptings. Harden not your heart when you hear that voice. The Spirit will leave you if you refuse obedience; every warning disregarded is a door closed against future progress. If you do not now the good which you can, the time will come when you cannot do the good which you would.

If we would receive the divine influence in its fullest measure and its greatest force, we must earnestly desire it. God will help no one in that in which he himself is indifferent; he will not give his Spirit except to those that ask it. Other gifts do not wait our entreaty; the common bounties of Providence are not withheld from those who neglect to ask for them; but prayer is an indispensable condition of spiritual gifts. By prayer I mean not a form of words, but an earnest desire and a fervent affection. No needed gift is denied to the prayer of faith. Every thing may be had by him who earnestly desires what he should. If we fail to receive the grace we implore, it is because we ask with a wavering mind, and a lazy desire, and a sluggish faith. It is because we ask as if we wished or expected to be denied; as a man asks a dentist to draw his tooth, or a surgeon to cut off a limb, or to execute any other painful operation which he supposes to be necessary, but would fain avoid if he could. "If we loved truly what we ask for daily," says Bishop Taylor, "we should ask with hearty desires and a fervent spirit. The river that runs slow and creeps by its banks, and begs leave of every turf to let it pass, is drawn into little hollows, and dies with diversion. So, if a man's prayer move upon the feet of an abated appetite, it wanders into the society of every trifling accident, and stays at the corners of the fancy, and cannot arrive at heaven. But, when it is carried upon the wings of strong desire and a hungry appetite, it passes on through all the intermediate region of the clouds, and stays not until it dwells at the foot of the throne, and draws down showers of refreshment."

Pray for the Spirit; for who in this world can do without it, — without its impulse, without its leaven, without its restraining and sustaining power? It has been affirmed that civilization and the progress of society are wholly and purely an intellectual product. To assert this is to forget the gift of God, and what it is that keeps the human heart from dying out, and all the powers from perishing through utter corruption. It is not our laws and our courts, not well-balanced constitutions and social devices, not science and steam and electro-magnetism, — not these alone that have brought us thus far, and made this world what it is; but beneath all these, and above them all, a divine impulse, never wanting to the race of men; a divine Spirit for ever haunting them with those two radical and universal ideas, — truth and duty, without whose penetrating and creative power not one stone would ever have been laid upon another of all our cities, no tree ever felled, no human implement fashioned for its work. And, if God should now withdraw his Spirit, this proud civilization, with its gorgeous palaces and solemn temples; this shining and sounding culture, with its traffic and its arts, its stately conventions, and fair humanities, — would tumble and dissolve; the wild beasts that are caged in these human frames, now awed and tamed by the presence of that Spirit, would creep forth, and rend, and devour; and the civilized earth revert to chaos and night.

The individual no more than society can dispense with the Holy Ghost. The rich requires it as well as the poor. He needs its promptings, and he needs its peace; he needs its strength, and he needs its consolation. He needs it in smooth prosperity, and he needs it in the struggles and straits of life. He is subject to assaults from within and from without; he is tempted to transgress the law in his mind, to obey the law in his members, to forsake himself, to swerve from the right. No earthly power can secure him against temptation, or deliver him when tempted. The Holy Spirit alone can bring him safely through the wars, and save his feet from falling and his soul from death. He is subject to calamity and sharp distress, to grief and bereavement, the loss of his beloved, the wreck of his hopes. No earthly power can avert these woes, or soothe their sting. The Holy Spirit is the only comforter that can reach him in those deeps, and make the night seem light about him. This same Spirit is nearer to us all, and more to us, than any soul can fully know in this world, or is willing to believe. What is it, in fact, but the hidden life, the self of our self, which now and then bursts into consciousness, and amazes us with a foreign presence in our private thought? Those lucid intervals in our experience, those clear spaces in our life, when the roar and rush of the world's torrent ceases, and the cloud-rack lifts, and a bit of the blue sky struggles through, with revelation of immortal deeps; — these are momentary realizations of the presence of the Holy Spirit, from which at no time we are otherwise sundered than by the wanderings of our own thought and will.

But suppose this earthly world could be traversed, and this mortal life lived, without the gift of the Holy Ghost, how will it be when the gulf yawns toward which we are momently drifting? No earthly power can bridge that gulf, or ferry us over it. There is no spring in this breast of ours by which it can throw off the clod that is laid upon it, and erect itself out of dusty death. There is no power in this soul by which to extricate itself out of the wreck of this mortal. Let philosophers say what they will, there is no natural immortality. If ever we rise again to conscious life, it will be by no native power, but by the operation of the Spirit of God on souls already possessed by it, and in some degree conformed to its likeness.

The doctrine of the Holy Spirit is peculiarly Christian. It is not a deduction of the human understanding, but a revelation from "the Father of lights." And, without this revelation, the name of God is only a name, a vague abstraction, having no relation to the heart or life. It is only through his Spirit that God becomes to us a person and reality. You may gather — who does not? — from the visible creation the notion of almighty power and beneficent design. From the course of human affairs you may get — who does not? — the impression of a superintending Providence and an all-present Love. From the experiences of your moral nature you infer — who does not? — a moral government and a righteous law. But all this does not constitute the God of the Christian revelation, the Father of spirits and of mercies. That idea could never be wrought out of those materials. The idea of God is a revelation of his Spirit; and unless the Spirit of God dwell in us, superstition may have an idol, conscience a law, philosophy a name; but the heart has no God.

V.

THE SPIRIT IN THE LETTER.

V.

THE SPIRIT IN THE LETTER.

ALL spirit, in proportion to the force there is in it, seeks to embody itself, and tends in time to become a letter. All spiritual movements, that are strong enough and true enough to last, end there. All revelations and reforms, after passing through the fluid stage, arrive at a solid one: after living and working as disembodied spirit for a while, they crystallize into stated, formal agencies, and settle down into scriptures and churches. Judaism was a spirit once, and became a letter; Christianity was a spirit, and became a letter; Protestantism was a spirit, and became a letter. Such was their providential destiny. Every letter, ordinance, organization, that now exists, was once a disembodied spirit; and every thought, sentiment, movement, which now agitates society, if genuine and destined to endure, will one day become a letter.

It will not do to quarrel with the letter: the spirit requires it. Spirit will not stay without a letter to hold it, as every one knows from his own experience. What avails your vision, your aspiration, your ideal? what avail your kind purposes and generous emotions, if they do not embody themselves? You have a vision of excellence; it fills your whole soul; your spirit is aglow with it; it is your spirit for the time; and could your spiritual interior at that moment be laid open and portrayed, as a photograph fixes the fleeting expression of the countenance, the portrait would be that of a hero or a saint. What boots it, if you do not embody that spirit in some word or work? It expires with the pulses of the breast; it evaporates with a breath, and no man is benefited by it: it was and is not, and no memorial of it remains to kindle aspiration in another, or to rekindle it in yourself. But express that spirit, record it in some way, embody it somewhere, and you add something to the spirit's life and the world's riches. As yet, it is a mere breath that steals over the soul, a possibility only; you are none the better for it, nor any one else, if it end so. And yet the spirit is good and holy and divine as that which fired St. Francis when he poured out his soul in measureless love, or that which flooded the heart of Jesus when he prayed for his enemies on the cross. But, divine as it is in possibility, it is nothing in reality, until it is embodied; and it may be worse than nothing, as exhausting sensibility in leaves without fruit, like the infructuous fig-tree, whose leafy and lying luxuriance availed nothing, but drew to itself a curse. As yet, it is a mere breath: shall it end so? — a passing wind whence coming you heed not, nor whither going? or shall it become actual, and a fact of life? Express it, actualize it in some way, and straightway it becomes life, a thing, a fact; insignificant in appearance, obscure in place, evanescent in time; but still, life, and a fountain of life to others, an influence in the world, and so an actual, constituent part of the world, inseparable, indestructible. The difference between it and spirit unexpressed is simply infinite, — the difference between something and nothing. I fancy that, when the soul reckons with us in our day of judgment, we shall burn less with the memory of bad acts or words, than of good designs unembodied, and worthy thoughts unexpressed.

All spirit, so far as it is good and holy at all, is a unity. The spirit which prays in any of us to-day, if the genuine fire of devotion is in us, is the same which discoursed in the Sermon on the Mount, and opened the eyes of the blind; which blew into the soul of Peter, and drove Paul like a rolling thing around the world, and built up universal Christendom, with its temples and its scriptures, its sanctities and its arts. The difference between the spirit that did all this, and the holy thought or generous sentiment that stirs my heart to-day, and remains unexpressed, is not in quality, but in outwardness, — the difference between the spirit *with* a letter, and the spirit *without* it. Theoretically, the spirit that originated these things might not have originated them (although providentially it must), and yet have been as holy and divine a spirit still. It was no more holy and divine than the spirit that has wrought in many an anchorite and recluse, and in many a Quaker Friend, which might have produced the like, but did not embody itself, — spent itself, rather, in private devotion and secret contemplation.

We are indebted to the letter as much as to the spirit, — to the spirit only through the letter. And when we consider how a piece of parchment in a registrar's office, which is not even looked at once in a lifetime, may fix the occupation of large portions of the earth's surface for thousands of years; and how a printed paper which they call a Constitution may determine the political condition of a nation, — the measure of external freedom enjoyed, or bondage endured, of millions of people; and how some leaves inscribed with tables of figures will enable a ship's company to find their way across the pathless sea, and to circumnavigate the world, — when, I say, we consider these things, and note the power of the letter, and the value of its function in the secular economy of life, we may come to think respectfully of its agency, as a power in religion.

It must be granted to those who argue the cause of the spirit as against the letter, that no existing letter can endure for ever, or continue for ever to hold the place which it once held in the spiritual economy. Every form in which the spirit clothes itself, every body it puts on, is transient; every existing organization is destructible, and to be destroyed. The spirit endures, the form perishes. Yet even here we must distinguish between form and type; that is, between the material form and the spiritual, — between soul and body. Every form of being which is not exceptional or transitional and accidental, expresses a type which will re-appear when the form that now embodies it is dissolved. In other words, the form will reproduce itself continually. The human body is fragile and corruptible: all the bodies in which humanity is now invested will soon be dust; but the human form will endure while heaven and earth remain; and when the heavens and the earth that now are have passed away. The human form is a letter that can never become obsolete. And so there may be types of the spirit in the present institutions and ordinances of religion, which will survive their dissolution, and reproduce themselves in new and similar ordinances, if ever the present shall pass out of use; as indeed the present are reproductions of elder rites. Sacrifice is as old as worship itself; but what a difference between the human sacrifices of ancient religions and the High Mass of the Church of Rome! And what a difference between that and the commemorative rite of our Protestant faith!

This also must be conceded, that in no letter is the spirit fully and perfectly expressed, and that the letter still requires the spirit to interpret its import, and to make it available and edifying to those who would use it. It is a medium of spiritual life to those only who come to it with and in the spirit. Without that touch of kindred life, it is dead and deadening. Then it is that "the letter killeth." The metallic wire which conveys your message to a distant friend, and his to you, possesses that capacity in a latent state. No manipulation can make it work to that end without the touch of the electric fluid which develops its secret virtue. Nevertheless, that metallic wire is a necessary condition of the communication desired: no other medium can supply its place, nor can the communication take effect without a medium. So is the letter without the spirit, and still an indispensable mediator of spirit.

It is an old controversy, the dispute concerning the

letter and the spirit in religion. All parties agree in asserting the supremacy of the spirit. There is no difference between Quaker and Romanist on that point. The only question is, whether any, and how much, of letter is essential to spirit. There is always a party in the Church who despise the letter and disparage ordinances and all external sanctities. They think they have Paul on their side, when they quote those words of his, "The letter killeth." But Paul is not to be so understood. He does not condemn the letter as such,—any and every letter,—but only the literality and empty formality which Judaism in his day had come to be. The correct application of this saying will depend on what we assume to be the object of the word "killeth." It is not the spirit that the letter killeth; on the contrary, we have seen that the letter is necessary to any continued life of the spirit;—not the spirit, but those who rest in the letter alone; those who separate the letter from the spirit, and make it supreme and final. The fault, then, is not in the letter, but in those who use it.

Men may rail as they please at the letter, and disparage what is outward in religion: but those churches are the strongest that have most of it; strongest not only in the way of efficient action and ecclesiastical power, but strongest in spiritual vitality. Out of them have come the sublimest examples of spiritual life; while those churches which have thought meanly of the letter, and sought to dispense with it, have languished and died out. George Fox and his followers were filled with perhaps as pure a spirit as ever animated a body of religionists. If spirit without letter could accomplish any thing, how much should have been accomplished by them! Here was spirit with a witness, spirit shed with boundless prodigality, — a river of God which was full of water. But for want of the letter, which it flouted and disdained, comparatively little was accomplished by this movement; while the Church of England, against which it contended on account of the alleged excess of the letter in its ministrations, has, through that letter, survived to this day, and still flourishes with undiminished vitality; and is at this moment to millions of souls an efficient medium of spiritual life. I am no friend to the Church of Rome. I believe it to be an enemy to social progress and intellectual freedom. But what a power it is! maintaining itself to this day, through so many revolutions of time and society; at this moment the strongest Church in Christendom, the strongest organized force on the globe. And, after deducting its manifold evils and corruptions, what a vast amount of spiritual good must still be conceded to it; of how much genuine piety and practical holiness, and good works, it is still the fruitful and constant source! What is the reason of this continued vitality? The Church of Rome, as a leader of human thought, has long since fallen from her pride of place; as a guide and law of the human soul, she has long been obsolete; the vision and the prophecy have departed from her: no longer capable of originating new thought or generating new life, her sole aim is to guard and perpetuate the life of the past. The reason of her continued vitality is the fulness and breadth of the letter, by which she subsists, and which supplies, at least, and will long supply, that traditional life. When the spirit of the living God was poured out upon this Church, in the days of her youth, it was gathered into these vessels, which are still so far impregnated with it that he who comes to them in the spirit of faith, by the power of that faith in himself awakens the spirit that is latent in them, and partakes of its life.

Where the letter killeth, the fault is not in the letter itself, though of that there may be, no doubt, an excess. The fault is the want of spirit in us by which to interpret its import, and reproduce it in our use. Whoever comes with the spirit in himself to the letter of his Church will find it living. So much spirit as he brings to it, so much spirit will he find in it, and give to it in his communications; as Jesus, when he took the traditional cup of the Passover at the Last Supper, flashed the light of his own spirit over all the ages that had handed it down to him, recovering its original import, and forward across all the ages that were to hand it down, reproduced with new import, to us. The letter killeth not the spirit, but the unspiritual; and the spirit maketh alive, not the spiritual only, but every letter which the spirit produced in times gone by. Much of the complaint which we hear of the oldness of the letter, and much of the impatience of rites and forms and scriptures, so far from betokening larger spirituality, is often but a proof of weakness of faith, — a want of power to penetrate into the soul of these things, to interpret their deeper import, and recover their latent life. Or it may be that spirit abounds in those who contemn the letter, yet not the spirit which gave the letter, but one contrary thereto.

"Try the spirits whether they be of God." Not every spirit that arises in the Church, and discourses of religion, is of that denomination. The world of spirits, like that of chemic forces, has its negative as well as its positive pole. The spirits of God are known by their affirmations; but there is a spirit which denies. So Goethe, in his immortal drama, makes Mephistopheles describe himself, "I am the spirit that evermore denies;" a necessary agent, no doubt, in the universal and divine economy; but beware of that spirit, — the spirit of negation, opposition, unbelief. Subsidiary, let it be, not dominant, in your scheme of life. The test of a true spirit is its productiveness. The spirit that can originate a letter in which men shall find their oracle and comforter and life, or that can interpret such a letter when it has grown dim, or re-animate it when it is old, — the same is of God.

In advocating the claims of the letter in religion, I am advocating the cause of the spirit. It is not a lifeless form, but a living body, as distinguished from spirit disembodied, for which I plead. Not letter and spirit are opposed, but literal and spiritual views and interpretations.

There is a literal and a spiritual way of viewing and handling the doctrines and ordinances of religion, as in Paul's day there was a literal and a spiritual Judaism. "The letter killeth" in doctrine and rite, when doctrine and rite are held and interpreted as letter alone, in slavish subjection to a formula which should be regarded as a servant of thought, and not as a law; an imperfect attempt to articulate truth, and not as the limit and measure of truth. Every doctrine which is not an individual conceit, but has the acceptance and sanction of the Church, expresses a truth, which, spiritually interpreted, maketh alive, but expresses it in a letter, which, held in its literal narrowness, killeth. It is always on the letter, and not on the spirit, that sects have split. For example, the doctrine of the Trinity, an ancient and generally received doctrine of the Church, — Father, Son, and Spirit, — conceived as a kind of theological arithmetic or ecclesiastical mythology, proposing three Gods, and calling them one, — this doctrine is death to reason and common sense; but conceived in the sense of those immortal leaders and interpreters of the Church, — Anselm, Thomas Aquinas, Lullus, and Abelard, — as expressing a self-communicating God, in contradistinction to the incommunicable one of Judaism and Mahommedanism, or as shadowing forth the encyclic completeness of the Godhead in its three chief aspects of Power, Wisdom, and Love; or Being, Truth, and Action; — although no part of the gospel, it is a quickening and edifying view of the divine nature. The divinity of Christ, understood, as modern orthodoxy too often conceives it, in a sense which violates the humanity of Jesus and insults the gospel record; which leaves us but this alternative, to conceive of God as a once-limited personality, or to conceive of Jesus as a mere apparition by which God was manifest; — so understood, I say, it is a letter which killeth. But conceived as ancient orthodoxy conceived and settled it, as expressing that unity of the human and divine which was realized in Christ, it is a truth which "maketh alive." The doctrine of the Atonement, conceived as an historical transaction or commercial arrangement by which God consents to waive the action of his penal law, in its application to human kind, in consideration of the meritorious death of Christ, is death to reason and the moral sense; but conceived as a mediating and reconciling influence through the ministry of Christ, by which the erring and alienated nature of man is restored to God, according to the saying of Paul, that "God in Christ is reconciling the world to himself;" — so conceived, the doctrine is life to mind and heart.

The letter killeth in sacraments and rites, where rigid conventionalism precludes spontaneity, or where a low utility assumes to be the measure of sanctities, or where the symbol becomes a fetish; or where the ordinance is viewed as compulsory observance, instead of a free communication or free-will offering. Why sprinkle water on a baby's forehead in any other name, utility asks, than that of personal cleanliness, — in any other way than that of physical ablution? Why, indeed, if those sprinkled drops are all that baptism means to you? If you see in baptism nothing but ritual water, it is a dead and deadening formality. But fill your mind with the awful truth, that the infant, born this day into this phenomenal and vanishing world, as one of its phenomena and passages, rising like a bubble on the great world-stream to fill a place among the shows of time, and to act a part in its processes, is also a child and heir of eternity, and is born, at one and the same moment with its time-birth, into a world of spirits that is real and eternal, a family of God, transcending the home-circle, and yet including it; a kingdom of God, transcending and including civil society; a universe of God, transcending and including the mundane sphere, and connecting this breathing creature of to-day, this palpitating human animal, with the farthest star that looks down on its cradle, with the Church of the first-born in the infancy of time and the Church of the last-born in time's completeness, and with God, the Judge of all, and the Mediator of his love, and which knows the life just cast on this shore, and claims it as its own, and yearns toward it out of all its heavens; — consider this, and you will see that some open and solemn recognition of this fact is no vain ceremony, but a just and becoming acknowledgment of the image of God bound up in that form, of the immortal destiny bound up in that life. And if water, the most universal of tangible creations, and therefore fit type of universality, is the given and accepted symbol of all this in your sphere and time, then should the water be sacred in your eyes that bathes a baby's forehead in the rite of baptism, administered in the name of the Father, the head of this spiritual All; the Son, the connecting link between him and it; the Spirit, its universal bond. And then is infant baptism not the mere dash of water on the brow: it is the solemn recognition of a new advent, the auspicious presentation of the new-comer to the general and august assembly of his spiritual home.

The sacrament of the Supper, like that of baptism, has its literal and its spiritual side. He who sees in it only a bit of bread and a sip of wine, of which a company of church-goers partake in common, will see only the letter that killeth, — a lifeless and killing formality. But lay to heart the meaning which lies in that word "communion," and consider that this spiritual All of which I have spoken exists for us only as we turn toward it the eye of our consciousness, and embrace it with our thought and aspiration, and you will see significance and sanctity in whatever promotes that consciousness or assists that aspiration. To him whose faith can take in the idea of the general assembly of our common humanity present as one man through all its epochs, in all its spheres, the Supper is no vain form, but the highest act of the consciousness of society. It is not the commemoration of an *individual* merely that gives this rite its true significance. The memory of Christ, as the summit of humanity, is a point of meeting for all souls. Whatever symbol recalls that memory is a door of communication with the Church universal and eternal, comprising whatever is noble and brave and wise and holy in the past and the present, in heaven and on earth. The thought which connects us dwellers in the dust with the noble army of the immortals who have shed their light on the course of time, and wrought their life into this our world, is one of the sublimest revelations of the gospel, and deserves expression in the rites of religion. This is the expression the Church has given it, showing us, in the Eucharist, our part and place in the common march and the sacred host. The bread and wine which it sets before us are the symbols of immaterial nourishment, — types of the constant daily feast of life, the same for all souls in all worlds, — the feast whose food is God's will in daily work, whose guests are the faithful of every faith and name, whose cheer is love, and whose song is praise.

The spirit in the letter, the spirit through the letter, is a lesson wide as human life, — the reconciliation of ideal and actual in human things. If the visible letter of our work be no dead letter merely, but a genuine fruit of the spirit, a service and a sacrifice, into which we breathe the aspiration and good-will, the faith and the love, which alone can make it and make us alive, it will be an epistle from the heart to the world of our time, in which all who behold it shall read the spirit that was in us, that possessed our thought and wrought in our will, and sought to express itself, not wholly in vain, in our activity. Therefore let the spirit that stirs in us, ere it evaporate in idle dreams, or degenerate into sickly sentimentality, hasten to record itself in some visible letter and condign work that shall give it effect. If love springs in the breast, let it rush into action; the vision in the brain, let it turn into deed; let the plastic present — the molten metal of the hour — receive the impress of our will before it stiffens into the past. The world about us is a standing admonition to this effect, stamped all over as it is with the letter of the spirits that have gone before us, and proving that the smallest deed whose grain is good is better than the noblest aspiration that dies in the breast.

VI.

SAVING FAITH.

VI.

SAVING FAITH.

The oldest controversy in religion respects the comparative value of faith and works. This contest pervades the whole history of man's spiritual progress from Abraham down. It arrayed that patriarch against the worshippers of Moloch, his contemporaries. It was the quarrel between Brahmanism and Buddhism in India. It was the quarrel between Judaism and Christianity; later, between Romanism and Protestantism, between the Orthodox * and the Liberal.

It was the earliest topic of dispute in the Christian Church. We find the writers of the New Testament at variance on this point, maintaining opposite sides of this question. Paul maintains the sufficiency of faith: James insists on the absolute necessity of works. Singularly enough, they both appeal to the same example in defence of their respective positions, — the example of the patriarch Abraham. Paul cites him as a supereminent instance of faith. "Abraham believed

* Belief in orthodoxy, when made a condition of salvation, is as much a species of "works" as pilgrimages or fasts.

God, and it was accounted to him for righteousness. Know ye, therefore, that they who are of faith, the same are the children of Abraham." James, on the other hand, magnifies Abraham's works — his acts — as the real, meritorious, justifying, and saving trait of the patriarchal example. "Was not Abraham our father justified by works when he had offered Isaac his son upon the altar? Seest thou how faith wrought with his works, and by works was faith made perfect?" To this plea it might have been objected, that Abraham, according to the story, did not sacrifice his son, although it was the fashion of that time and country to do so. Parents, in that country, sacrificed their first-born, as a matter of course. Custom demanded it; religion enjoined it: it was the old Canaanitish worship. What distinguished Abraham from his contemporaries was, that he did *not* sacrifice his first-born. It must have cost him a struggle to resist the universal custom; but he did resist it: and he did so, not from excess of parental fondness, but from a deeper, truer faith. He had such faith in God as to believe, contrary to the general voice, that a man might be justified without that unnatural sacrifice. He believed in the sacredness of nature; he believed in the still small voice of the heart, and God speaking in that; and, though his first impulse was to comply with what seemed to be the dictate of religion, his second and manlier thought was to refrain. If at first he seemed to hear the voice of the Lord, saying, "Take now thy son, thine only son, Isaac, whom thou lovest, and get thee into the land of Moriah, and offer him there for a burnt-offering," he listened again in a higher and healthier mood, and heard the command, "Lay not thine hand upon the lad, neither do thou any thing unto him." So I interpret the old tradition. Abraham did not sacrifice his son: he believed that he might forego the sacrifice; and it was "accounted to him for righteousness." If faith was shown by a willingness to make the offering, it was still more signally proved by withholding it. For which requires the greater faith, — to comply with custom and tradition, or to refuse compliance? Nonconformity, no doubt, may sometimes arise from irreligion and unbelief; men may neglect a religious ordinance from want of interest and want of faith; but when it is faith that impels dissent, as in the case of such earnest and heroic and devout natures as are sometimes found in that predicament, that faith is unquestionably greater than the faith expressed by any works of conformity and tradition. There can be no question that the faith of Paul was something superior to that of the Jews of Damascus, or the silversmiths of Ephesus; or that the faith of John Huss was superior to that of the bishops who assisted at the Council of Constance; or Luther's to that of Leo X.; or the faith of George Fox to that of the magistrates of Manchester and Worcester.

Paul but puts into words what Abraham, three thousand years before, had uttered in action, when he says, "The just shall live by faith."

When we speak of salvation by faith, we do not mean that a man is saved by his orthodoxy. Else were the greater part of the world irrevocably doomed, — all the pagan world, and the greater part of the Christian, — the greater part, and, I fancy, the better part; so that the remnant saved would not much commend the salvation, or exalt the Saviour in the world's judgment. There is no saving power in orthodoxy; there is no saving power in mere belief of any kind, except as belief may be symptomatic, indicating a receptivity of mind; and that receptivity a vitality which certainly is saving, — say, rather, which is salvation. Then, however, it is not because the belief is dogmatically correct that it saves. It may not be correct, and yet be saving, so far as the state of mind in the believer is concerned. Setting aside the influence on the life, a man shall as soon be saved by believing with the Hindu in the incarnations of Vishnu, as by believing with the Christian in the Word made flesh.

Salvation by faith means two things. It means that man's destiny is determined by what he is, not by what he does; and it means that confidence itself is salvation.

1. A man's destiny is determined by what he is, and not by what he does. In other words, being is more than doing. This is the Christian view of salvation, as interpreted by Paul. And so truly and specifically Christian is this view, that I am tempted to call it a discovery of Christianity, — a spiritual truth which Christianity first brought to light. Not what we do, but what we are. The old theory, the childish, pagan, Jewish theory of salvation, — the theory which still most widely prevails, even in Christendom still prevails, — is precisely the reverse of this: it puts doing before being; it reckons by works; it tries a man by tale and stint, as a task-master tries a slave. Now, it must be granted that human judgments are necessarily

based on the standard of action. What a man does, that he is, we say, and say truly; for, generally speaking, we know men only by their works. Nay, more, in judging of *ourselves*, we have to apply the same test. For who dare flatter himself that he is wise and charitable and devout, when all his conduct bears witness to the contrary? But observe that this test is safely applicable only as a negative criterion: it is a very doubtful one if we apply it positively. In the absence of all works, or where the works are only evil, we are safe in inferring moral deficiency or moral corruption; but we cannot reverse the criterion, and rate the internal goodness of the man by the external goodness of the act, which may or may not be the genuine offspring of the heart.

False religion puts doing before being: it reckons by works. It has always been so. I account for it thus: The sense of accountableness is instinctive in man, and suggests a Power which punishes and rewards, and whose punishments and rewards the childish mind conceives to be regulated by the same standard which governs earthly authorities, — the parent, the task-master, the governor, in appointing theirs, — compliance or non-compliance with external requirements. This is the first rude conception of moral accountableness, — something done to please God, to win his favor and avert his wrath. Hence the inquiry, — perplexing, doubtful, anxious, — What must I do to be saved? the feeling that something is to be *done* to satisfy and gratify Almighty Power. Hence the idea, — so natural, so universal, so hard to eradicate, — salvation by works.

Judaism was no wiser in this than other religions, though wiser and better in so many respects. The Jewish idea of human accountableness was that of a God who sets his people stints, and rewards and punishes accordingly. So Paul described it: "The law is not of faith; but the man that doeth them shall live by them." The Jewish religion was a tariff of duties levied on its subjects, with corresponding forfeitures, exacted *ad valorem*, for every article omitted or transgressed. The Christian religion, in its principle and essence, averse to all this, as interpreted by Paul, was yet converted into this by the misapprehension and misguided zeal of the ages following. And, because the gospel had set no stints, the Christians of the East, and, after them, the Christians of the West, began to stint and task themselves with works by which they hoped to earn salvation. They made their dwellings in deserts and caves; they spent their lives in saying prayers; they subsisted on the scantiest and poorest food; they wore haircloth; they scourged their flesh, and in every way made life as uncomfortable as bodily privation and hardship could make it. In process of time, the Church authorities took it upon themselves to prescribe these works and impose these stints on their subjects. The Church had its tariff of good works, and dispensed the salvation of which it assumed the administration and control, in conformity with it. All Judaism came back with the penances and fasts, the pilgrimages and mulcts, and other prescriptions, of the Church of Rome. Instead of Christ being "the end of the law of righteousness," as Paul had predicted, a new law of righteousness (or a new law-righteousness) was instituted in his name. The exploded principle, "He that doeth them shall live by them," was revived and adopted by the recreant Church as the Christian rule. So inveterate is man's proclivity to materialize in religion, to convert the most interior concerns of the soul into formalities and business transactions, to look abroad for that which only the heart can give, to trade in the unmerchantable. Every revival of religion is a protest against this one everlasting mistake. When Luther, in his younger days, as a pious monk and obedient son of the Church, was climbing on his knees, according to prescribed usage, the sacred staircase of the Lateran Church, he recalled the saying, "The just shall live by faith." With that recollection began a crisis in the history of religion. Christianity was new-born in that hour, — the end, once more, "of the law of righteousness to every one that believeth."

Has Protestantism, then, entirely outgrown this error in all its applications? We have ceased to rely on ecclesiastical good works, on pilgrimages and fasts: do we not still cherish the belief in salvation by moral? The Pauline principle applies to these as well as those. Moral works are as valueless as ecclesiastical, when undertaken upon speculation, as means and conditions of salvation. Temperance, chastity, charity, are saving graces when they exist as genuine fruits of the Spirit: they lose that saving quality when adopted as expedients and means to an end. Action, like belief, is merely symptomatic. The best acts are valuable and saving only as authentic exponents of the moral life. If they do not truly express that life, if they have any other source than that life, they are spiritually worthless, like promissory notes from an empty vault.

Not what a man does, but what he is, is his justification or condemnation. Doing may be copied, being cannot. All the graces can be imitated; but grace is original in every man in whom it exists. Works may be borrowed; but the heart is man's own.

Every religion, in turn, repeats the illusion about salvation as a bargain with God, a good to be purchased with a price. But what price can purchase heaven, if we come to the question of equivalents, — of value earned by service rendered? Who is sufficient for such a trade? Who so rich and strong and good as to offer an equivalent for heavenly gifts? Who has that which God so needs, and has so much of it, that God will think it worth the while, as a matter of profitable trade, to sell him eternal blessedness therefor? The best of us can do no more than pay, as he goes, for all that he receives and has received during all the years when he could do nothing. Can the best of us do even that?

But, though our good works can be no equivalent, may they not be still a condition of salvation, — the terms which God has seen fit to exact in return for that great boon? Suppose it to be so, what are those terms? If there is such a covenant, expressed or understood, what is man's part in the contract? Nothing less, surely, than obedience to God's law. Now, if God has made our well-being to depend on strict obedience to the moral law, then our moral welfare is forfeited by disobedience to that law, not only by gross and continued disobedience, but by all disobedience whatsoever. Every violation of the moral law violates the contract. This is Paul's argument. But every one does violate it. "There is none righteous," in that sense; "no, not one." "They are all gone out of the way." It is impossible not to violate it. Perfect obedience is practically impossible. It is what no one has yet accomplished, or will accomplish. It is impossible, because man is not a machine, but a spirit. You may construct a machine with such precision that it shall perform a given work in a given manner. You may construct it with such precision that the action of the motive power on each part shall be reduced to a certainty; the function of every wheel and screw may be determined and controlled, — so far and no farther, so much and no more in a given time. Such a machine may be made for a while to perform its whole duty, and nothing but its duty. But even a machine will become disordered in time, and sin against the law written in its constitution, by neglect or transgression. But man is not so fashioned, and cannot be so managed, or so manage himself. He cannot be made to perform all possible duties, and keep the whole law of God, with that mechanical exactness with which the hands of a clock perform a certain number of revolutions in a given time. Let him try the experiment for a single day. Let him undertake for one whole day to fulfil the law in every minute particular, positive and negative, in thought as well as deed; to do every thing which he ought to do, in the way in which he ought to do it; and to do nothing, say nothing, think nothing, which he ought not. Let him at night subject the history of that day to a rigorous scrutiny; and, if his conscience is but moderately enlightened, he will discover, that, with the best intention, he has not been perfect for one whole day, — that the day might possibly have been better spent than it was. With the best intention and the uttermost endeavor, he has still come short of the mark. Man is a poor creature, if he is to be judged in this way; he is less perfect than a steam-engine or a watch. "By the deeds of the law shall no flesh be justified; for all have sinned, and come short of the glory of God." The Mohammedans have a fable, that the soul, before it can enter paradise, must cross a bridge, narrow as the edge of a sword, over a gulf of fire; and that no one can be saved who does not endure this test. A good illustration, this, of the doctrine of salvation by works. To attempt to win heaven by this method is like the attempt to cross a gulf of fire on the edge of a sword. Forlorn would be our prospect, perdition our doom, if our destiny depended solely on our works.

To remedy this difficulty, to complement this deficiency of human virtue, theologians, still clinging to the notion of a law to which perfect obedience is the one indispensible condition of salvation, have proposed a substitute in the person of Christ. At first, it was the perfect obedience of Christ which answered, instead of other men's obedience, and satisfied the law on their behalf; more recently, it is the death of Christ, which, received as the penalty of sin, serves instead of the punishment of sinners, and insures their salvation in spite of transgression. It is not my purpose, at present, to criticise these views. The error lies in the prior assumption, that salvation is made by divine decree to depend on perfect and exact obedience to the moral law; that is, on works: in strange and direct contradiction to the teaching of Paul, who shows that the ground of salvation is faith.

Not what we do, but what we are, is the strength of our present, and the hope of our future, if any strength there is in us, or any hope for us. There are cases, no doubt, in which the actions of men are better than their hearts. Whited sepulchres there are, fair without, not wanting in good works, but inwardly full of treachery and uncleanness. What are the acts of such natures worth? Suppose them to be ten times fairer than they are, can their works save them?

But most men, it is to be hoped, are a great deal better than their works. Their inward life is more divine than all the manifestations of it that have yet appeared. The best of men would seem to us less perfect than they do, did we not impute to them a goodness exceeding all their actions. Jesus would not be to us the pure ideal that he is, did we not suppose him to be better than his life, divine as that is. We feel that what he did was a very small part of what he was; his nature was not all expressed in his works: there was more virtue in him than went out of him. The exigencies of his condition did not exhaust all the fulness of his divine humanity; the mould was not equal to the form. He stands in our apprehension immeasurably great behind his works, more honored for what he was, in our ideal, than for what he did. Most of us, it is to be hoped, are better than our works. It is to be hoped there is more goodness in us than appears. The conduct is a very imperfect exponent of the inner life. Still, if the inner life is sound and strong, it will sooner or later justify itself in action, and justify the actor. But the justifying power is not in the act, but in the faith that produced it. The virtue resides not in the fruit, but in the tree. You value the trees in your orchard for their fruit-bearing power, not for the fruit that hangs on them at the time. That tree must be a poor one, which is not worth more than its present crop.

Being before doing, — this is the interior truth which lies in the doctrine of salvation by faith. And another thing is meant by it. It means, —

2. That confidence in salvation, in one's own salvation, is essential to salvation; nay, more, that it is salvation. Does this statement seem questionable? I see very clearly the abuse that may be made of it; nevertheless, it is the doctrine of Paul, if I rightly understand him. It is the doctrine of Luther, the best interpreter of Paul, because interpreting him out of a kindred spirit and similar circumstances.

Believe that you are saved, and you are saved. Such a belief must be the result of an inward experience which justifies it. But may there not be a false confidence, an overweening pharisaic conceit, like that recorded of the Rabbi Jeremias? "I saw the sons of the Feast; they are very few in number. If there are a thousand, I and my son are of the number; if a hundred, I and my son are of the number; if there are two, I and my son are they." To this I reply, Conceit is one thing, and belief is another. The faith which this view supposes is not born of conceit, but of verity.

It is easy to put cases which shall seem to make the doctrine ridiculous. There is Graceless, whom we all know, a thorough worldling, selfish, hard, sensual, mean. Suppose that Graceless fancies his salvation sure, is he therefore saved? The presumption is, that Graceless bestows no thought upon the matter: but, if he does, you may be sure he feels no such confidence as you suppose; you may be sure that salvation to him looks very problematical.

There are cases of indifference, — of what may be called a negative confidence, the taking-for-granted of ignorance and unbelief. And there are cases in which the moral life is apparently too feeble to weather the crisis of death, and survive the dissolution of the mortal frame. If ever souls so destitute of spiritual life can recover themselves from the wreck of mortality, if they are to assume a conscious existence hereafter, it is only through sore pangs and bitter travail, if at all, that the moral life can be born again. There are also cases of superstitious terror, of doubt and despair, experienced by very worthy people, induced by false religion, where the spirit of adoption and filial trust has not yet replaced the spirit of bondage and of fear. All that is disease. All anxiety about salvation, all fears about the future, fears of death and judgment to come, in really good people, in those who love and seek the right, are morbid affections. The healthy soul casts off all that. Conscious of right purposes, believing in God, it never troubles itself about the hereafter: it commits its future, without misgiving, to the infinite Father, not doubting that the Power which has brought us thus far, and kept us hitherto, will be as near to us in every coming state as here and now, and equally able and equally willing to guide and to bless.

The perfection of spiritual growth gives us back the unconsciousness of primitive man, when life flowed on from its source to its close without question or fear of the hereafter. I figure to myself a state when this unconsciousness, like some lost paradise, shall be regained; when the emancipated spirit, having realized its own nature by complete development, and having outgrown the dreary period of self-questioning, shall be conscious of no obligation, shall never hear the "stern daughter of the voice of God;" but follow its own impulse with absolute freedom, and never stray; shall gravitate to good by divine necessity, and know not that it is good, and know no merit in seeking it, because there is no evil in its consciousness with which to contrast it. A seraph at work is a child at play, combining the earnestness of settled purpose with the freshness of immediate impulse, and the glow of a momentary mood. Will such an one ask, "What shall I do to be saved?" Will the sun desire to know the method of its shining, or the stars how far to cast their ray; or the rushing and rejoicing river, the meaning and purpose of its course? The emancipated spirit has outgrown all questions; it derives its knowledge, not through the troubled medium of the questioning, groping, prying, doubting intellect, but directly from the fountain-light of the purified, perfected will. It knows by doing, and in knowing does. Knowing, doing, willing, loving, are no longer the severed and unequal functions of a halting and distracted life, but one undivided, spontaneous action of a life as serene as the source from which it flows.

VII.

THE AGE OF GRACE;

OR,

ATONEMENT WITHOUT EXPIATION.

VII.

ATONEMENT WITHOUT EXPIATION.

"Die Vernichtung der Sünde, dieser alten Last der Menscheit, und alles Glaubens an Busse und Sühnung, ist durch die Offenbarung des Christenthums eigentlich bewirkt worden.* — NOVALIS.

THE years of the Christian era are technically styled years "of grace." The term is used without, I suspect, an adequate sense of the import and fitness of that designation. The word "grace" — synonymous with "pardoning mercy" — denotes a special and characteristic trait of the Christian religion; a fundamental distinction between it and other religions. I know of no other religion in which pardoning mercy forms a constitutive, organic element, — none which assures forgiveness of sins to penitent souls on the simple condition of repentance, and so absolves from the superstitious fears which other religions connect with the thought of God and the hereafter.

I find in other religions the principle of propitiation, which is quite a different thing. When the gods of

* The proper effect of the Christian revelation is the annihilation of sin, — the ancient burden of humanity, and of all belief in penance and expiation.

the Gentiles were supposed, by their votaries, to be incensed by neglect or transgression, the only way to pacify them, to bring back the averted eye of their blessing, was to offer animal sacrifices. So only could the Powers be propitiated and the sin atoned. Even this method was not always effectual. The wrath of the *Numen*, as we read in the old myths, would sometimes continue to burn with immitigable fury against the offender, and even against his remote posterity, as in the case of "Pelops' line." And, when effectual, the result was not forgiveness, but expiation; not grace, but quittance; not pardoning mercy, but satisfied ire. So the Jehovah of the Hebrews is represented as propitiated by sin-offerings and trespass-offerings, which the priest was required to offer with exact and complicated rites for the sins of the people, that they might be remitted. For without blood, by the Law of Moses, there was "no remission." The writers of the New Testament, and especially the writer to the Hebrews, transfer this idea of sacrifice from the old dispensation to the new. They represent the blood of Christ as the substitute for the blood of bullocks and of lambs. By such representations they describe the subjective fruits of Christ's ministry, — of his death as the consummation of that ministry, — not the objective nature of his work, viewed in its relation to the Godhead. The language is figurative, not dogmatic. I see not how any other interpretation could ever have been put upon it by Christians. Nothing in the history of opinions is more marvellous than that Christian theologians should fail to see, that by treating Christ's death as the satisfaction of a debt, whether in the sacrificial sense of expiation, or the governmental sense of a shift or compromise, they rule out of Christianity precisely that which constitutes its most distinctive feature, — Grace. They reduce it to the level of the elder religions, in which law and sacrifice were predominant elements. In what sense can grace be said to have come with Christ, if the Christian's God, like the Jew's and the Gentile's, is a Being whose enmity is provoked by sin, and propitiated by sacrifice? with this remarkable difference, that, while the Gentile or Jewish Divinity was alienated from individuals and tribes, by individual and ancestral transgressions, and reconciled by the blood of bulls and rams, "the God and Father of our Lord Jesus Christ" is represented as alienated from the entire race of man by the moral infirmity of the first pair, and reconciled only by the blood of a man. Surely, on this supposition, the Christian's God is less gracious than any other. Instead of living under a dispensation of grace, we are under a dispensation of inexorable law. Instead of a Heavenly Father, we have only a Hebrew Jehovah or Olympian Jove.

The gospel was meant to be a message of glad tidings: any system of theology which makes it a message of bad tidings, carries falsehood on its face. Its message is grace; and its grace is peculiar to it, — the grace of God, which by faith and repentance absolves from sin, and redeems from the terrors of divine wrath, which the consciousness of sin awakens in the soul.

Religious terrors are incident to all faiths, and common to all nations. Christianity alone reveals the grace that delivers from this torment; the perfect love which casteth out fear. Let us glance for a moment at other dispensations, and compare them with the gospel in this particular.

If there is any nation of antiquity which might be supposed to be exempt from spiritual terrors, it is the Greeks, — a cheerful people, who seem to have lived a life of the senses, thoroughly at home, and perfectly content with this visible world; caring little for any other; having no faith and no interest in the spiritual, except a poetic and an artistic one. Such is the character of the Greeks as represented in poetry and art. But go behind these manifestations, inquire from other sources the state of mind of the Greeks on the subject of religion, and you will find that, where atheism had not neutralized the idea of God, the mind was haunted by religious fears. Wherever there was enough of belief in Divinity to constitute religion, there was superstition. A Latin poet praises the atheist Epicurus for being the first to deliver men from this fear. Atheism, in his view, was the only salvation. Plutarch, whose writings bring us nearer to the mind of the ancients than any others, has depicted superstition in a way which shows what the terrors of religion must have been, with no revelation of divine grace to mitigate their gloom. "The victim of spiritual terrors," he says, "has no hiding-place, no refuge. Polycrates was the scourge of Samos, and Periander of Corinth; but one could escape both, and find shelter in some free and equal government. But he who fears the divine government as an inexorable, implacable tyranny, whither can he remove, or whither can he flee? What land or what sea can he find where God is not? Miserable man! in what corner of the world canst thou be so concealed as to think thou hast escaped him? Slaves are allowed by the law, when despairing of their freedom, to demand another sale, in the hope of obtaining kinder masters. But superstition allows no change of gods; and where could he find a god whom he would *not fear, who dreads his father's and his own? A slave* may fly to an altar; and they that are pursued by an enemy think themselves safe if they can but lay hold of a statue or shrine: but the superstitious fear and tremble there most where others, even the most timid, take courage. Death itself puts no end to this foolish dread. It extends its fears beyond the grave; and, after the sorrows of this world, looks forward to sufferings that never end. Then open I know not what gates of hell from beneath, rivers of fire, Stygian torrents, judges and tormentors, ghastly spectres and endless woes."

Such was the religion of the most polished nation of antiquity, in the experience of those who were spiritual enough to regard religion as any thing more than a civil institution. It was a religion of fear, in which no voice of grace spoke comfort to the stricken and trembling soul, overwhelmed with the terrors of the invisible.

Still more remarkable is the absence of grace in the two great systems of Eastern and Southern Asia, — Brahmanism and its offspring, Buddhism. In these religions every sin is unpardonable, and must be expiated by a separate life in some new state whose conditions are determined by the errors of this. When the soul is separated from the body by death, it migrates into some new body, — it may be of a man, or it may be of a brute, — in which it must bear the penalty of some particular sin, committed in some former state. According to the Buddhist conception, all life is penal. The life which we lead in this body is charged with the penalties of past transgressions, of which the soul has been guilty in unremembered lives antecedent to this; and the life that now is, has its own transgressions to be atoned for in lives to come. Thus the soul passes from life to life, from body to body; through form after form, grade after grade, of humanity and animality; through princes and beggars, and cats and dogs, and creeping things, — ascending and descending; now soaring into spiritual day, now steeped in thickest night of sense; still atoning, and sinning and atoning again; until, after ages of mundane experience, every sin expiated, every blot wiped out, the pilgrim spirit arrives at last at its destined goal. And that goal, — the end of all these wanderings, the fruit of all this discipline, — what is it? Hear, O Christian! and compassionate the infinite despair which lurks in the doctrine. Annihilation! The privilege of non-existence; extinction of the individual being, absorption in the universal Being; the soul dissolved in blank unconsciousness, which, if not absolute annihilation, is personal decease in every practical sense of the term. The gospel says, "The wages of sin is death;" but the faithful soul "is passed from death unto life." Buddhism says, "The wages of sin is life; but the perfect soul passes from life to death. Life is penance; extinction is salvation."

I find in all these religions no sign of pardoning mercy, no trace of those ideas so prominent in the gospel, — the efficacy of repentance, and forgiveness of sins.

These ideas, it is true, are found in the writings of the Jewish dispensation; and, although the religion of Moses is characterized as "law" in contrast with the grace which came by Christ, the Old Testament contains the nearest approximation to the gospel, the most clear and emphatic declarations of forgiveness to be found in any of the elder religions. "The Lord is merciful and gracious, slow to anger, and plenteous in mercy. He will not always chide, neither will he keep his anger for ever. He hath not dealt with us after our sins, nor rewarded us according to our iniquities." "Let the wicked forsake his ways, and the unrighteous man his thoughts, and turn unto the Lord, and he will have mercy upon him; and to our God, and he will abundantly pardon." — "If the wicked will turn from all his sins that he hath committed, and keep all my statutes, and do that which is lawful and right, he shall surely live: he shall not die."

But let it be remembered, that these utterances are no part of the Mosaic Law; the spirit which they breathe is not the spirit of Judaism. They are glorious anticipations rather of the grace that was to come, and such anticipations as were possible only to a prophet of the race of Shem; to a Hebrew standing where Moses stood, and seeing, from the spiritual Sinai to which the lawgiver had brought his people, — its thunders all hushed, its blackness and darkness and tempest rolled away, — more clearly even than Moses saw, the deep things of God. Such anticipations were possible only to the shepherd-king whose musing youth the Shepherd God had lodged in the green pastures, and led by the still waters of his grace, and anointed with the oil of gladness above his fellows; to the rapt Isaian, whose eyes in the midst of "a people of unclean lips" had "seen the King, the Lord of hosts," and whose mouth the seraphim had opened with a coal from the altar; to the brooding exile, to whom, in the land of the Chaldeans, by the river Chebar, the heavens were opened.

What was rapt vision, and rare, prophetic apperception, known only to elect and inspired souls, under the old dispensation, is become the staple and commonplace of the new. Christianity is the first and only religion that teaches forgiveness of sins on the simple ground of repentance, as a fundamental element of its doctrine. It is the only religion that makes adequate provision for the troubled conscience, and redeems from bottomless despair the soul that is penetrated with a poignant sense of sin. That overpowering conviction of sin which lashes into madness the souls it masters; which the Greeks impersonated in the fable of the Furies, — that malady was proof against all the remedies of the ancient religions. It yields only to the healing grace of the gospel.

It is true, Christianity enhances the consciousness of sin. "I had not known sin," says Paul, "but by the law." Not Moses' law merely, but every clear revelation of righteousness, develops this knowledge. The clearest revelation of righteousness comes by Christ; consequently the profoundest consciousness of sin. No one who has not experienced conviction of sin, whether in the way of remorse for actual transgression, or a general sense of unworthiness, can understand Christianity aright. But the same ministration which causes the disease supplies also the homœopathic remedy. If the gospel awakens consciousness of sin, it is also charged with healing virtue. The soul that is drawn with reverential faith and love to the manifestation of perfect love in the Crucified, is made partaker of that love; it feels itself relieved of its crushing weight: as the heavy-laden, staggering pilgrim, in the beautiful fable of Bunyan, when he came at length to a place "where there stood a cross, and a little below, in the bottom, a sepulchre, his burden loosed from off his shoulders, and fell from off his back, and began to tumble, and so continued to do till it came to the mouth of the sepulchre, where it fell in."

The higher the revelation, the clearer the consciousness of sin; but the clearer also, and the fuller, the absolution.

But is not forgiveness of sins a doctrine of "Natural Religion" which the common understanding is competent to discover, and would have discovered without other illumination? It is time this phantasm of a "Natural Religion" were exploded. There is no natural knowledge of divine things, as the word "natural" is commonly understood. We can judge of what might be, only by what has been; and we know that the keenest and profoundest minds of antiquity did not attain to this idea. Plato, in whom, if anywhere, the student of antiquity might expect to find it, knows it not. The Hebrew prophets alone attained, before Christ, to the vision of unconditional grace and atonement without expiation.

But, while we claim for the Christian religion the peculiarity of a dispensation of grace, it must be confessed that the gospel has not been so received and so interpreted by the Christian Church. The grace that was in it was soon forgotten, and overlaid with dogmatic additions and ecclesiastical inventions. It would seem as if the Church had made it her special aim to obscure and obliterate this characteristic trait of our faith, — to assimilate the religion of Jesus to other religions, by engrafting upon it a sacrificial, expiatory element entirely foreign to its spirit. So completely has the Church of Rome misconceived the spirit of Jesus in this particular, that her authorized version of the Scripture substitutes for the word "Repent," in the New Testament, the perverse rendering, "Do penance." "From that time Jesus began to preach, and to say, Do penance; for the kingdom of God is at hand." That one word indicates the change from a religion of faith and grace to a religion of legality and of works.

But this vital truth of the gospel was too deeply rooted in the heart of Christendom to be quite choked by the tares of theology, or eradicated by priestly tampering. The *sentiment* of the Church re-acted in a very remarkable manner on its doctrine. The grace which was banished from its creed re-appeared in its mythology. It incarnated itself in the Virgin Mary — the supreme object of Catholic devotion, more than Christ himself, the divinity adored and implored in the homage and prayers of the faithful. The Virgin Mary of the Roman Church, the Queen of Heaven, the Mother of God, is a providential embodiment of divine grace. However we may liken her to the female divinities of other religions, Phœnician, Egyptian, Hindoo, Greek, with all of which undoubtedly she has some affinity, the most zealous Protestant must confess that the Christian goddess represents a character, expresses an idea, entirely distinct and infinitely removed from any conception embodied in any other religion. It is not beauty, nor wisdom, nor purity alone, nor even the union of virginity and maternity, — however peculiar to Christian mythology, — that Mary represents; but the infinite grace of God, stooping down to human infirmities and sins; raining pity from eyes of love on the erring and abandoned, on the slave of sense and the victim of passion; the exorable mother of the inexorable, coming between the sinner and the law, softening the terrors of absolute rule, directing the applications of abstract justice, making justice but means to an end, — the means remedial, the end salvation.

I say, this embodiment was providential. It fulfilled an important office to the Christianized Pagan in an age that must of necessity have other objects of worship beside the Supreme. It was the most effectual, if not the only way, in which the idea of divine grace could be presented to the unreflecting mind of the time. I believe that this benign form has often stood between the sinner and despair. Often, in sorrow and perplexity and imminent peril, prayer to the Virgin, and faith in the Virgin's intercession, has sustained the sinking soul when the thought of the infinite God was too awful and too remote for support. The Mother seemed so much nearer and more real than the Son! The devout Catholic instinctively flew to her in all time of trial, as the child flies to its natural mother for relief.

Protestantism purged religion of idolatry; but it failed, in its early stages, to replace the image of the

Virgin with any adequate representation of divine grace in its creed. Protestantism, in some of its communions, developed the ideas of Expiation and Vicarious Satisfaction and Propitiation of divine wrath, with such bleak emphasis, with such unrelenting rigor, as to dissipate the idea of grace more effectually than even Romanism had done; and to give us, instead of an evangile or message of glad tidings, a bloody cartel of vengeance and of doom.

But one thing Protestantism has done, for which Christendom owes it everlasting thanks. It has restored the written word. It has given us the Scriptures, and with them the way of escape from its own entanglements. It uncovered the well of divine truth on which twelve centuries had piled their traditions; and, though the spring was troubled at first by the process, and reflected only distorted images, there have not been wanting — Heaven be praised! — persistent spirits who stayed by the waters, and gazed till the troubling angel had passed away; and then saw in the crystal depths a human image, and the sun-grace of God, and the pure, unfathomable heavens bending over, serenely inviting, and ready to embrace.

Grace is the innermost sense and soul of the Christian revelation; the Alpha and Omega of the "New Covenant;" the hidden pearl of the parable, for which, when found, the theologian is willing to give up all his theology. A false theology has long ignored it; but it could not remain for ever concealed. May its lustre become ever more apparent to Christian faith, until the Church of the Crucifixion, which has hitherto prevailed in the Christian world, shall be replaced by a Church of the Resurrection! And as Christendom has borne in its body "the dying of the Lord Jesus" in its doctrine of Expiation, so may "the life also of Jesus be manifest" in its future grateful recognition of a grace without expiation!

VIII.

THE "DOUBLE PREDESTINATION."

VIII.

THE "DOUBLE PREDESTINATION."

THE first glance at society discovers a vast inequality in the outward condition of men. A second and nearer view reveals a less portentous, yet very considerable, difference in human desert, or what we call desert,—a difference in the moral character and life. If the former of these differences exactly corresponded with the latter; if high and low, rich and poor, fortunate and unfortunate, happy and wretched, were identical with moral good and moral evil,—these contrasts would not much trouble us. To the greater part of mankind, they would seem quite natural and proper: the why and wherefore of them to most minds would present no difficulty. The common judgment would be, that some are righteous, having chosen righteousness, and therefore deservedly blest; and that others are wicked, having chosen wickedness, and therefore deservedly wretched.

But if any should consider the matter more curiously, and inquire more minutely into the causes of that moral difference which has wrought this difference of outward condition, to such the common answer, that the good and evil have chosen respectively to be what they are, would not suffice. A further question would suggest itself: "Why have they chosen thus? why have they not rather all chosen what is best, and will bring the greatest satisfaction?" And if to this it were answered, "These have chosen thus because they were wise, and those have chosen otherwise because they were foolish," a new question would immediately arise, "Why were these wise, and those foolish?" And the answer to that question would carry the inquirer beyond the actors themselves, and beyond the present condition of society, back, and still back, from circumstance to circumstance, and from generation to generation, — back to the first man. And here a portion of these inquirers would halt. The first man, they would say, explains every thing. The first man had it all in his power, — the future history of the race, the character and condition of all his successors. He made a mistake; he did the wrong thing; and all his posterity have contracted a taint from his guilt, and inherit from his fall an irresistible proclivity to evil, by which they slide to sure destruction, excepting those whom God by his grace shall see fit to elect, and snatch from the common doom.

But some there would be who would not stop here. They would ask again, "What possessed the first man to blunder so foully, consigning himself and his offspring to everlasting death? Something must have ailed him to choose as he did." They would seek the reason of his mistake in his constitution, which was not made proof against such folly; that is, they would seek it in the author of that constitution. They would go beyond the first man, and never stop till they reached the First Cause, and would stop there only because they must; because the will of God is the adamantine boundary-wall of the mind, which no wit can penetrate, and which no imagination can scale.

In thus describing the natural and probable course of inquiry concerning the differences in the nature and condition of men, I have indicated the actual history of the doctrine of "Election," or rather of "Predestination," which includes "Election" as one of its terms, and includes "Reprobation" as the other.

It is true, the conditions of the problem are not precisely such as I have supposed. The difference in the outward condition of men does not exactly correspond with the differences in their moral nature. Moral good and temporal good, moral and temporal evil, are by no means identical or commensurate, the one with the other. Prosperity and vice are sometimes conjoined, and righteousness is sometimes wedded to adversity. But all this, in the eye of theology, is very superficial and transient. The doctrine of Predestination overlooks all this as insignificant; it takes its stand in eternity, and sees there a portentous and overwhelming difference in the human condition. It sees an eternal state of outward blessedness on the one hand, and of outward misery on the other, corresponding with and compensating moral good and evil.

In the system of religion received by our fathers, originating with Augustine in the fifth century, developed by Gottschalk in the ninth, revived by Calvin in the sixteenth, and consummated by Edwards in the eighteenth, — that system which once reigned in this country with despotic sway, which overshadowed the New England of the Puritans, and in the shadow of which many now living were born and bred, — in that system the doctrine of Predestination maintained a conspicuous place. It was held, that God had chosen a limited portion of the human race to be for ever blessed; that he chose them before they were born, while as yet they existed only in idea; chose them from all eternity, and without regard to any future and foreseen merit on their part; chose them of his own free grace, undetermined by any quality in the object, or by any consideration out of himself; chose them by an act of irresponsible, absolute will. And this will was irresistible. No one who was fore-ordained to eternal life could fail of his destination, or forfeit the blessedness in store for him, through any slip or fault of his own. He might sin as other men sin, but his sin would do him no mortal harm. His "effectual calling" would triumph over all the defects of his nature, and all the evil of his life, and carry him to heaven in spite of himself by the "final perseverance" of divine grace.

There is nothing revolting to the moral sense in the doctrine thus far. Had it never been developed beyond this point, or if nothing more were implied in it, it would have had no stronger objection to encounter than its want of foundation in the universal consciousness, and its want of support from the Scripture. This is the favorable side of the doctrine, — "Jacob have I loved." Some modern theologians have pretended that it goes no farther, and involves nothing more; that all men are capable of attaining that which the elect are sure of attaining. All are called, if few are chosen. All are furnished with the requisite means and opportunities, — the only difference being, that some are left to win the prize by the unaided exercise of their own powers, while others are goaded to it by an irresistible compulsion, stronger than their own wills, and than all the powers of a hostile world. But this was not the doctrine held by the fathers. That doctrine had a dark and repulsive side, — "Esau have I hated." The Church could not fail, in the course of her inquiry, to discover, that predestination and extraordinary action of divine grace are superfluous, if every man, by the ordinary powers of his nature, is capable of attaining that for the sake of which this special action is put forth. The doctrine, as consummated in the formularies of the ninth century, was, that every man who attains to everlasting life does so by a special act of grace, electing him thereto; and that no man attains to it who is not so elected. It follows, that the elective grace is an exclusive grace. In the act of choosing a part, is included the act of rejecting the rest. And since it is undeniable that God might have elected the whole race, as well as a part, — no respect being had to the qualities and claims of the chosen, — it follows further, that Predestination is as much an act of hostility to the many who are excluded, as it is of favor to the few who are chosen. Again, the Church was too acute not to see, that what God alone can prevent, and does not prevent, that he ordains. If none can be saved without the special election of God, then every one who is not elected is condemned by him to endless misery. Hence the horrible doctrine of the "Double Predestination" (prædestinatio duplex), taught by Gottschalk, and confirmed by the Synod of Valence in 855, — the doctrine of Calvin and Edwards.

Double Predestination includes Reprobation as well as Election. Reprobation is the other side, the complement of Election; the latter is incomplete without the former. Reprobation means that a large portion of the human race are foredoomed, for no fault of their own, by the arbitrary will of God, to endless misery. I say, by no fault of their own. The guilt contracted by the sin of the first man was assigned as the reason and justification of this decree. But the reason is no reason at all, so far as the justice of God is concerned. A thorough inquiry will not stop, and did not stop, with the sin of the first man. It demands, and demanded, the cause of that sin, the reason of its permission, the justification of a liability in which such portentous consequences were involved. Besides, Reprobation is not the necessary consequence of hereditary sin: if it were, then none could be saved. If God could elect some to be saved in spite of that sin, then he could elect all to be saved in spite of it. And if he did not, then Reprobation was purely an act of arbitrary will, undetermined by moral considerations.

After some vacillation of opinion, St. Augustine denied all efficacy to the human will, and ascribed the work of salvation to God alone, whose grace and election are entirely independent of any merit or quality in the subject. In other words, he maintained an absolute Predestination. His antagonist, Pelagius, starting from different premises and reasoning from a different experience, maintained, on the contrary, the power of all men to become good and holy. The Church decided in favor of Augustine, and the doctrine of Pelagius was repudiated as heresy. Augustine, however, did not consummate the doctrine of Predestination. His opinion was rather a practical than a speculative principle. After the lapse of three hundred years, the discussion was revived by a German monk, — a man of subtler intellect, if less elevated nature, than Augustine, who applied the principle of Predestination not merely, as heretofore, to the good, but also to the wicked. The one, he maintained, follows necessarily from the other. If a portion of the race are predestined to salvation, the rest are as certainly predestined to damnation. This Double Predestination was finally adopted by the Church. It was re-affirmed by Calvin after the Reformation, and carried out to its last results by Jonathan Edwards, who frankly admits that the doctrine makes God the author of sin.

There is something sublime in the uncompromising and inexorable consistency of this doctrine, and in the heroic disregard of consequences with which those who taught it carried out their reasoning, and pursued their principle to its final and legitimate result. And they seemed to find a ground and warrant for their doctrine in the sacred books. "For whom he did foreknow, he also did predestinate. . . . Moreover, whom he did predestinate, them he also called." There is a kind of election affirmed in the New Testament. Christians are called the "elect of God." They seemed to be singled out from the rest of mankind, and made the recipients of peculiar and exclusive privileges and blessings. This election is justified by Paul, who finds a precedent for it in Hebrew history, in the case of Jacob and Esau.

Before Jacob and Esau were born, consequently without regard to the character of either, it was ordained that the elder should serve the younger. "The children being not yet born, neither having done any good or evil, that the purpose of God, according to election might stand, not of works, but of him that willeth." "As it is written, Jacob have I loved, and Esau have I hated." That is, according to the true rendering of the Hebrew idiom, Jacob have I preferred before Esau, and distinguished with peculiar blessings.

Here was an instance of actual Predestination or Election in the world's history. It stands forth the representative of many others, — an instance of what has been in the world's history, and what is still, — an example of preference and divine favor wholly irrespective of personal merit. Jacob is no better than Esau; in many respects he is worse, — cunning, perfidious; a man entitled to no preference on the score of merit; and yet he is preferred. He is made inheritor of the promises; he is placed in the line of divine communications; through him is transmitted the Abrahamic blessing, while his brother is set aside, — ignoble head of an inferior line.

St. Paul adduces this instance, by way of precedent, to illustrate God's method in the distribution of civil blessings. It was an instance of what was then taking place in the election of those who were called to be disciples of Christ. Christians were called without regard to any previous claim, — Gentile and Jew, those who had performed the works of the law, and those who were without the law, — that the elective purpose "might stand, not of man's works, but of God's will." — "For he saith to Moses, 'I will have mercy on whom I will, and compassion on whom I will.' So, then, it is not of him that willeth, nor of him that runneth, but of God, that showeth mercy." This was the order of Providence then, and this is the order of Providence now. God's government is not a system of equality as it regards the privileges and blessings enjoyed by different orders of men: on the contrary, it is a system of seeming partiality, — so far as we can see, of arbitrary election; that is, an election entirely irrespective of the qualities and claims of the chosen, and undetermined by any law intelligible to us. All creatures have by nature an equal claim on the Universal Love; all are children of one Father; but how different the rank assigned to them in his household! One is created an angel, another is created a worm. Or, confining ourselves within the limits of the human family, some are elected to the highest culture and the noblest works of which human nature is capable; others are condemned to life-long ignorance and vice.

Observe this election on the large historic scale, as manifested in the lot of nations. One nation is set in the van of humanity, nurtured in Christian schools and churches, and blest with every advantage of moral and scientific culture; another is overshadowed by gloomy superstitions, and crushed by inexorable despotism. Compare our Protestant Christendom of to-day with the polities of some rude Polynesian tribe, and learn how wide the scope and how vast the distinction embraced in the scheme of divine election, as applied to nations.

But the fact and import of this election are most striking when we view it in its application to individuals. Suppose two souls, two individual entities, not yet incorporated in human frames, existing as yet only in the vision and will of the parent Mind. Both are equal in the sight of God; neither possesses any claim above the other, "being not yet born," as the apostle says; "neither having done any good or evil." What shall be the calling and destination respectively of these two souls? The one shall be launched into life in a civilized land, illumined by the light of the gospel, ennobled by science, adorned by art, rich in historic traditions, rich in sacred memories, abounding in the means of culture, affording scope and supplying motive to the nobler faculties of mind and heart. It shall draw its earliest nurture from the bosom of Christian parents, and come forth taught and stimulated by sages and poets and heroes and saints, imbued with all human learning, instituted in all useful arts. The other shall be cast on a savage shore, among savage children of the desert, in some unexplored island of the Indian Ocean, or some African wild, neighbor to the tiger and the ape; where hopeless night broods over the mind, and God's truth is quenched in thick superstition which not a ray of the everlasting light can pierce; where no science is learned but that which teaches the fingers to fight, no art acquired but that of fashioning and handling the bow and the spear, no calling known but that of violence, and no good pursued but the gross satisfactions of appetite and lust. Or, again, the one shall be lodged in a sickly and deformed frame, and crawl through life with labor and sorrow, and a crushing sense of inferiority;

the other shall incarnate itself in strength and beauty, and, with full command of its powers, rejoice in the buoyancy of perfect health, — every sinew tense, and every nerve in tune, — a body worthy to be the temple of the Lord. Yet, again, the one shall be born into the lap of wealth and social refinement, born to high station and command; the other shall enter humanity by the way of penury and want and grovelling vice, and see no way open but that of shame and guilt. These are no imaginary differences, but well-known and familiar facts. They present a curious theme for contemplation, when we think what a different value life is likely to have for individuals so divided in the circumstances of their lot. But they assume a more serious aspect, — these inequalities, if we attempt to trace their consequences in the moral destiny of those who are thus distinguished. Consider the influence of circumstance on character. Suppose two youths just entering the world, — the one a child of intelligent Christian parents, well circumstanced, able and willing to give their offspring such an education as shall best secure his moral well-being; the other sprung from the bosom of want and vice in some squalid den of a populous city, brought up in the daily contemplation of evil examples, — every known influence that acts upon him unfavorable to moral growth. What are likely to be the lives of these two subjects? Let any one attempt from these elements to calculate their future history; what will he predict? For the one, a useful and honorable career, life-long progress in well-doing; for the other, a life of infamy and shame, constant declension into gulf after gulf of depravity and ruin. But this is not all; it is not the worst: it might seem to be the least and most favorable part of the calculation. We are taught that the consequences of our actions extend beyond this mortal world; that this life delivers us over to another, like this in its moral conditions, subject to the same law, taking up and carrying on the same process of development; that the next world finds us as this world leaves us: he that leaves this with pure habits, unspotted by sin, enters a circle of pure spirits, and engages himself to eternal purity hereafter; he that leaves it in sin, in sin begins his future course; and every step which he takes in that course, binds him to inextricable entanglements of guilt and woe, and renders his recovery more difficult and doubtful. So that, for aught that we can see, the eternal destiny of a human soul may be determined by the accident of his earthly condition. According to the circumstances of his birth, he might seem to be fore-ordained to eternal life, or foredoomed to endless woe. And is not this the very election and predestination which the fathers taught; put in a different shape, deduced by a different process from different premises, but the same in substance and effect? So it would seem; and it may be that some such contemplation of the facts of life, some deep impression of the huge inequalities of the human condition, lay at the foundation of the old doctrine, or was intimately connected with it. But this view of life, so far as the happiness and moral destiny of the individual are concerned, is a mere illusion, a fallacy, which confounds the certainty of the facts observed with the certainty of the inferences from them. The facts are certain; the inferences are merely plausible, and will not bear examination. The election affirmed in the New Testament is election only as to means and opportunities and external condition. And this is not a theory, but a fact; an election actually observed; a matter of history. But this is all. The distinction goes no further than outward advantages and blessings. No other election is taught in the Scripture, no other is inferrible from the facts of life. A closer examination will show that this election is quite superficial; it does not touch the interior life. It does not affect, or does not necessarily affect, in the way supposed, the happiness or moral destiny of the chosen or rejected. Happiness and character may bear an inverse ratio to circumstance. The most favorable, as we reckon, may prove the least so.

1. As it regards happiness, who that has studied human nature and human life does not know that happiness is a thing which defies calculation? It is found in greatest abundance there where there seemed least reason to expect it. It has nothing to do with circumstances. It would even seem as if a kind God, by way of compensation, had bestowed most of it there where circumstances are most forbidding; so that the poorer and the more degraded a man's condition, provided the poverty and degradation are native, and not a reverse of fortune, the happier he is; and, on the other hand, the higher we ascend in the scale of life, the more thoughtful, serious, ay, the more sad, life becomes. Indeed, I figure to myself the blessedness ascribed to higher natures, the blessedness of heaven, to be very different from what we call happiness,— as far from glee as from mourning. A divine compensation is for ever equalizing the human condition, reconciling its opposite

extremes, and awarding to each individual, in his interiors, so much and no more of secret satisfaction as his own consciousness enables and entitles him to receive, without respect to circumstance or person. When the tide rushes inland, every channel is flooded; the river which bears a thousand tons on its bosom is no fuller than the creek on which the schoolboy launches his mimic craft. When the dew of heaven distils, all plants partake of the blessing, — the vilest weed that lifts its despised head above the soil, as well as the queenly rose and the trellised vine. And the mercy of God is that tide and that dew which floods and blesses all, both small and great, both splendid and vile, with its equal and impartial largess. Nothing is more delusive than to judge of another's consciousness by his visible condition. Do you wonder how the beggar, the prisoner, the slave, the maimed and diseased, can endure the burden of being; or whence, in their hard estate, they derive so much of satisfaction as the heart requires to maintain its life? — ask where the berry in the arid rock-cleft, with its minimum of earth and moisture, finds the sweetness that circulates in its veins? — ask whence the flower that springs from corruption gets its spotless raiment and its balmy breath? — ask whence the pearl-fish, in the unsunned darkness of the deep, derives the rainbow hues that paint the walls of its cell? The heart is a chemist, more subtile than berry or flower or pearl. In the hardest and most arid conditions it will find some nurture. If the world of its surrounding yields nothing, it will push its roots through into another, and draw in heaven by the mighty attraction of a mighty need.

Happiness is not confined to the favored of fortune. Jacob may be preferred before Esau; but Jacob is not therefore the happier man. The actual, historical Jacob of the Old Testament, we know, was not. Turn to the record, and see. He triumphed over his brother; but his triumph had a root of bitterness which avenged its wrong. He stole a blessing; but a curse went with it. He was doomed to be most sorely afflicted there where chiefly he had garnered his heart and hope; and he spoke the bitterness of his soul when he said, "Few and evil have been the years of my pilgrimage." On the other hand, Esau may be postponed and cast out, but not therefore for ever miserable. What did the Esau of history when he found himself defrauded of his rights? "He cried with an exceeding bitter cry, and said unto his father, 'Bless me also, even me, O my father!' And he said, 'Thy brother came with subtlety, and hath taken away thy blessing.' And he said, 'Hast thou not reserved a blessing for me? Hast thou but one blessing, my father? Bless me also, even me.'" This is the cry which still goes up from the poor, the injured, the oppressed, to the mercy-seat. "Bless me also, even me also, O my Father! Though poor and vile, let not me be excluded from a share in the general joy." And the prayer is heard. The Father has other blessings besides outward distinctions and the prizes of the world. He opens a compensating fountain of joy in the heart of the desolate, over which the world has no power, and entertains it with the hope of deliverance: "And it shall come to pass when thou shalt have the dominion, that thou shalt break thy brother's yoke from off thy neck." So much for the influence of circumstance on happiness.

2. As it regards the character and moral destiny of the individual, these two are less affected by the inequalities of fortune — that is, they are less affected by adverse circumstances — than we are apt to suppose. There is a superficial morality induced by prosperous fortunes, — a correctness of deportment; an external decorum which cannot be too highly prized in its social bearings, but which has no relation, or an inverse one, to the inner man, — which is not the fruit of the heart, but its covering. So there is a superficial depravity induced by adverse circumstances, a contempt of law and social conventions, an external flagitiousness, which looks bad, and which society must punish in self-defence, but which does not necessarily involve any great depravity of heart. Many a one who leads a profligate life, from having been "to the manner born," may be less infected with sin in the core of his heart, than a hundred others of decent reputation all around him. Jesus, who knew what was in man, who could see murder and adultery in the heart, beneath a canonical robe, and who could see a soul of goodness in the fallen prostitute, told the wealthy and respectable Pharisees of his day, "Behold, the publicans and the harlots go into the kingdom of heaven before you." The moral worth and the moral destiny of men are not determined by the means of moral culture, allotted or withheld, or the manners corresponding thereto; but by something in the heart, which only God can see; by a certain proportion, which only God can estimate, between the means and the life.

But suppose a deeper corruption of the moral nature, instead of this superficial depravity. Suppose the victim of adverse fortune to have sinned, not only against social conventions, but against the witness in the heart, and to have perished in the midst of his sins. What right have we to limit the redeeming power of God to the present life, or to think that, because the requisite means of reformation have not been afforded in this world, they will not be afforded hereafter? For that very reason, that this life has not furnished them, there must be some state that will. There must be some provision in the immeasurable future, some crisis there must be in the history of that soul, which shall reach its necessity, and place before it the same opportunties of moral culture which Heaven has vouchsafed to the most favored in this world. So, too, I can see no reason why the character which has never been sorely tempted in this world may not be so tempted in some future state: on the contrary, I see every reason to suppose that it will. That virtue is of little worth, — it can never be a heaven and a fountain of life to the soul, — which has not been tried to the uttermost point of endurance. Somewhere in the course of its history, every soul must enjoy the means of grace; and, somewhere in the course of its history, every soul must be tried with fire.

An equal Love has ordained the inequalities of life. Esau is as dear to God as Jacob. He loves the wild Ishmaelite as well as the polished Israel of the old covenant or the new, the vagabond and the outlaw as well as the saint. Meanwhile, these inequalities are lessons to us of courage, and patience, and gratitude, and trust. They teach reliance on the Wisdom that arranges the conditions of life, allotting to each the portion most needful for the discipline of each, whether prosperous or adverse; they admonish us to make the most of our position by brave endeavors to meet its requirements, by patient endurance of its evil, and by free communication of its good.

IX.

THE CHRISTIAN IDEA OF IMMORTALITY.

IX.

THE CHRISTIAN IDEA OF IMMORTALITY.

"Dust and clay,
Man's ancient wear,
Here you must stay,
But I elsewhere!" — VAUGHAN.

It is commonly supposed, that the doctrine of a future life is one of the specialties of the Christian revelation. Gibbon ascribes to it, among other causes, the early conquests of the gospel. But had the historian been challenged to produce from the gospel record the statement of this doctrine, in clear and explicit terms, as a universal spiritual truth, embracing the whole family of man in its import and application, he would have been at a loss to recall a proposition answering to his own impression of the place which that doctrine occupies in the Christian scheme. Had he turned to the New Testament to refresh his knowledge of its teachings on this subject, he would have found the resurrection of Christ asserted by all the four Gospels, pervading the Acts of the Apostles with its glad report, and enlivening the Epistles with its heavenly promise. But a critical examination would have shown him, that the promise was bounded in its application by the household of faith, and had no validity in the apprehension of the writers of the New Testament beyond those bounds; that when Jesus says, "Because I live, ye shall live also," he is thinking only of his own; and that Paul had only believers in view when he wrote, "As in Adam all die, so in Christ shall all be made alive." He would find the immortality of the soul, as a universal psychological fact, if seemingly intimated, nowhere explicitly declared. I recall, at this moment, but two passages in which that doctrine is even intimated. One is that saying of Jesus, in which he deduces the fact of a future life from the phrase, "The God of Abraham, of Isaac, and of Jacob." "God is not a God of the dead, but of the living; for all live unto him." A most noteworthy saying! "All live unto him." The world of past generations is not a charnel, or world of dust, but a world of life and thought, of energy and love. The Spirit of God strikes through it and enfolds it no less than our human world of to-day. The other instance which occurs to me is a passage in the well-known 15th chapter of 1st Corinthians, "If there be no resurrection of the dead, then is Christ not risen;" words which represent the truth of the resurrection of Christ as depending on the general fact of a resurrection, — which make it a particular instance under a general law.

Elsewhere in the New Testament, so far as I remember, the future life is regarded, not as a natural event, — a consequence resulting from the nature of the soul, — but as something achieved by faith, or communicated by God through Christ.

Thus envisaged, the doctrine of a life to come unquestionably occupied a large place, and constituted an active ingredient, in the consciousness of the early Church. You can hardly open the New Testament without lighting on some allusion to it, or some hint of the speedy coming of the Son of Man, whose advent was to raise his departed followers from the dead. The Church of that age, still glowing with the recent Sun which rose on the first great Easter morning with a right ascension, and, it may be, still ascends, appears to have lost the consciousness of death. For Christians it did not exist. They might "fall asleep in Christ," as Paul termed it, but only to "be caught up with him in the clouds." Their sun of life might decline, but only as the sun of the arctic midsummer skirts an horizon where evening and morning club their splendors to furnish an unbroken day. In their horizon there was no dissolution of the continuity of life. Day blossomed into day, mortal was swallowed up in immortality. Friends who had seemed to depart, putting off this corruptible, came beaming back, and swelled the cloud of immortal witnesses that filled the Christian's heaven. Believers felt that they had come "to an innumerable company of angels;" that there was but one "family in earth and heaven;" and one of them was bold enough to say, that Christ had "abolished death."

These heats could not last; the vision faded; the senses resumed their sway, doubt returned, and death returned; and, even within the covers of the New Testament, we hear the complaint, "Where is the promise of his coming? for, since the fathers fell asleep, all things continue as they were from the beginning of creation." We cannot, in our age, appropriate with the fervor of young Christendom the brave saying, that Christ has "abolished death;" but this we may say, that the modern Christian world is possessed with a better view of the future of the soul, and a better hope, than the ancient. The ancients believed in a life to come; but it was not the hereafter contemplated by the Christian. The difference between the two is fitly expressed by the word "resurrection;" understanding by that term, not the resuscitation of the mortal body, but the resurrection of the soul from Hades. The state of the departed, as conceived by the ancients, — except for the few who were raised to the fellowship of the gods, — was no improvement on this present life. It was human life relieved, indeed, in the case of the good, from mortal cares and pains; but still occupied, in a dim and dreamy way, with earthly pleasures and pursuits. Its locality was not like the Christian's heaven, the dwelling-place of divinity; it was not above, but below, in the bowels of the earth, or in distant isles of the sea, from which there was no return. With all its delights, which were mostly sensual, it was still a prison; at best, a peaceful asylum whose inmates lived in the past, and dreamed over again the scenes of their mortality, with no development and no progress, — an after-shine of the sun that was set, or pensive moonlight, not a new day. The Christian hereafter is *Resurrection;* that is, spiritual new-birth, life more abundant, intenser action, endless progress, — the mortal life quickened into life eternal.

I am speaking of the Christian ideal of the future destiny. A very different thing is the Church doctrine of the life to come. The doctrine of the Church, in most of its communions, is that of a *bodily* resurrection, — a simultaneous resurrection of all the dead at the end of the world, accompanied by a general judgment, which shall fix the condition of each soul for all coming time. The state of the departed previous to that event is a question on which different communions hold very different opinions. The Church of Rome affirms the existence of an intermediate spiritual world, in which all but the saints are confined until the general resurrection. The doctrine of Protestant sects in relation to this point — of those, I mean, which hold the resurrection of the body, and do not admit the intermediate world — is painfully confused and wavering. The more consistent among them suppose that the soul exists in an unconscious state; that it sleeps with the body until with the body it is raised at the last day. This is the view embodied in the popular hymn, —

> "Unveil thy bosom, faithful tomb!
> Take this new treasure to thy trust."

Others conceive that the disembodied spirit enters at once on a state of happiness or misery, according to its character and life in the flesh, — a view which nullifies the point and significance of the doctrine of a bodily resurrection and the general judgment, by making both seem ridiculously superfluous. For, if the soul can exist for ages, and fulfil the conditions of a moral agent without a body, why should the perished body be revived and re-annexed? And, if it has already reaped the reward of its deeds, of what use the verdict after the award?

This diversity and confusion in the doctrine of the Church is due, in part, to the conflict of views represented in the New Testament itself, and the vain attempt to combine in one theory the civil and personal elements in these representations, — the passages relating to the great historical crisis in human society, and passages relating to individual destiny. It is impossible, I believe, to deduce from the Scriptures of the New Testament a doctrine of the life to come, which shall fit all the texts and satisfy all the requirements of the subject; which shall harmonize the Apocalyptic vision of the "new earth" and the New Jerusalem upon it, with Paul's conception of being raised from the dead and caught up into the clouds to dwell with the Lord in the air; which shall harmonize any doctrine of final resurrection with the words of Jesus to the thief on the cross, "This day shalt thou be with me in Paradise."

Whilst the doctrine of the Orthodox Church, mistaking the import of the resurrection, and substituting a bodily rising for a spiritual one, perverts and degrades the Christian idea, the popular belief in those communions which reject the dogmatic impositions of Orthodoxy is false to the moral aspects of that idea, in supposing that immortality is the natural heritage of man, — that man is born to it as the sparks fly upward; that life eternal is the sure destination of every soul; that for every soul the attainment of the highest and best is only a question of time; in other words, that in every human animal, not only the possibility but the fact of a spiritual man is enfolded. This representation wears, to the superficial thought, an aspect of plausibility which vanishes on closer inspection. What is gained in diffusion is lost in depth. What is gained in popularity is lost in aspiration. On its Godward side, the Universalist doctrine embodies a precious and momentous truth; to wit, the impartiality and limitless scope of divine love. On its human side, it errs in not recognizing the proprieties and fatalities of the individual soul.

The Christian idea of immortality is essentially a moral idea. Only the moral and spiritual in man is supposed by it to be capable of resurrection; whatsoever is not concluded in that category is mortal. So I interpret that saying of Paul, "As in Adam all die, so in Christ shall all be made alive."

Adam and Christ represent respectively different sides of human nature, — different phases or principles in man, — the natural (or animal), which is mortal; the spiritual, which is immortal. We cannot say, that the spiritual in man, as source and ground of everlasting life, originated, historically speaking, with Christ; that before the Christian era there was no spiritual, eternal life. By Christ we must here understand, not the historical, but the eternal Christ, the ideal man, the divine man. What is put chronologically, we must understand spiritually. "In Christ shall all be made alive." In Christ all *are* made alive. In and through the spirit which Christ represents, man is made partaker of eternal life; all men — whether nominally Christians, or whatsoever name they bear; whether contemporary with Jesus, or ages after or ages before — who partake in that spirit, in the degree in which they partake of it.

Immortality is a thing of degrees. All souls are immortal in some sense; none are utterly annihilated at death. Even animal souls are not annihilated, but survive, with unknown conditions, the dissolution of the bodily frame. I assume the existence of the entity called "soul," and that what we so name is not, as some have pretended, the result of organism, but rather the foundation and cause of organism, — the central force of the system it inhabits. The greater this central force, the more perfect the organization, the more immortal the soul, though, perhaps, the more mortal the body. In animals of a low type, the weakness of the central principle is compensated by increased vitality of the members. Instead of a single regent soul, these forms are pervaded by a general diffusive life, or multiplicity of inferior, unconscious souls, distributed equally through the whole economy. The unconscious vitality is great, even to the reproduction of perished members; but the individual, voluntary energy is small. The snail and the earthworm, it is probable, do not define their own individuality by an act of consciousness embracing the entire organism, and distinguishing it from other bodies. Immortality cannot be predicated of such natures in any other sense than the indestructibleness of the atoms which compose them.

As we rise in the scale of being, life becomes more central and individual; one monarch soul possesses and dominates the entire frame, subjecting and subordinating all its organs, and enduing all its members with its own vitality. That soul, we may suppose, is immortal in a higher sense than that of essential indestructibleness. Not only is it indestructible in its essence, but it enters after death, as soul, as central vital principal, into new forms of animal life.

The immortality which we ascribe to the higher animals, we cannot of course deny to the natural or animal man. But neither can we attribute much more to the animal man in this regard than we concede to other animals. His intellectual superiority, the faculty of speech, the powers by which he acquires and applies scientific knowledge, his philosophic insight, his capacity for abstract truth, his converse with ideas, creative genius, poetry and art, — all the mental traits and endowments which distinguish a Shakspeare or a Raphael prove nothing on this head. These have no immortality other than that of the works they produce, and confer none other on the author of those works than the deathless name which they hand down. Splendid as these endowments are, they contain no germ of everlasting life, no intimation of their reproduction in a future world. There is no reason to suppose that the Shakspeares and Raphaels of this life will be Shakspeares and Raphaels in the life to come. The qualities of genius are rightly termed "gifts;" they are not the soul's own, not spiritual property, not part and parcel of the inmost nature; but extrinsic, incidental, like personal beauty, muscular strength, an ear for music, or a sweet voice; they are not of the nature of substance, but of accident; they are detachable; they pertain to the tabernacle that is dissolved, to the natural and corruptible which is put off in death, not to the spiritual which is raised.

Only through his moral and spiritual nature can man become partaker of an immortality essentially different from that of the brute, — the immortality of which Christ is the prototype, "the first-fruits." Only through the spirit does he lay hold of everlasting life. Only the highest can inherit the highest. The Holy Spirit is the summit of all being, the top of all imagining; the source and mark, the beginning and the end of life eternal. Whatever holds of that, whatever co-operates or sympathizes with it, whatever ranges in the same line with it, is immortality of that supreme type of which the apostle says, that "in Christ all shall be made alive," and which justifies the contrast, amounting to antagonism, which the apostle sets between the destination of man in Adam, and the destination of man in Christ. Even in Adam all is not mortal. The soul of man, independently of those spiritual experiences and acquisitions which alone insure, which alone mediate eternal life in the gospel sense, possesses a kind of immortality. That mysterious, indivisible entity, that insoluble something which we call "soul," must survive in some sort the dissolutions of death; albeit, in some cases of extreme depravation or limitation, it may not be able to recover itself from the mortal shock, and to take up again the conscious life which it had in the flesh; it may lack sufficient force to collect together a new system of particles, and to organize a new body, of which it shall reign the central, life-giving power. It may only survive as one of the constituents of such a system, with no independent, conscious individuality; — subordinate, not chief, in the new economy to which it belongs. In most cases, however, one would fain believe that the soul is raised *as soul*, — as regent, conscious principle again. In the case of the strong men of history, the men of might, who have stamped their image on their time and filled the world with their deeds, it is impossible not to believe that the power which wrought with such mighty effect will continue to work in a new body, with new conditions. Yet even here, in so far as the power put forth was mere self-assertion,—the power of egoism, working for private and selfish aims, — it dies with the death of the body. All egoism dies; world-conquering, world-coveting ambition must not expect to push its adored self across the gulf, and resume its conquests on the other side. No self so sought is raised again. All efforts, wishes, and pursuits that terminate in self are self-limited, and end with the grave. Constantine the Great rebuked the covetous ambition of one of his courtiers, by drawing with his spear the man's figure on the ground. "Within that space," he said, "is contained all you will carry with you when you go hence."

Even in Adam all is not mortal; and yet, as we survey the world of which Adam is the type; as we follow the changes of time, and cast our thought along the line of the quick succeeding generations that have occupied, each in its turn, the populous past, — there comes to us from that survey a savor of death. The sentiment impressed upon us by the contemplation of Adam's line is a sense of mortality.

> "He lived: he died. Behold the sum,
> The abstract, of the historian's page!"

The march of humanity across the fields of this planet is a funeral procession; the planet itself is a moving cemetery; the ground we tread is saturated with the dust of our fathers. So true it is, that in Adam all die.

But look again; glance at the world as it is in Christ. I mean not the technically Christian world, but this human world, in so far as any portion of it has been illumined, enriched, regenerated, sainted, by that spirit of truth and love, which, while it dwelt without measure in Christ, has dwelt and wrought, in varying measures and degrees, in countless others before and since, — in how many prophets and heroes of the Old Covenant! in how many martyrs and saints of the New! in how many lights of the Gentile world, — the Sakyas and Zoroasters, the Socrates and Antonines of other faiths. When we so gaze, there is nothing that speaks of mortality; nothing that breathes of dust and decay. The thought here is not of death, but of faith triumphant over death; of the victories of the spirit, of everlasting life. The mind recalls a venerable host whose names are written in heaven, — prophets, evangelists, patriots, apostles, benefactors of every kind, differing widely in power and grace, and the worth of their work, as one star differeth from another in glory; but all agreeing in this one trait, that they labored, not "for the meat that perisheth, but for that which endureth unto everlasting life." They gave themselves up with unwavering faith and uncalculating love to some worthy object in and for which they lived. Their creeds were many; but the same mind which was in Christ was in them all. They wrought with differences of administrations, but in them wrought one and the self-same spirit, asserting itself in all diversities of operations as holy and divine. We cannot think of these as dead and dust. They are with us still by the witness of the spirit that was in them: vital forces in the realms of faith, —

the spirit's own, they live unto God and they live unto us, witnessing and working with us and for us until now. So I interpret the saying, "In Christ shall all be made alive."

As we trace the presence and the working of that spirit in human history, we open an interminable gallery of the pious and brave, whose unselfish aims and devoted lives have raised them to the sainted seats of the world's undying reverence and love. Some by wisdom and some by charity, some by patience and some by daring: but all, in the spirit of Christ, have been lights and saviours in their generation. Some have wandered through desert lands, and some have traversed the ocean waste; some, who were born to wealth and rank, have renounced their heritage of earthly splendor, and spent their lives in poverty and obscurity, companying with rude and ignorant men, perhaps with savage children of the forest; some have perished for their country's rights; some have laid down their lives for the truth; some have been eyes to the blind, and feet to the lame; some have burst the bonds of error; some have broken the fetters of the slave; some have brought truth and newness to the understanding; some have brought truth and newness to the heart: but all these, in their kind and degree, have been made alive with the life that never dies.

This is the Christian idea of immortality, of the "everlasting life." It is not a "natural," but a moral growth; not universal, but special; not a heritage, but an acquisition. It is something which appertains, not to the natural man, but to the spiritual. I do not question that it may be developed in another state, in cases where contrary influences have made its development impossible in this. I only deny that it is or will be developed in all cases as a matter of course, — developed by the accident of death. I deny that, without development and without an effort, it will be imparted to the grovelling soul; that where it has not been attained, or even sought in this world, good angels wait to confer it in the next, or that God will hand it over as a birthday gift. We do not tumble into everlasting life when "our feet stumble on the dark mountains." Only the moral and spiritual in man is capable of conscious immortality. "Flesh and blood cannot inherit the kingdom of God; neither doth corruption inherit incorruption." There are human creatures with whom it is impossible to connect the idea of immortality, — children of earth, whom it is impossible to conceive of as starting up at once from the bed of death into new and immortal life. On the other hand, when we see a man noble, generous, active in good, we can hardly imagine such a spirit and such an energy suddenly and for ever extinct, when the blood has ceased to circulate in the mortal frame in which and through which it wrought. The soul in its essence is indestructible; but indestructibleness is not immortality. The soul as an entity may and will survive; but the soul as a conscious agent may, nevertheless, suffer death.

Only the fulness of the spirit can "abolish death," as it did in that affluent dispensation of it in the early days of the Church. Brave souls may look upon it undaunted; philosophic minds may comfort themselves with the thought, that this is a fate which strong, brave men, and feeble men, and women, and little children, have been through; that we can bear what these have borne, sustained by the everlasting love co-present to all the exigencies of being. But only the spiritual eye, instructed by faith, and conscious of immortality, can look through the gloom, and dissolve it in its own supernal light. "If a man keep my sayings," said Jesus, "he shall not see death." The spirit cannot see death, no more than the sun sees the shadows which it casts behind it.

The Mussulmans have a fable about Moses, that, when the hour of his departure was come, God sent the angel of death, who appeared before him and demanded his soul. Moses greeted the angel with a friendly salutation, but questioned his right to touch a soul that had had communion with God. The death-angel was baffled by such assurance, and knew not how to proceed; for death and Moses, it seemed, had nothing in common. Then the Lord deputed the angel of Paradise to convey to him an apple of Eden. And, as Moses inhaled the immortal fragrance, his spirit went forth from him, and was borne upon the odors of Eden into the presence of the Lord.

This is the Mussulman's parable, and this is the interpretation of it. The assurance which disputes the power of death is the spirit's unconquerable faith in spirit; and the apple of Eden is that full and untroubled vision of immortality, whose strong attraction conquers death.

X.

CRITIQUE OF PARTIALIST AND UNIVERSALIST VIEWS OF PENAL THEOLOGY.

X.

CRITIQUE OF PENAL THEOLOGY.

"Ein jeder muss seine Hölle noch im Himmel und seinen Himmel noch in der Hölle finden." — LESSING.

IT is a matter of comparatively little moment to a right-minded man how speculative theology may figure the awards of the life to come. No dogma relative to this subject can be more offensive than that whole system of views concerning the moral order of the universe, in which the ideas of punishment, and escape from punishment, (partial or universal) play so prominent a part. The objection to this system is, that it turns the mind from that which is primary and vital, and fixes it on that which is secondary and subordinate, — turns it from the everlasting substance, and fixes it on the accidents; that it puts happiness above goodness, and puts goodness as a means of happiness.

The first and last and only question which this system propounds to the individual is, how to escape the eternal damnation to which it supposes him doomed by the fact of his humanity; i.e. by the measure of sinfulness proper to human nature as such. The question is, not how to escape the sin, but how to escape the damnation incurred by it. The system makes the whole essence of revelation to consist "in the discovery to man of a new means by which, without any previous eradication of sin, sin can be pardoned." The aim of a true religion is, not to escape damnation, but to lay hold of everlasting life. These aims may seem to coincide in effect; but the difference between them is heaven-wide. The one is dictated by selfish fear: the other springs from exceeding love. The former is ascetic in its tendency and method; it delights in scrupulous correctness of deportment, it accomplishes wonders of self-denial, but all for self's sake, to escape damnation; as the miser denies himself the gratifications of sense for the sake of increasing his store. The other is a self-forgetting, a losing of one's self in some worthy object for its own sake. It is written, "He that will lose his life for my sake" (not for the sake of his own soul, but for *my* sake, for the sake of truth and righteousness and human weal) "shall find it." And who can doubt, that one who devotes himself, a living sacrifice, to some great and good work, without troubling himself about the salvation of his soul, or spending a single thought on the subject, is in quite as salvable a condition as one whose single aim in life has been to save his soul from death? A very poor soul it may be when it is saved, and very little comfort he may have in it. However free from positive vice, however unspotted from the world, it may not have expanded, not developed; it may never have fairly come out of itself in one true act of self-abandonment. A very little soul after all, and scarcely worth the pains it has cost.

A true religion will rather aim to make us forget ourselves in the love and pursuit of noble ends, than seek to occupy us with thoughts of the hereafter, — our part and lot in another world. Let theologians say what they will, that is not the first and great concern, but a very secondary one. What we want of religion is to develop in us the principle of love. Without this no soul can be truly blessed, and this the fear of hell will never awaken. The uttermost that the fear of hell can do, is to keep the life unspotted from the world. It can never kindle the flame of love; it can give no hold of eternal life. What we complain of in this system is, that, instead of taking us out of ourself, it drives us back upon ourself, in self-tormenting introspection. Instead of showing us spiritual beauty in forms that shall win and command our affections, it turns a magnifying-glass on our sins and unworthiness. It aims to frighten us with our lost state. If it does not succeed in that, it leaves us weaker than before. If it does succeed, the remedy it proposes to our fear is, not eradication of the sinful principle, but a transfer of the penalty. It makes more of the penalty than it does of the sin. The salvation it offers is salvation from the consequences of sin, rather than from sin itself.

The various opinions which have been entertained regarding the moral future of souls may be reduced to these two: 1st, That of the Universalists, who suppose that all souls, after a purgatory longer or shorter according to the exigency of each case, or even without purgatorial discipline, will be eternally blest; 2d, That of the Partialists, who suppose that only a select portion will be so blest, and the rest consigned to eternal punishment, either in the way of annihilation or of conscious endless suffering. From the earliest period of the Church, these two parties have divided, very unequally, the Christian world. These two, and no third. No sect has maintained that all will be lost. An eschatology so desperate, however agreeable to the Church Despondent, involves too violent a theory of life for the hardihood even of penal theology. It seemed absolutely necessary that some should be saved, and that hell should have its correlative heaven, were it only for the sake of perspective. Simple theism required thus much. A God who creates only to destroy, or, creating to save, is balked in that intent by the wilfulness of his creatures or the power of Satan, and cannot so much as save one soul, would be equivalent to no God, and would answer no theological purpose. It was therefore conceded (not without seeming reluctance in some cases) by even the most zealous of those who identified the majesty of God with revenge for violated law, that a special effort of grace would be made by way of showing what Mercy could do if Justice would.

Universalist and Partialist — both of these systems, with proper modifications, that is, with a reasonable extension of the penal discipline on the one side, and a reasonable allowance of saving grace on the other, are plausible; but neither is demonstrable, neither possesses the certainty requisite to constitute it a positive doctrine of religion, nor is it in the power of theological learning or human wit to establish any thing definite on this subject. Theology here must content itself with generalities; religion must rest on those everlasting laws which compose the framework of the moral universe, and which include, together with this earthly life, the heavens and the hells in one dominion.

If we suppose, with the Universalists, that all souls are predestined to everlasting blessedness in the world to come, we must suppose a fitness or capacity for such blessedness on the part of the subject, already existing or to be hereafter acquired. Without this fitness on the part of the subject, blessedness in any state is inconceivable. No man in his senses believes that happiness hereafter will be thrust upon him in spite of himself, and against all the habits and antecedents of the soul. But to change that condition of the soul by an external force, in order to make it receptive of happiness, would be to annihilate one soul, and to create another in its place. If we say that this capacity already exists in the subject, — in all subjects, — we are contradicted by the plainest facts of nature and life. It may be urged, that the present unfitness arises from causes which cease with death; that death will make all men blest by removing the obstacles to blessedness which abound in this world, and which belong to this world alone. This plea supposes an efficacy in death which we have no right to assume. It is thought by some, that the body and the physical or other external influences by which we are conditioned in the present life are the cause of all evil; and that every soul will be found fit for happiness when once divested of its mortal covering, and disencumbered of its present relations. But are there no evils beside those which arise from physical and terrestrial relations? Granting that a portion of our sins and our sufferings have their origin in the flesh, there are others which cannot with any propriety be traced to that source. Some organizations, no doubt, are more favorable to moral rectitude than others: but experience shows, that moral rectitude may exist under all conditions; that the most favorable, so far as we can judge, do not secure it; that the most unfavorable, so far as we can judge, do not preclude it. We have, therefore, no authority from any grounds in our present experience, and certainly not from any other source, for supposing that vice and misery belong to the body alone, and will cease with the ending of this bodily life. Moreover, in its extreme form, — the supposition of immediate and universal happiness hereafter, — the Universalist theory impugns the disciplinary character, and confounds the meaning and aggravates the mystery of this human world. If all men are morally fit for happiness now, it is difficult to understand why this world has not been so arranged as to yield that happiness now; and why we are doomed to reach, by the long and circuitous route of mortal experience, and through the miracle of death, a good to which, in our present capacity, we might seem to have a present claim.

Or, adopting the modification with which the Universalist theory is commonly held, if we suppose that the fitness and capacity for happiness which exist not now will arrive hereafter, will arrive to all, — that all souls are destined to eternal blessedness after such probation as each may require, we still stretch the right of conjecture. We suppose a remedial and restorative influence in the air of hell, or (lest the theological term should mislead) in the future transmundane penalties of sin, which may possibly belong to them, but of which we know nothing, and which seems to be assumed for the sake of the argument. Our observation does not detect this medicinal quality in the penal sufferings of the present life. There is virtue in sorrow to educate and perfect the good, but none that we can see to reclaim the wicked. It does not appear that punishment in this world has always the effect, or has in the majority of cases the effect, to reform the sinner; contrariwise, it is notorious that men continue to sin and suffer to the day of their death. What authority have we for supposing that this process is arrested hereafter? or for not supposing that the sinner will go on sinning and suffering everlastingly, or till evil becomes so predominant in the soul as utterly to quench its moral life, and conscious suffering ends in everlasting death? Who shall say, that sin, once established, may not grow to be supreme and ineradicable, — that the habit of transgression contracted in this world, and confirmed by every fresh transgression, may not become a necessity of nature strong as fate and deep as life?

Thus, in either of its species, — that of immediate emancipation from sin and suffering by death, or that of final restoration to holiness and happiness by remedial suffering, — the Universalist theory concerning the future destination of the soul is pure conjecture, undemonstrated, incapable of demonstration.

Moreover, although, in a matter like this, individual authority is of little account, we cannot conceal from ourselves that the weightiest names in the realm of speculation, both within and without the Christian Church, are found on the side of eternal retributions. Of each of these classes suffice it to name one. Of ethnic sages our example shall be Plato, the supreme name in ancient philosophy. Plato, in the "Gorgias," delivers himself, through the mouth of Socrates, to this effect: "It behooves that every one who suffers punishment, if justly punished by another, should either become better and be benefited, or should serve as an example to others, that others, seeing him suffer the things which he suffers, and being afraid, may reform. Now, there are some that are profited when punished, both by gods and by men: these are such as have sinned with curable sins.* Nevertheless, by torments and sorrows cometh their benefit, both here and in hell; for it is not possible otherwise to be freed from wickedness. But others have been wicked in the extreme, and on account of such wickedness are become incurable. Of these examples are made: they themselves are no longer benefited, being incurable; but others are benefited, seeing these suffer on account of their sin the greatest, the most afflictive and most terrible woes *eternally*,† being regularly fixed as examples there in the prison of hell, as shows and warnings to the wicked perpetually arriving."

Our modern and Christian example shall be Leibnitz, the optimist, — an authority second to none in metaphy-

---

* ἰάσιμα ἁμαρτήματα. † τὸν ἀεὶ χρόνον.

sical profundity, or in logical acumen or conscientious love of truth. Optimism and eternal damnation are things hard to reconcile; but Leibnitz, in the "Théodicée," after glancing at the Universalist theory, proceeds to say: —

"Holding, then, to the established doctrine, that the number of human beings who are damned eternally will be incomparably greater than that of the saved, it behooves us to say, that the evil would still appear as almost nothing in comparison with the good, when we consider the veritable magnitude of the City of God. . . . The ancients had narrow ideas of the works of God; and St. Augustine, through ignorance of modern discoveries, was sorely put to it when the problem was to excuse the prevalence of evil. It appeared to the ancients that our earth was the only inhabited sphere: they were even afraid of the antipodes. The rest of the world, according to them, consisted in some luminous globes and crystalline spheres. At the present day, whatever limits may be assigned or denied to the universe, we cannot overlook the fact that there are innumerable globes as large and larger than ours, which have as much right as that to be the abode of rational beings, although it does not follow that those beings are men. . . . It is possible that all the suns are inhabited only by happy beings; and nothing obliges us to believe that there are many damned among them, since few examples or patterns will suffice for the use which the good may derive from the evil."*

This reasoning, it must be confessed, is very weak, and altogether unworthy of such a mind. Its fallacies are too obvious to need any comment. Nor need we

* Théodicée, Partie I. 19.

stop to inquire how far Leibnitz was hampered by the wish to avoid controversy on secondary points with the theologians of his day, or what mental qualifications may have neutralized his exoteric admissions. I cite the passage only as showing that so resolute an optimist and so penetrating a thinker as Leibnitz believed the principle of eternal punishment, in some sense, to be compatible with the goodness of God and a best possible world. And this belief is more unequivocally expressed, as well as more ably vindicated, in another passage of the same work: —

"There is, nevertheless, one species of justice, and a certain sort of rewards and punishments, which seems less applicable to those, if any such there be, who act from absolute necessity. It is that species of justice whose object is neither amendment nor example, nor even reparation. The only foundation of this justice is the fitness which demands a certain satisfaction, by way of expiation, for an evil act. The Socinians, Hobbes, and others, do not admit this punitive justice which is properly vindictive. . . . Nevertheless, it is founded in a relation of fitness which contents, not only the offended party, but also the wise who behold it, as beautiful music or a fine piece of architecture contents well-constituted minds. . . . One may even say that it carries with it a certain indemnification to the mind, — that the disorder would offend if the punishment did not contribute to re-establish order.* . . . . Thus the pains of the damned continue then, even when they no longer serve to deter from evil." †

* "Et on peut même dire qu'il y a ici un certain dédommagement de l'esprit, que le désordre offenseroit si le châtiment ni contribuoit à rétablir l'ordre."

† Théod., Partie II. 73, 74.

Turning now to the opposite view, we shall find that Partialism has its own peculiar difficulties. We encounter here obstacles different in kind, but equal in their way to those which embarrass the view we have been discussing.

If we suppose, with the Partialists, that only a select portion of human souls will be finally blest, and the rest consigned to everlasting punishment, we are met on the threshold by a strong objection drawn from the idea of God, — a God all-merciful and all-wise, — and a universe formed and ruled by Infinite Wisdom and Mercy. This idea seems to require that adequate provision shall be made in the constitution of things and the soul for every case of sin and suffering which the universe contains; it seems to demand from the infinite resources of the Spirit a remedial force commensurate with every exigency of spiritual life, a power of nature or of grace by which the most corrupt may be reached and restored. It does not help the matter to say, that the sinner sins of his own free will, of his own free will persists in sin, and so dooms *himself* to endless perdition. That a being should have been created with this liability in his constitution, capable of so sinning and suffering eternally, — this is precisely the difficulty in the case. This it is which piety finds it so hard to adjust with the cherished idea of a Father of spirits and of mercies. In that word "Father," it seems to see a refutation of Partialism.

The old defenders of this theory associated with it a doctrine of predestination, importing, as they interpreted that phrase, that the sinner sins by strong necessity, acting as his evil nature prompts, incapable of acting otherwise. Modern orthodoxy, anxious to relieve the idea of God of the odium of damning predestined sinners, shifts the responsibility of the act from the Creator to the creature, and, by substituting the notion of free-will for the dogma of Predestination, seeks to devolve on the damned the burden of his own destiny; while at the same time, retaining the partial Grace of the old system, it claims for God the undivided merit of salvation. But the shift is a failure, so far as the honor of God is concerned. The justice of eternal damnation is not vindicated by the theory of free-will. If human free-will is capable of abuse to such an extent as to be the occasion of endless misery, and if God foresees that abuse of it in any subject, then no theology can exonerate God from the consequences of that fatal endowment, and the responsibility of such a doom. The difference is merely nominal between a God who destroys by his own immediate act, and a God who puts into the hands of his creature an instrument by which he will certainly destroy himself. "It is as sure a method of killing a man," says Bayle, in his comments on this point, "to give him a rope with which one knows for a certainty that he will hang himself, as to stab him or to have him stabbed with a dagger. His death is willed as much by one who uses the former method, as by one who employs either of the others;" nay, "il semble même qu'on la veut avec un dessein plus malin puisqu'on tend à lui laisser toute la peine et toute la faute de sa perte."

Theology must not think to escape this dilemma by taking a high tone, and insisting on the power which the Creator has over the creature. "Hath not the potter power over the clay, of the same lump to make one vessel to honor and another to dishonor." * True, O Paul! Nevertheless, the question is not of power, but of right. The Being who possesses this almighty power has created in me a sense of justice which demands justice of the Maker, — has established in me a judgment-seat by which his own acts are inevitably tried. The answer quashes the plea, instead of refuting it. It may silence the objector, but does not satisfy the objection. Unquestionably the potter possesses power over the clay. Unquestionably the Maker possesses the power to make one man wicked and miserable, and another righteous and happy. But Christianity has taught us to know God, not as absolute Power merely, but as Justice and Mercy. "Shall the thing formed say to Him that formed it, Why hast thou made me thus?" The thing formed in this case is the human heart; and that heart is so constituted by its Author that it craves to know, and must and will ask, concerning the purport and end of its being. And if to such questioning it receives this answer, "Thou wast formed to be wicked and eternally damned," shall not the thing made then say to Him that formed it, "Why hast thou made me thus? Why thus, O thou Infinite! who hast all power to make and mould, even as the potter has power over the clay, — why hast thou made me, thy helpless vessel, to be the subject of such deep dishonor and boundless wrong?" It will so ask, and will not be content to receive for answer the absolute will of God as the sole and sufficient reason

* Rom. ix. 21.

for such ordination. Could it really believe in such ordination, on such grounds, the heart would feel that it had no God; for, verily, absolute power does not make a God. And the heart would sink into itself with a grinding sense of infinite cruelty and almighty wrong, or re-act on oppression like the chained Prometheus of the old Greek fable, — profound symbol of oppressed but unyielding manhood, — and scorn omnipotence dissociated from justice. But the fact is, the heart can never truly believe in such an ordination and in such a God. The Divine has written his nature too deep in man to be extinguished by a dogma. It is possible to human piety to love God without demanding his favor in return; * but true piety knows by its own deep sympathy with the Divine, that God is love, and that in that love there is no distinction of persons, — that all being is embraced in its boundless affection. No one felt this more profoundly than Paul. No one more ready to confess it, notwithstanding the words just cited. When, in this same Epistle to the Romans, he declares his belief that "all Israel shall be saved," together with the "fulness of the Gentiles," he discovers the real conviction of his heart.

We may say, then, speaking as critics of the Partialist theory, that that theory militates with the infinite love which reason compels us to ascribe to God, and which seems to require that to every creature of God its existence shall be on the whole a blessing, — that no creature shall be called into being for whom in any

* "Qui Deum amat, conari non potest, ut Deus ipsum contra amat." — SPINOZA: Eth. V. 19.

case it would be better that he had never been born. It matters not how widely we extend the circle of the blest, or how greatly we reduce the tale of the lost. The principle is the same, and no arithmetic can alter it. Suppose all saved but one, the difficulty still remains. Humanity demands that one; it mourns an imperfect heaven where that one is not, it hears a wail in the Alleluia whose choral symphony lacks that complemental voice. Indeed, the smaller the number of the damned, the heavier the damnation, and what is gained in one way by such concession is lost in another. What is gained numerically is lost qualitatively. It may even be questioned if the old doctrine which made damnation normal, and salvation exceptional, be not, on the whole, a more rational view than that which saves the mass and abandons the few. For, if the happiness of the world to come is purely a matter of grace, the free gift of God's love, entirely irrespective of the merits of the subject, then the few who are excepted from that grace would seem to be more hardly dealt with, and to have more legitimate ground of complaint, than the multitude of the lost, where perdition is the rule, and salvation a rare and exceptional favor. But if, on the other hand, the hereafter is determined by moral conditions, the few who shine with pre-eminent holiness are more broadly distinguished from ordinary degrees of moral excellence than the few superlatively wicked are from the general mass of unworthiness.

The insufficiency of those distinctions on which the rewards and punishments of the future state are presumed to be based, is another of the difficulties which embarrass the Partialist theory. If we suppose, what that theory commonly assumes, that the state of the soul is unalterably fixed at death, — the wicked precluded from all chance of reform, the good secured from all danger of lapse, — the disproportion between the moral distinctions of this world and the different fortunes of the next is too monstrous for reason to contemplate. The infinite difference between right and wrong must not be urged in defence of such a doctrine. The infinite difference between right and wrong is one thing; an infinite difference in the characters of those who, during the years of this mortal life, have done well or ill, is quite another thing. If we subtract from the character and life of the righteous all that may be termed good fortune, natural temperament, the native strength of the higher faculties, the comparative weakness of the baser appetites, education, social influences, opportunity, absence of strong temptation, — who can say that what remains of a purely moral nature is sufficient for eternal life, or even a sufficient guaranty that the individual who has borne so fair a character in this world will preserve the same in another, — that he will not change from saint to sinner when placed in new circumstances and solicited by new relations? So, too, it is impossible to say with certainty how much of the crimes of this life may be due to external conditions; how far the circumstances of the sinner may have tended to suppress the good in his nature, and to bring out the bad; and how far the good may be elicited and the bad counteracted by a different position hereafter. We are not warranted in ascribing all sin to circumstance; yet much that we call sin, and that makes the apparent difference between the moral and immoral classes of society, may have this origin, and the good and bad of this world may change places in the next.

It avails not to say, in vindication of the dogma of eternal damnation, that God inflicts no positive pains on the sinner, but simply "withdraws," and leaves the wicked to their own devices. This withdrawing is precisely the thing which God cannot do, — one of the limitations of his omnipotence. Out of him no creature can exist; in him and by him all being subsists, the hells not less than the heavens. The mystic *Yggdrasil* is rooted in him as well as crowned by him.

Verily, the strength of the Orthodox heaven does not consist in its exclusiveness, or the rule by which it excludes. The rough Norseman, on the eve of regeneration, when the priest, to his inquiry, disclosed the different future of Christian and heathen, withdrew his foot from the water, and declined the baptism which would separate him from the cherished heroes of his house and heart. Many, not wholly depraved, except in the theological sense, will sympathize with the honest sea-king in this, less tempted by what the ecclesiastical salvation offers, than pained by what it excludes. Even from its heaven blows the east-wind of Orthodoxy.

St. Augustine affirms of divine anger and forgiveness, that God does not change, but his creatures. He is changed to them in their sufferings "as the sun to sore eyes is changed from mild to harsh, and from pleasant to oppressive, while he himself remains the same." * And, speaking of the blessedness and misery

---

* "Illi potius quam ipse mutantur, et cum quodammodo mutatum in his quæ patiuntur inveniunt: sicut mutatur sol oculis sauciatis et asper quod-

of the future life, he identifies the one with a clear vision of the truth, — the other with ignorance and unreality. There are two opposite kinds of affection, he says: "one by which the blest are ravished with the purest cognition of their Author; the other by which the wicked are plunged into the deepest ignorance of truth. The latter will suffer real punishment by means of unreal images; the good will enjoy real beatitude in the contemplation of realities." *

In like manner, Maximus, the contemplative theologian of the seventh century, makes the nature and punishment of the wicked to consist in want of reality. "They who wisely meditate the divine words," he says, "call by the name of Perdition, Hell, Sons of Perdition, and the like, those who make to themselves, according to the affection of their mind, a reality of that which is not, and so come in all things to resemble phantasms." † But, above all, John Scotus, the intel-

---

ammodo ex miti et ex delectabili molestus efficitur quum ipse apud seipsum maneat idem qui fuit."

* It must be confessed, that St. Augustine has maintained in his writings as grossly material views of the sufferings of the damned, and of the physical constitution of the life to come, as have ever been propounded by the Christian Church. See, for example, the second, ninth, and tenth chapters of the *De Civitate Dei*, which treat of hell-fire. But, when he speaks of the joys of the blest, it is always the Beatific Vision that predominates in his conception. "Quapropter cum ex me quæritur quid acturi sunt sancti in illo corpore spiritali, non dico quod jam video, sed dico quod credo. . . . Dico itaque, Visuri sunt Deum in ipso corpore." — "Ibi vacabimus et videbimus: videbimus et amabimus; amabimus et laudabimus." — *De Civ. Dei*, lib. xxii. cap. 29 and 30.

† "Qui divina sapienter meditantur verba perditionem et infernum et filios perditionis et similia appellant eos qui quod non est, sibimet et secundum mentis affectum subsistentiam faciunt et sic phantasiis per omnia similes fiunt." — Quoted by Scotus Erig. in the *De Divisione Naturæ*, lib. v. c. 31.

lectual wonder of the ninth century, who treats these matters more profoundly than any one else, has developed in all its bearings the idea of the vision and participation of the Truth as the chief distinction between the good and the wicked hereafter. Both, he says, will have their intellectual images, as it were, the expressions of so many faces. (*phantasiæ veluti facies quædam expressæ*). The just will see God in different appearances, according to the *altitude of contemplation* attained by every saint. The wicked, on the other hand, will see different and false appearances of mortal things, according to *the diverse motions of their evil thoughts*. As the deified ascend through innumerable grades of divine contemplation, so those who depart from God descend ever through the different declensions of their vices into the deep of ignorance and into outer darkness. But *the general, natural goods of humanity*, he maintains, *will be common to all*. "These are given from above, coming down from the Father of lights, generally diffused among all, from whose participation no one is excluded, of which no one is deprived, since no one can exist without them; no demerits can impede the gift, no merits promote it; they anticipate all merit; by the sole, abounding, divine plenitude of goodness, they flow to all, everywhere, in unexhausted effusion; in none are they increased, in none diminished; the property of all alike, the good and the bad, they are *withdrawn* from none; eternally and substantially they will endure in all, free from all corruption and independent of all contrary passion."*

* "Hæc sunt data de sursum a Patre luminum descendentia, in omnes, generaliter diffusa, quorum participatione nemo excluditur, nemo privatur,

Hell-fire, he maintains, is not penal in itself, nor designed for penal purposes; it is a part of the universal good, an element which the blest will inhabit as well as the wicked; what is torment to the one will be health and joy to the other.

I said the weight of authority is on the side of the Partialists. It must not be forgotten, however, that the other view has had its advocates in every period of the Christian Church, and among them has numbered some of the best voices of the Church, from Paul to Schleiermacher. The opinion of Origen on this subject — his doctrine of an ἀποκατάστασις, or general Restoration* — is well known. It subjected him to persecution during his life, and to heavy condemnation after his death. Gregory of Nyssa, and Theodore of Mopsuestia, both eminent in the Trinitarian controversies of the fourth and fifth centuries, inclined to Universalism. St. Jerome, while insisting on the irrevocable and everlasting damnation of the heathen, expects a milder fate for Christian transgressors.† The Christian poet Prudentius, in the fourth century, proba-

---

cum nemo sine his subsistit; nullius mali meritis impediuntur ne dentur, nullius bona merita præcedunt, quibus præstentur; omne meritum præoccupant; sola divina bonitatis largiflua plenitudine omnibus per omnia universaliter inexhausta effusione manant; in nullo augentur, in nullo minuuntur; æqualiter omnibus insunt, et bonis et malis; a nullo retrahuntur, æternaliter in omnibus et substantialiter permanebunt, omni corruptione contrariaque passione absoluta." — *De. Div. Nat.*

* It ought to be stated in this connection, that the Restoration of Origen was not a finality, but only one stage in a great revolution, to be followed by a new lapse.

† "Sicut diaboli et omnium negatorum et impiorum qui dixerunt in corde suo, Non est Deus, credimus æterna tormenta, sic peccatorum et impiorum et tamen Christianorum, quorum opera in igne probanda sunt atque purganda, moderatam arbitramur et mixtam clementiæ sententiam."

bly expresses the prevailing sentiment of his time, when, in one of his hymns, he makes eternal damnation a rare exception to the universal Benignity, —

> "Idem tamen benignus
> Ultor retundit iram
> Paucosque non piorum
> Patitur perire in ævum."

The prevalence of Universalism in St. Augustine's day may be inferred from the fact, that several chapters of the "De Civitate Dei" are devoted to its refutation. After that, with the doubtful exception of John Scotus, above named, who rather hinted than confessed his heresy,* its traces are lost in the barbarism of the Middle Age. "Dismiss all hope" was written over the entrance of the mediæval hell; and, until the Reformation, theology seems scarcely to have questioned the legend. And since the Reformation, the authorities, in number if not in quality, preponderate on the side of Partialism. If questions in theology could be settled by the votes of theologians, the truth of Partialism would be established by an overwhelming majority. But, in such matters, one original thinker and independent critic outweighs a hundred traditionalists, — one fresh voice, a hundred echoes.

Will any maintain that the Christian Scriptures have decided this question beyond dispute for all who receive them as final authority? That they have not done so appears from the fact, that opposite opinions concerning

* "Divina siquidem bonitas consumet malitiam, æterna vita absorbet mortem, beautitudo miseriam, ... nisi forte adhuc ambigis dominum Jesum humanæ naturæ acceptorem et salvatorem non totam ipsam sed quantulamcunque partem ejus accepisse et salvasse."

it are entertained by different sects, each claiming to be Christian, each professing to receive the New Testament as final and divine authority. The testimony of the sacred books on this subject is not uniform: the voices conflict. The doctrine of Paul in the Romans, as we have seen, is Universalism: other portions of the Scripture emphatically assert the opposite view. The language in these passages is strong, yet not so strong but that modern criticism, sharp and trenchant as a two-edged sword, will pierce between the words and the doctrine supposed to be contained in them.* Indeed, what language can be made so strong as to be impervious to the sword of criticism, when many transcribers, and many mediating witnesses, and many centuries, and a foreign language, intervene between the writer and the critic? What language can be made so strong as to bind for ever thought and faith? The purpose of revelation is not to settle speculative questions depending on the nice interpretation of words, but to infuse a new spirit into human things, to illustrate great principles of practical import with new sanctions. The principles are eternal; the dogmas in which they are embodied are limited and transient.

The question is one of the *antinomies* of theology,

---

* We attach little weight to the verbal criticisms on the word *αἰώνιος*. Granting what has often been alleged, that this word, in its strict and original import, is not equivalent to our "everlasting," it is nevertheless probable that the New-Testament writers connected the idea of endlessness with it. But the plea, that whatever is deducted, in the interpretation of this word, from the duration of hell punishments, must also be deducted from the duration of future bliss, — a plea as old as Augustine, — is utterly futile (as De Quincey has shown) as an argument for the eternity of the former.

— a question of which affirmative and negative are equally debatable and equally doubtful. It is a question on which sentiment and reason are divided. Our heart is with the Universalists; but reason is shocked by the violence of the hypotheses which Universalism — theological as well as philosophical — seems to necessitate. Theological Universalism supposes a too forcible interference of Almighty Love in the normal processes of the individual soul, bringing the Divine into self-collision. Philosophic Universalism assumes an inevitable triumph of self-recovery, — a fatality of goodness in man which seems to be based on no analysis of human nature, which certainly is not warranted by any mundane experience, and whose only voucher, so far as we can see, is a brave hope, which, however honorable to those who cherish it, is of no great use in the critical investigation of this subject. Theodore Parker, one of the ablest representatives of philosophic Universalism in this country, states the doctrine with his usual vigor: "But there is no spiritual death, — only partial numbness, never a stop to that higher life. The soul's power of recovery from wickedness is infinite; its time of healing is time without bounds. There is no limit to the *vis medicatrix* of the inner, the immortal man. To the body, death is a finality; but the worst complication of personal wickedness is only one incident in the development of a man whose life is continuous, an infinite series of incidents all planned and watched over by Absolute Love. . . . In all the family of God there is never a son of perdition." This is fine, had the author but legitimated it by some demonstration of the grounds of his prophecy beside general reference to the revelation of the "Universe," from which he professes to have derived it. "I think there is not in the Old Testament, or the New, a single word which tells this blessed truth, that penitence hereafter shall do any good. . . . But the *Universe* is the revelation of God, and it tells you a grander truth, — infinite Power and infinite Love, time without bounds for the restoration of the fallen and the recovery of the wicked."

I am far from questioning the fact of conversions and reformations in the world to come. On the contrary, I believe that to countless profligates who perish in their sins, opportunities and appeals and gracious influences, denied in this world, will be vouchsafed hereafter, and will tell with saving effect; and that many who were last, will be first. But does it follow that all will be converted? that saving influences will act with compulsory force? that the soul, as such, is fatally bound and predetermined to goodness? that every Borgia is a Carlo Borromeo in eclipse, and every Brinvilliers an undeveloped Elizabeth Fry? Has this pleasant fancy any foundation but its own pleasantness, any authority but an undefined conception of the possibilities of Divine government? It is not a natural consequence, not a development according to cause and effect, but a monstrous accident, a wild interposition of juggling miracle which we expect when we so dream. The most distinguished of American philanthropists, with large experience of human nature and reformatory discipline, expressed to me his conviction that some natures are beyond the reach of moral influence, — proof against all discipline, — moral incurables. What reason to expect a moral revolution in such characters hereafter? If any derived from the nature of the human soul, let psychology declare it. The divine mercy? It is easy to talk of divine mercy; but the question is here of divine power. The question is of possibility; it is whether Omnipotence itself can reform such characters without so violating their idiosyncrasy, without so traversing their normal developments, as in effect to destroy their identity; and whether it would not better comport with divine economy to substitute at once another soul. A conversion which, instead of developing a native good, should impose a foreign one, would not be a reformation, but a *metaktizosis*, a transubstantiation. But we are supposing a case, in which there is no good to be developed, if not a case of entire depravity, — the existence of such cases may be denied, — yet a case in which the will is irrecoverably divorced from good, and bent on evil. Schiller describes the hero of the "Robbers" by saying, that he would not pray, if once so resolved, though God should appeal to him in person with the offer of immediate heavenly bliss. I fancy this conceit expresses a possibility of human nature, that the soul may arrive at a point of antagonism where the pride of self-hood shall resist all appeals, and a self-centred wilfulness shall say, "Evil, be thou my good." When that point is reached, we can see no remedy, no way of restoration, that would not compromise the soul's integrity. Yet even these cases are scarcely more hopeless than those of weak and unstable souls, swift to repent, and equally swift to transgress anew, whose existence oscillates between contrition and indulgence. The moral influences which recoil from the solid resistance of the former character, glide infructuous from the smooth facility of these.

If, therefore, we allow that Universalism is a natural and legitimate inference from the moral nature of Deity, we must qualify that inference, admitting here, as in every general principle, possible exceptions. Universalism is true in the general principle, that future blessedness is the normal destination of man. God will have all men to be saved, in the sense in which he wills that all fruit-germs shall become fruits, and all human embryos, well-formed, healthy men and women. But this destination is not always accomplished: * resistance or defect in the stuff, collision of forces, or what not, produces abortions in the one case; and defect or contradiction of the will may produce them in the other. The world of souls may have its failures, as well as the world of forms.

Supposing, then, that some individualities shall prove intractable and insalvable, what, in the final event, is to be the destiny of these abortive and exceptional souls? The idea of a state of endless, positive, unmitigated, conscious suffering, such as the old theology prescribed for them, we, in this age, have no hesitation in repudiating, as utterly inconsistent with all just views of divine government and the nature of the soul. However imposing the authorities in favor of a doctrine which numbers a Plato and an Augustine among its advocates, we cannot so affront the more imminent authority in

---

* "It is true," said old Meletius of Mopsuesia, "that God will have all men to be saved; but it is evident that the human will does not always coincide with the Divine."

our own breast as to symbolize with them in this particular. Though a vast majority of the Christian Church affirm it, we pronounce the doctrine *unchristian*, contrary to the spirit of Christ, however it may seem to accord with the letter of the gospel. Orthodoxy may steel itself to approve an immortality of woe, and even, as in the case of Tertullian and of Edwards,* imagine a satisfaction in the contemplation of it; but mature reason and the unperverted heart alike and instinctively reject it. Moreover, I hold such a state to be psychologically impossible. Satisfaction, in the way of fruition or of hope, is the *pabulum vitæ* without which no soul can permanently subsist: the result of continued suffering must either be an accustomedness which will make it tolerable, or an intolerableness which will overpower and extinguish consciousness. "No soul," says Lessing, "is capable of a pure sensation; that is, of one which even in its smallest moment is only pleasant or painful, much less of a state in which all the sensations are thus unmixed, whether of the former or the latter kind." † More elaborately, Schleiermacher, in his trea-

---

* See a Sermon of Jonathan Edwards entitled "The End of the Wicked Contemplated by the Righteous, or the Torments of the Wicked in Hell no Occasion of Grief to the Saints in Heaven." — "The miseries of the damned in hell," says Edwards, "will be inconceivably great. . . . The saints in glory will see this, and will be far more sensible of it than we can possibly be. They will be more sensible how dreadful the wrath of God, and will better understand how terrible the sufferings of the damned are; yet this will occasion no grief to them. They will not be sorry for the damned; it will cause no uneasiness or dissatisfaction to them: but, on the contrary, when they have this sight, it will excite them to joyful praises." — *The Works of President Edwards* (Worcester edition), vol. iv. p. 290.

† Theologische Aufsätze.

tise on Christian Faith,* has shown the irreconcilableness of a state of perpetual torment as well with the constitution of the human soul as with the supposition of an opposite state, appointed for the good, of perfect and everlasting blessedness. If the torment, he says, be supposed to consist in physical pains, the conscious power of enduring such pains is itself a mitigation of the suffering. If remorse be the punishment, conscience must be active in the sufferer, and that activity of conscience supposes a change for good, and is in its nature remedial; — if consciousness of forfeited joys, the ability to figure those joys implies the capacity of like enjoyment, and that capacity a partial reformation. On the other hand, if such a state be considered in relation to the opposite state of the blest, it is vain, he argues, to deny to the blest a sympathy with souls in torment which must effectually disturb their felicity; it is vain to contend that eternal pains, if decreed, must be just, and that the contemplation of God which constitutes the blessedness of heaven must include the contemplation of his justice; that contemplation does not exclude and cannot neutralize sympathy with suffering; and we even demand of the righteous "*a deeper compassion for merited pains than for unmerited.*"

In discussing these matters, one principle is of last importance; namely, that the future, whatever its character, will be a necessary consequence of the present, the natural result of causes now at work, the fruit of a good or evil life. Much of the error which prevails

* Der Christliche Glaube nach den Grundsätzen der Evangelischen Kirche (ed. 1836), vol. ii. p. 163.

in relation to the future state must be ascribed to a disregard of this principle. The essential truth involved in the figurative language of Scripture has been confounded with the pictures which envelope it. Hence, in the doctrine of the Church, the natural results of character have been converted into rewards and punishments, these into states of rewards and punishments; and these states have been conceived as entirely distinct from each other, each perfect in its kind and eternal in duration. Such, to this day, are the popular heaven and hell of the Christian world. The consequences of men's actions are eternal. Let us keep this principle in view, and we shall see that the future state of the wicked can hardly be one of pure suffering. For who so depraved that no good has ever mingled with his earthly life? This good, however scanty, is not lost: it must bring forth fruit according to its kind, and yield its consolation in eternity. If any shall object, that, according to this principle, the good must have their sorrows in the world to come, and that "Heaven" is not the unmixed rapture represented by the popular faith, I have no wish to avoid this obvious conclusion. On the contrary, I frankly confess that the popular representation seems to me to err as widely on the one side as on the other; the idea of a heaven into which no sorrow can enter, — a broad, unchastened day, —

> "Shining on, shining on, by no shadow made tender,"

seems to me just as absurd as that of a hell whose Stygian hold no joy can penetrate, and no hope relieve. The heavens and the hells interpenetrate each other; and the souls of men, with few exceptions, hereafter as here, for a time at least, will inhabit both or harbor both. The difference between the wicked and the righteous consists, not so much in the funded good or evil of their respective natures, as in the tendencies — good or evil — established in their wills. These tendencies, once established, will draw their subjects contrary ways, with progressive divergence sundering souls, the good from the bad; attracting the former to the Infinite Good, and impelling the latter — shall we say to the Infinite Evil? There is no infinite evil.

What, then, is the final destination of incorrigible and exceptional souls? Not endless torment, but everlasting (spiritual) death, utter extinction of the moral life. All the analogies point to this conclusion, all true deductions from the moral nature confirm it; and, for those who demand the warrant of the letter, what conclusion more just to the letter of the Scripture which declares that "sin, when it is *finished*, bringeth forth death"? Conscience (or self-consciousness) is the life-principle of moral natures. The tendency of sin is to weaken and corrupt, and finally to mortify and destroy, that principle. When, accordingly, in any soul the evil tendency exceeds a certain stage of development, the soul loses the power of self-recovery, and — the evil tendency still proceeding — arrives at last to rest in evil as its good, and to sin without compunction, or any inward restraint or contradiction.* Then — the evil tendency still proceeding — commences a process of mortification, which involves, as its final consummation, loss of consciousness; for consciousness supposes a ca-

* This is the stage of Devildom, or "Evil Spirits."

pacity of distinguishing good and evil, and loss of voluntary power, for voluntary power involves also a moral element. Sin is then finished, and has brought forth death. The soul, as a moral agent and a conscious individuality, is extinct: as a *monad* it still survives. No longer a person, but a thing, its condition thenceforth is not a question of psychology, but of ontology.*

The view here offered is by no means new, but has never obtained extensive currency in the Christian Church. Yet it is the one which seems to me most defensible, as being less violent in its hypothetical assumptions than Universalism, and more in harmony with just conceptions of Deity and divine rule than other forms of Partialism. The only point we may regard as established in this matter is the immortality of the moral nature, and a moral connection between the life that now is and the life to come. All else is mere speculation; and so little is gained by speculating on a future state, that the wise, after sounding in vain, to the extent of their line, this uncertain deep, will bound their inquiries by such practical conclusions as are best adapted to our moral wants. No reform in theology is more needed at present, than one which shall teach us how to prize, and how best to possess, this mortal world. We make too much of death and hereafter. We seem to be wandering at the foot of a mountain, behind which lies the land of our dreams. And the mountain

* To those who are curious in such speculations, the Gnostic cosmogony of early Christendom, which was afterwards unconsciously revived by Jacob Böhme, — the cosmogony which supposes the material universe to be the wreck of a foregone spiritual creation, — may suggest the possible uses of lost souls.

casts its long, dark shadow across our earth-life, obscuring its import and veiling its glories. The mountain exists only in our conceit: the land of our hopes and our fears is in the soul. We carry within us the "Judgment" to come, and the Judge, and all the hereafter. To be in eternity is not to be personally translated, but spiritually transformed; it is not to be disembodied, but disenchanted, *unselfed*. To fill the moment worthily is everlasting life.

XI.

THE TWO TYPES.

XI.

THE TWO TYPES.

WHEN the gospel was first delivered to the world, it had to encounter two contrary tendencies, represented by two different classes of minds. It encountered religious prejudice on one side, and philosophic pretension on the other. The former of these tendencies was represented by the Jews; the latter, by the Greeks. No two minds could be more unlike than the minds of these two nations, — the one perversely straitened, bigoted, intolerant, but firm; the other liberal, expansive, but curious, fickle, doubting. The one demanded external authority; the other demanded philosophic justice. The one required that a doctrine or system should be authenticated by some visible token; the other required that it should be scientifically legitimated. With the one, the question as to every doctrine was, "Hath the Lord spoken? hath the Lord said it?" And the evidence that the Lord had said it must not be internal, but external. It was not the nature of the doctrine itself, but some prodigy or supernatural circumstance attending its first annunciation. With the other, the question was, "Is it philosophical? Is it logical? Is it capable of demonstration? Does it harmonize with this or that school?

The Jews were a nation taught by prophets, who claimed a divine commission for what they uttered. They delivered their doctrine with an introductory, "Thus saith the Lord." The Greeks were taught by sophists and philosophers, who claimed no authority but that of reason for their opinions. They questioned nature, questioned the soul, analyzed their impressions, and gave forth the results of their inquiries in the form of scientific propositions, subject to criticism, to be received or rejected as criticism should confirm or refute them; not as the burdens of the Lord, to be received, without question, in the Lord's name. Their wisdom was reflective, not intuitive; it was elaborated, not inspired. They surveyed, according to their light, the entire field of human inquiry; they investigated all the questions which have ever agitated the human mind. All the tendencies of modern thought were anticipated, all the schools of modern philosophy are represented, in their speculations. When these speculations were brought to bear upon Christianity, they encountered a new and opposing element. Christianity would not accommodate itself to the wisdom of the schools. The schools could not adjust themselves with Christianity. To Greek philosophy Christianity seemed "foolishness." As little could the Jews, on the other hand, reconcile Christ with their traditions. They could not, or would not, see their Messiah in the Crucified. To Jewish prejudice, a gospel sealed with the cross was a "stumbling-block." But the gospel, ordained to be a new wisdom and a new power in the world, pursued its way, regardless of Jewish traditions and of Greek philosophy. "To the Jews a stumbling-block, to the Greeks foolishness," it proved itself to those who received it, "the wisdom of God and the power of God unto salvation."

The Jew and the Greek, as Paul found them, have passed away from the stage of this world; but these two tendencies remain. There are still these two classes of minds,—the Jew and the Greek; and, corresponding with them, two different forms of religious thought and life, — a Jewish and a Greek Christianity. Neither of these is complete in itself; neither expresses the whole truth of the gospel; each serves as a check on the other; each is the other's complement. True Christianity is the reconciliation of the two. Let justice be done to both!

1. The prevailing type in theology is Judaism. In the Christian Church, as everywhere else, the majority depend on external authority for their opinions, especially their religious opinions. In settling for themselves the question what is true, they look outward, and not inward. The doctrine which shall gain their assent must have some other basis than reason, or than *their* understanding. Is it the doctrine of the Bible? Is it the doctrine of our sect? Has the Conference or the Council endorsed it? Does this or that preacher accept it? If you inquire the grounds of their belief in Christianity, they refer you to the signs which accompanied its first promulgation. The miracles of the New Testament are more to them than the evidence of the spirit in the doctrine and life of

Jesus. They appeal to the Scriptures. If you demand of them, "How do you know that the Scriptures are true?" the answer is, "Because they are inspired." "And how do you know them to be inspired?" "The Church says so." The "says so" of the Church carries greater conviction to their minds than the evidence of the spirit in the word itself. If you could convince them that the miracles of the New Testament are not true, Christianity, in their estimation, would lose all its authority. The doctrines might still be true, but they would cease to have any special value. If you could convince them that the Scriptures are not inspired, in that technical and half-material sense which they connect with the term; that, though full of a divine spirit, they are not exceptional compositions,—convince them of this, and the Scriptures would seem to them to be deprived of all their significance. In short, truth to them is not a relation between their own minds and a given proposition or aspect of a subject, but a relation between them and some authorized person or persons, or institutions. It is not an act of perception, but an act of homage; not an individual experience, but a foreign *dictum*. They are constitutionally averse to *new* opinions, or such as have the aspect of novelty. And, when they assail such opinions, it is not by reason, but by authority. They call for a sign, and triumphantly appeal to their own. "To the law and the testimonies" is their cry. And what they cannot find in the law and the testimonies, according to their interpretation, or the interpretation of their sect, they not only reject, but reject with scorn. The asserter of such opinion is not only an errorist, but antichrist. It is not enough to disallow his doctrine: they rise against it. Not content with ignoring it for their own particular, they denounce it as an offence; and, where the times will permit, they punish it as a crime.

These are the Jews in religion; in modern phrase, the "Orthodox." They are the conservative force in the Church, the safeguard and bulwark of Christian doctrine; without which it would run wild, and lose itself in endless perversions. If not philosophic and rational, they are politic and practical. If not progressive, they are all the more steadfast. They are "constitutional." I intend by that phrase, so familiar in political life, the same quality or the same attitude in religious matters which is commonly expressed by it in relation to civil. We say that a statesman, or public officer, or public act, are "constitutional," when they conform to the written instrument on which the State is founded, and by which it is agreed that the legislation of the State and the administration of its affairs shall be ruled. The constitution is not infallible: it may be faulty in some of its provisions, it may need revision and amendment; but, so long as it *is* the constitution of the State, it is very evident that wisdom and the public good require its observance. It is easy to see what mischief must ensue, what disorganization and dissolution of all bonds and proprieties, what confusion, what hazard to life and goods, if the people of the State, and especially those in authority and public trust, should wholly disregard its provisions, and conduct themselves as if no such instrument existed, as if nothing were settled, but every thing left to the private discretion of each individual. It is obvious that the State could not stand on such a basis as that. There must be some kind of constitution, written or understood, to secure the well-being, to secure the existence, of society. And there must be constitutional men to maintain and execute its provisions.

The Christian Church is a spiritual society, associated for spiritual ends on the same terms, as regards the point we are now considering, on which the State associates for civil and temporal ends; that is, on the terms of a mutual understanding as to aim and action. And, since the greater part of the business of the Church is the communication and inculcation of religious truth, it follows that there must be a mutual understanding on *that* point, — on the question, What is truth, or what is the truth which the Church has to teach? That understanding, expressed or implied, is the constitution of the Church. And when I say the Church, I mean each particular branch of the Church, by whatsoever name it may be called. Each branch of the Church has its constitution, which serves as the basis of its action, and the maintenance of which is essential, not only to its prosperity, but to its very being. Suppose that no such understanding existed; that the doctrine of the Church, of any Church, were wholly undetermined; that not so much as a fundamental proposition, or general outline of Christian faith, were admitted or understood; that every proposition which might offer, from whatsoever quarter, of whatsoever import, were equally entitled to call itself Christian, and to be received as the doctrine of the Church; that, instead of a constitution, the Church presented a blank tablet, on which each might inscribe his own theory and call it Christianity, — suppose this, and what follows? It is easy to see, that Christianity, as a form of faith, would soon become extinct, overlaid with the speculations of all who incline to speculate, with the visions of all who are given to dream. The Christian Church, instead of the "Bride of the Lord," would become the harlot of every reformer who might wish to dally with her; the temple, instead of a fane for Christian worship, would become a pantheon for all the divinities of all religions, or a pandemonium for every abortion of the human mind. Thanks, therefore, to the Jewish party, the Orthodox, the conservative party in religion! They are the body-guard of the Church; they stand by the record; they guard the ark of religious truth from the wildness of fanaticism on the one hand, from insidious speculation on the other. Let them have their dues. If unfriendly to inquiry, and indifferent to absolute truth, they are fervently attached to what they suppose to be "the faith once delivered to the saints." If limited in their views, and bigoted in action, they are serious and devout. If wanting in liberality, they excel in zeal.

At the same time, we must not, in justice to Christian truth, conceal from ourselves the radical vice of the Jewish type. Having no interest in truth as such, but interested only in the forms that embody it, and in them only as something given, as fixed facts and institutions, minds of this class refuse to perceive that no existing forms or institutions contain the whole truth; that truth cannot be thus confined; that the forms of one age become inadequate to the wants of the next, — the human mind, with its capacity for truth, for ever growing, while forms and institutions remain stationary. The Jews in religion are unfriendly to progress; they oppose themselves to progress; and, had it depended on them alone, religion would have made no progress in the world, and humanity none. The same zeal which levels its ban at every new word in the Christian Church would ban Christianity itself, if Christianity were a new dispensation just offering itself to the human mind. One cannot help feeling, that the Jews who require a sign at the present day, and admit nothing without authority, are the genuine descendants of the Jews who required a sign in the days of the apostles, and would not see it when it was given. One cannot help feeling, that these Orthodox, who contend so zealously for the old way, had they been contemporaries of Jesus would not have been among the number of his disciples. It was the Orthodox party in the old Jerusalem Church that demanded the crucifixion of Christ. It was the Orthodox party in the early Christian Church that resisted the propagation of Christianity among the Gentiles, except they first became Jews, and would have kept it, if possible, a national privilege, confined to the children of Abraham. It was the Orthodox party which all along, from the final establishment of Christianity in the fourth century until now, has uniformly resisted every attempt to reform the doctrine or the polity of the Church. It was the Orthodox party which clamored for Mary-worship and the worship of images, and raged against all who sought to abate or to banish these corruptions. It was they who sent hell among the Vaudois, and presided at the Council of

Constance; who choked Savonarola, and would have choked Luther; who unsepulchred the bones of Wickliffe, and kindled the fires of Smithfield, and instituted the blood-bath of Huguenot France. It was the Jewish party in the English Church which enacted the Act of Conformity; which wielded the Star Chamber and the Court of High Commissions against the Puritans. It was the Jewish party in Puritan New England that hanged and scourged the Quakers, and re-enacted in the New World, the ruthless rigors of the Old.

In fine, the Jews in religion are no friends to truth as such. Though fanatically jealous of what they call truth, they value it not for its own sake, but only for authority's sake and tradition's sake. They value it, not as wisdom, but as a sign; not as the bread of life to be nourished by, but as show-bread to swear by. They value it, not as something to use, but as something to hold. If the formulas which they guard so jealously, express the truth, it is accidental, so far as they are concerned. Any other formulas which should happen to have been delivered to them would answer the purpose just as well. They might as well have falsehood as truth in their creed, as to any life which they draw from it. It is not truth that they want, but authority.

2. If, now, we turn to the Greek type in religion, we shall find it to be the exact reverse of the foregoing in all its essential features. "The Greeks seek after wisdom;" that is, philosophy, knowledge, understanding. Conviction, with them, is not based on authority, but on insight. They make little of authority, and little of tradition; they want, not only to believe, but to com-

prehend. It is not enough that a doctrine is delivered to them by the Church. They cannot receive it on that ground, unless it shall approve itself to their investigation. They subject it to critical analysis; and what analysis confirms, that only they receive. The first question with them is, not what has been delivered, but what is true; not what the Church teaches, but what Reason affirms. They are not careful to abide by the Past; they do not believe that all truth is embodied there. They believe in progress; they believe that truth is progressive, that more light is to break forth, and new discoveries to be made. They seek truth in all directions, and welcome it, or the promise and semblance of it, from whatsoever quarter, whether it be the School or the Church. They love to supplement the word of revealed truth with the teachings of secular philosophy, and to reconcile and blend them both in a more comprehensive view than the current theology, in their judgment, supplies.

This is the Greek element in religion, — liberal, inquiring, receptive, progressive, apt to learn, eager to comprehend. A very important agent it has been in the Christian Church. Whatsoever of progress, of freedom, of light, of enlarged and comprehensive vision, the Church has attained, has come to it through this medium. Without it, the Church would never have emancipated itself from Judaism, from Romanism, from any other form of doctrine or discipline which has once been impressed upon it. Each successive development of Christian doctrine is directly or indirectly the product of this element. Personally, it is an indispensable condition of a living and productive faith. Without it, faith is a blind instinct, on which no reliance can be placed; which stimulates without directing; which makes fanatics, but never discreet and effective servants of the truth. We may believe without understanding, as we may also understand without believing; but the highest form of religious life is that in which reason is guide to faith, and in which believing is an act of the intellect as well as the heart.

But while we honor the Greek in religion, with his search after wisdom, and while we rejoice that this type has never been extinct in the Church, we must not overlook its essential defects, nor blink its perversions. We must bear in mind, that the very trait which constitutes its merit and its glory is peculiarly liable to abuse, and, when abused, is more mischievous than bigotry itself. There are two sides to the love of knowledge. It may be a dutiful desire for the truth, as spiritual nourishment, as means of growth, as something divine to be realized in life; and it may be mere curiosity, a thirst for mental excitement amusing itself with mental images, as a child turns over the leaves of its picture-book, or pulls its playthings to pieces, with a scrutiny in which there is more of the love of marvel than of wise research. There is a seeking after knowledge which looks upwards, and aspires to the light, — aspires to it as divine manifestation and divine guidance; and which, with earnest speculation in its eye, still acknowledges the God-ordained limits of human vision, and reverently accepts the everlasting mystery in which the Absolute hides itself from finite apprehension, and restrains intrusive fingers where it seems to see the handwriting of God, "Thus far, and no farther." And, again, there is a seeking after knowledge which looks not up, but underneath and behind; which pries and peeps and peers; and, not satisfied with the radiant and majestic face of truth, puts forth its impious hand to detect the forbidden form. Its desire is not for light and manifestation of the Godhead, and heavenly guidance; but for penetrating into dark corners, and disembowelling sacred mysteries. It is not to face instruction, but to go behind it. It tolerates nothing hidden, and is for ever peeping beneath the veils which the course of revealing Providence has not yet removed; and which science, by legitimate methods, has been unable to lift. For all that is to be known is not yet revealed, and not yet revealable. The language of God to the human mind is, "I have many things to declare unto you; but ye are not able to bear them yet." For every revelation, and for every discovery, there is a time; and no real progress is made, or insight gained, by empiric groping, where neither revelation points nor science leads the way. If it were possible to anticipate truth by prurient speculation, it would not be truth in effect. For truth is not an entity, but a right relation of the mind with the objects presented to it. And that cannot be a right relation in which the natural and divine order is violated. The rash disciple of Egyptian mysteries who uncovered the veiled image at Sais, was not instructed, but smitten with madness, by what he discovered.

Observe, too, that the Greek propensity in religion, so far from securing the inquirer against that excessive credulity which might seem to be the peculiar attribute of the Jewish mind, is itself especially liable to this weakness, and not unfrequently terminates in grosser illusions and wilder superstitions than ever authority imposed on those whose faith requires a sign. It was the Gnostics, among the early Christians, — that speculating sect for whom Christianity was not sufficiently intellectual, and who sought to piece it with their philosophy, — it was they who received the spurious "Gospel of the Infancy," with its foolish tales of miracles wrought by the infant Jesus. Lord Herbert, of Cherbury, believed in a special revelation vouchsafed to encourage him in a work in which all revelation was denied. And, in our day, many who professed philosophic doubts of Christianity, and could not accept the alleged improbabilities of the gospel history, have given unhesitating credence to pretended visitations from the spirit-world, of which table-tipping and anile gossip have as yet been the only fruit.

The propensity of the Greek mind is to require a reason for every truth. And it needs the critical action of this propensity to distinguish truth from falsehood in the doctrines presented to the mind; to secure the mind from error and superstition, and that unlimited credulity which is practically no better than unbelief. But let it be remembered that truth is not the product of reason; and that there are truths for which no reason can be given, but the reason assigned for the being of God, "I am because I am." This divine *because* is the terminus of human inquiry in religion and philosophy, beyond which speculation is fruitless, and where reverent minds will bow submissive, and inquiry yield to faith.

A mind indulging this bias, and pushing this propensity without heed and without check, will be very likely to lose its self-possession, and either to founder in the realm of inanities, without bottom and without goal; or, what is equally bad, to entangle itself with life-long, inexorable bondage. These are the minds that riot in ultraisms. The complexion of their ultraisms depends on accidental conditions. In one direction they become brawling infidels; men who glory in having no God and no hope, no calling but corruption, and no destination but the grave. In another direction they become vehement schismatics, disorganizers, destructives; anti-church, anti-state, anti-law; implacably hostile to every thing established, and, above all, to established peace and good-will among men: or if, as sometimes chances, they land in the Church of Rome, they find special satisfaction in all the extreme and most offensive features of that religion; they urge its exclusive principles with a rigor which exceeds the consciousness of native Romanism. They out-fulminate the Vatican, and complacently surrender to damnation their former acquaintance, and the greater part of mankind.

Such are the vagaries incident to minds of this class. They are liable to either and any extreme of superstition or unbelief. Seeking after wisdom is a brave pursuit; but the truest wisdom comes not by the Greek method. None so likely to depart from wisdom as he who seeks it through the understanding alone. I picture to myself the course of such a spirit diverging ever farther from the Source of truth, turning from the sun in quest of light, and losing itself in endless aberration.

The Greek mind inclines to metaphysic subtleties, and delights in curious speculations and abstract questions, which have no bearing on practical life. It was the Greek that introduced those perplexing questions of speculative theology, those controversies respecting the nature of the Godhead, and the nature of the Word, which rent the early Church, and which still divide the Christian world. It was the Greek Fathers who first mingled metaphysic subtleties with Christian doctrine. All those weary disputations — Arian, Homousian, Homoiousian, Heterusian, Monophysites, Monotheletes — which confuse the records of primitive ecclesiastical history are of Greek manufacture. And whatsoever of scholastic theorizing and metaphysic speculation, rationalistic, Calvinistic, transcendental, in later time has perplexed the Christian mind, has in it something of the old Greek element.

The Jew and the Greek — both types have existed in the Church from the beginning, and will continue to exist. Each has its merits and its dangers: either, when exaggerated, is fraught with evil; the one resulting in bigotry and superstition, the other in bleak negation or mystic aberration. Unhappily, they are found too often disjoined. If we look around on the world of our acquaintance, among those whose minds are active in religion, we find the Jew and the Greek each marked and distinct, — on the one hand, the rigorous conservative, the slave of tradition, the stickler for the letter, narrow, repulsive, hard; on the other, the rash innovator, the wild theorist, transcendentalist, mystic, genial and quick, but loose, uncertain, vague. A true religion unites both elements. The co-action of both is required for a healthy spiritual growth. We need the Jew; we need the sign, — external, supreme authority. We need the ultimate appeal of a given word to make our Christianity something more than a system of philosophy, a human invention, a fabric of the brain; to make it a faith, a religion, a certainty, a spiritual rock in the flood of thought and the tide of time. And we need the Greek; we need the reflective, intellectual element to make religion something more than a charnel and a sleep; to give it a propulsive and quickening influence; to give us in it and through it an abundant entrance into the everlasting; to make it a progress and a life.

Let each supply what the other lacks. Is your religion of the Jewish type, — a religion of authority, of rigid literality? Endeavor to enlarge your thought and to liberalize your mind by intercourse with minds of a different cast; converse freely with thinkers of every name; make yourself familiar with the literature and philosophy of religion beyond the limits of your School and Church. Add to conviction, insight; to tradition, reason; to dogma, charity; to the letter, life. Let ever green nature and loving humanity twine their tendrils around the walls of your Zion, and relieve with a gracious tolerance the harsh angularity of your creed.

Are you a Greek in religion, — rationalistic, studious of knowledge, addicted to speculation, impatient of authority, seeking in the human understanding alone the grounds of belief? Consider that if mortal wit were equal to all the wants of the soul, and to all the problems of spirit and life, no historic dispensation would have been vouchsafed; no church would ever have been established in the world. Reason as you will, examine, question: but overlook not the necessities of human nature; accept the limits of human insight, and temper the boldness of speculation with reverent regard for the manifest course of Providence in the education of the human race, and with something of respect for the faith of mankind.

"The Jews require a sign, and the Greeks seek after wisdom;" but Christianity comprehends and embodies both wisdom and sign. Christianity is larger than Jewish authority, and deeper than Grecian philosophy; and when in its infancy it burst upon the world, it swept away both; it bore down synagogue and academy; it floated Gamaliel and Plato, resolved them into itself, and, preserving what truth was in each, reproduced it in its own reconciling and transcendent kind. So it will do in all time to come with the sects and schools that have sprung from its bosom. It will absorb them all, — will survive them all. That steady flood will swallow up all our creeds, philosophies, organizations, reforms, — all our prophecy, all our knowledge; while, forcing its way through the heart of the world, it bears humanity on from truth to truth, and from life to life.

XII.

THE MORAL IDEAL.

XII.

THE MORAL IDEAL.

DIFFERENT ages and religions entertain very different notions of moral excellence, which they express in the models propounded for the admiration and respect of mankind. In many of the religions of the world, human models have been exalted into objects of worship. In the Greek and Roman cult, a considerable part of the rites of worship consisted in honors paid to deified men. The Herakles who forms so prominent a figure in the Greek mythology, is an instance of this deification, the prototype of many worthies, — part historic, part mythic, — whom their virtues raised to the company of the gods. The ritual name by which these worthies were designated was "hero;" a term which expressed the highest conception then entertained of human excellence.

The Christian Church, in its Roman branch, adopted the same practice. What in ancient Rome was Apotheosis, in modern Rome is Canonization. Canonization is the declaration of the Church of Rome, by her constituted authorities, that a certain individual is a holy person; one who, having passed directly to heaven without enduring the pains of purgatory, is to be invoked with prayers and honored with appropriate worship. The ritual name by which these Christian heroes are designated is "saint;" a name which expresses the highest ecclesiastical conception of human excellence. This is the present technical meaning of the term as applied to worthies of the Christian Church. The ancient apostolic use was different. Wherever the word "saint" occurs in the New Testament, it means simply Christian, without the attribution of personal merit. And after the time of the apostles, for more than a century, Christians without discrimination were called "saints." By that term they were distinguished from Jew and Gentile, but not from each other.

This change in the use of the word is very remarkable. It indicates the different view, entertained by different periods, of what constitutes holiness. In the view of the early Church, holiness resulted from position, — the position given by the Christian calling. In the view of the later Church, position results from holiness. In the former case, Christians were regarded as "called" in a special sense. It was not so much their own deliberate choice, as it was the special favor of God, that had made them Christians, according to the saying, "Ye have not chosen me, but I have chosen you." Being chosen, called from amid the great mass of the profane world, they were a separate and select race: "Ye are a chosen generation, a royal priesthood, a holy nation, a peculiar people." Their separation was their sanctity. As the age advanced, and Christendom extended its borders; and Christianity, instead of a specialty and a separation, became an empire and a world, — this view of sanctity got obsolete. Christian and saint were no longer synonymous. The idea of holiness was then transferred from a providential state to a voluntary act, from calling to character, from the lot to the life. But still the Church so far maintained the original idea as to recognize no holiness outside of the Christian fold. And, as being within that fold was purely providential, — a matter of nativity or opportunity, — holiness was still, in part, external and accidental. Accordingly, the saint of the Christian Church represents the two elements of fortune and character, — an accidental and a moral element: the fortune consisting in the circumstance of Christian nativity or Christian opportunity; the character being his own developed and disciplined will.

Regarding the moral element in the Church idea of the saint, we have here a type of character differing widely from that represented in the objects of Gentile adoration. The deified men of the Gentile Church were the strong, the brave, the beautiful, the eminent, and such as were distinguished by worldly success. The canonized worthies of the Christian Church were men and women, distinguished by moral exactness and religious devotion. Here, then, we have a point of comparison by which to estimate the different tendencies of the Gentile and the Christian mind. Here we have their respective ideals of human excellence, the characters to which they paid the highest honor, the hero and the saint, the powerful and the good. Out of this one difference it would not be difficult to develop all the moral differences which distinguish the two religions.

The hero was the saint of ancient worship, the saint is the hero of the Christian Church. And observe that the same qualities which the Greeks adored in their heroes and demigods were also embodied, and constituted the distinguishing traits, in their higher divinities. The Olympian gods were deified Force, Beauty, Cunning, Art.

In the city of Rome, in the early period of the Christian era, the two religions encountered each other, and contended together in a deadly conflict, which resulted in the overthrow of the Gentile and the triumph of the Christian worship, of the Christian ecclesiastical power, also of many Christian ideas, and among them the recognition of the Christian type of character. There remain, as monuments of this conflict and this triumph, some ancient temples, once consecrate to Gentile divinities, which, after the overthrow of polytheism, were purified, re-dedicated, and converted into Christian Churches, and which still survive as such. The most remarkable of these is the great pantheon of Agrippa, a temple erected near the time of the birth of Christ; and dedicated, not to one deity only, but to all the divinities of the Greek and Roman faith. Early in the seventh century, Pope Boniface IV. new consecrated this splendid fane, cleared it of the symbols of polytheism, replaced the ancient statues with representations of Christian worthies, and devoted it to the Virgin Mary and all the martyrs. It still exists under this designation, the most perfect monument which modern Rome contains of ancient architectural art. This venerable temple of two successive ages and religions affords, in the contrast of its present symbols, images, and decorations, with those of ancient time, an apt illustration of the change which religion has wrought in the moral ideals of the people of Rome. A writer * in the interest of the Catholic Church, defending it against the charge of Paganism, supposes an ancient Roman, who had known this temple in his lifetime, to revisit it in its present form. "The first thing which would strike him, instead of the statue of Jupiter, which once stood fronting the entrance, would be the image of Christ crucified, which now occupies that spot. On the right hand, the picture of one whom men are stoning, while he, with uplifted eyes, prays for their forgiveness, would rivet his attention; on the left, the modest statue of a virgin with a child in her arms would invite him to inquiry. Then he would see the monuments of men whose clasped or crossed hands express how they died with unresisting patience, and the prayer of faith in their hearts. When he should inquire into the character of these men, he would learn that they were not such as had been crowned with worldly success, or whose achievements had won for them the applause of their contemporaries; not victors in battle, not rulers and potentates, but men whose highest distinction was their humility and devotion, — men who were persecuted for righteousness' sake; who resisted not evil, but returned blessings for cursing, and submitted themselves to a painful death rather than deny their faith." — "I fancy," says this writer, "it would be no difficult task, with these objects before him, to expound and fully develop to him the Christian faith; and I think this ancient Roman would

* The late Cardinal Wiseman.

get the idea of a religion immensely different from that which he had professed, when he should see the substitution of symbol for symbol,—the cross of ignominy with its unresisting victim for the haughty Thunderer, the purest of virgins for the goddess of lust, the forgiving Stephen for the avenging god of war. He would conceive the idea of a religion of the meek and humble, of the persecuted and suffering, of the merciful, the modest, and devout."

In this change from the old to the new, from Gentile to Christian, the most marked and remarkable and indisputable sign of spiritual superiority on the part of the Christian is the irrecognition, the sublime disregard by the Church, of all adventitious, external, splendor and renown, of all pomp of circumstance, of all conventional distinctions of rank or place, of all physical endowments, such as beauty or strength, of all celebrity won by merely animal or merely secular or intellectual prowess or enterprise. The qualifications for ecclesiastical saintship have been precisely those qualities which the gospel commends, — humility, meekness, patience. The gospel announced itself as a power that was to "exalt them of low degree." — "Blessed are the poor in spirit, for theirs is the kingdom of heaven," "He that humbleth himself shall be exalted," is its spirit and promise, its all-pervading idea. This idea and promise the Church of Rome has strikingly and nobly fulfilled. Mistakes she may have made in regard to the claims of some whom she canonized; but one mistake she did not commit, from one abuse of power an impartial judgment must pronounce her wholly and signally free. In the canonization of her worthies there has been no respect of persons; no regard was paid to earthly rank or glory. However, in her policy toward the living, she may have truckled to rank and power, in the administration of her rites and duties to the dead she has known no man according to the flesh, and recognized no claim but holiness. There is no aristocracy in the Christian calendar but the aristocracy of good works and moral desert. There is no Julius there, no Augustus, no Antinous, much less a Caligula. If any crowned heads are there, they are such as Olaf and Edward, and Princess Elizabeth. If any nobles are there, they are such as St. Theresa and St. Charles. It is creditable to the Church of Rome, that she has canonized very few sovereigns, only one or two popes, and those not the most distinguished, nor the most devoted champions of ecclesiastical power; — not Hildebrand nor Innocent III., although one would say the temptation to canonize these must have been very great. On the other hand, the Church has freely and gladly exalted them of low degree, and raised them to sainted seats, where, after due investigation, the claim of holiness could be satisfactorily made out. In that calendar there are worthies whom some of their votaries would not have deigned to meet, while living, on equal terms, — would have deemed it beneath their dignity to consort with in the flesh, whose contact they would have shunned, to speak affably to whom would have seemed condescension, by whose side they would not have chosen to sit in public places. Servants are there, and beggars are there, and negroes are there; and their worshipful and aristocratic contemporaries are not there. The former are honored and adored, and invoked with prayer: the latter are forgotten and unknown. In this exaltation of the low, and neglect of the mighty, — where lowliness was coupled with holiness, and greatness was not, — the Church has done nobly, and carried out the idea of Christ. For if there is any thing which Christianity honors, it is humility; and, if there is any thing which God hates, it is exclusiveness and pride.

Thus much it seemed fitting and right to say in vindication and commendation of the ecclesiastical type of moral excellence as represented in the calendared saints of the Church. But when, from the positive side of this type, we turn to the negative, we perceive a certain narrowness, a one-sidedness, which renders the saint of the Church of Rome not altogether satisfactory to the liberal and philosophic mind. We are struck with the fact, that the heroes of the calendar are all Christians. I use the word in the technical sense. Those whom Rome canonizes must all have been within the pale of the Church; since the rupture of the Eastern and Latin Churches, they must all have been within the pale of the Church of Rome. No outsider, no ancient Gentile, no heathen of Christian ages, and, not only so, no Protestant Christian, can be in that calendar, — can be a saint, however pure and lowly and devout. I should be sorry to believe that there are not as many saints, ay, and a great many more, according to the highest Christian standard of excellence, outside of that calendar, than are in it, both among the dead and among the living. My calendar, were I authorized to frame one, would be a great deal larger than that of Rome. Not to speak of ancient worthies, of Socrates and Epictetus and Antoninus, there are numbers in our own age who by every principle of Christian right should be in it, and are not; men and women among the departed, to whom, were it lawful to address supplication to any below the Supreme, I would certainly as soon pray as to any Augustine or Chrysostom, ay! or the blessed Virgin herself. The Church of Rome could not be expected to know of all the holy without her own pale; but some she did know, and should have recognized, and would have recognized and canonized, had a wise and liberal piety guided her decisions; had she duly considered the words of the Master, "Other sheep have I who are not of this fold;" had she not been more influenced by ecclesiastical exclusiveness than by all her reverence for piety and holiness. Will the Church be more scrupulous than her Lord? She knew of Gentiles in the old world; she has known of heathen and Jews in the new, in whom was the very spirit of goodness and of Christ, to whom nothing was wanting but the accident of Christian baptism — a mere external, physical experience, a material sign — to constitute them as true Christians as any within the pale. These are not only excluded from the company of saints, but are not even salvable according to the Catholic theory of salvation.

The Protestant Church, with truer sympathy and broader charity, accepts for the most part the recognized saints of the Church of Rome, while she wisely refrains from establishing any canon for herself of either Catholic or Protestant worthies. But the private heart has a canon of its own, independent of the Church, and needing no decree of ecclesiastical councils to give it sanction. In that rubric of the heart are written many names unknown to Rome and unknown to the world. How many men of pure minds and spotless lives, whose daily record has been a registry of good deeds, and whose course through the world a river of blessing! And, oh! how many women, self-sacrificing, unpretending, uncomplaining, whose only art was loving-kindness, in whom was no thought that did not turn on others' need and others' weal, who have borne with patience and unconquerable faith the heavy burden of a thankless service and an unblest house, — the very incarnation of the charity which "hopeth all things, believeth all things, endureth all things"! Calendar or no calendar, our faithful rubric shall recognize these as booked and enrolled in that sacred host whose upper ranks and whose earthly platoons "but one communion make;" fellows and heirs in the peerage of holiness, "partners with the saints in light." Our highest mood will gratefully canonize all such, and praise the All-giver for that most needful and divinest blessing, good men and good women in every-day life, — the saints of the workbench, the saints of the office, the saints of the kitchen, the saints of the needle, the nursery, and the hearth.

I said that the Roman-Church type of the saint was too exclusive on its negative side. I must also add, that it seems to me somewhat narrow on the positive; a little too contracted in its moral aspect. Lowliness, purity, abstemiousness, devoutness, which constitute the chief ingredients in the composition of the calendar saint, are priceless qualities, no doubt; still, they are not the only virtues, nor the sole conditions of holiness. Sincerity, frankness, cordiality, liberality, cheerfulness,

— these also are Christian graces, and essential constituents of human excellence. And these are qualities which the Church canon makes little account of; which are often wanting, or not apparent, in the Church's saints. The consequence is, that the Church's saints, save here and there a Francis of Assisi, a Philip Neri, and a Francis Sales, are rather objects of reverential wonder than of cordial, affectionate sympathy, or enthusiastic emotion. I fancy the image conveyed to most minds by the word "saint" is that of a drooping, emaciated, wobegone figure, of sad countenance, "as the hypocrites are," or perhaps of a stern, repulsive look; not that of a healthy, eupeptic, cheerful, humane, and genial nature, such as one would choose for companion or friend. At best, it is an image of rapt, devout looks, "commercing with the skies," as of one who has no part or lot in things below. Nor can it be denied, that the saints sometimes have been men of narrow minds and narrow hearts, of limited views and sympathies; formal, unlovely, severe, — men in whom the religious sentiment has had a morbid and unnatural development, not carrying the other sentiments along with it, running to formalism, not blossoming into a large humanity and generous expansion of the heart, but contracting the affections, and seeking its food in asceticism instead of charity. Such examples have made the saintly character suspicious and repulsive to men of the world. The world will tolerate faults in its heroes, but not in its saints. Or, if there be faults, they must be such as spring from over-softness, not from defect of charity. No character is more repulsive than that in which religion is divorced from humanity.

The fact is, there are two quite opposite theories of moral excellence: we may term them the humane, and the ecclesiastical. The one makes goodness a natural growth; the other, an artificial product. The former discerns it in a healthy nature healthily developed, seconded by divine grace: the latter regards it as the substitution, by divine grace, of a theological and ecclesiastical conscience in the place of the natural heart. In the one view, grace re-enforces nature; in the other, it supersedes nature. According to one conception, goodness is self-manifestation; according to the other, it is self-alienation, — manifestation of an alien power.

In the fifth century of the Christian era, the two theories, represented respectively by St. Augustine and Pelagius, were brought into sharp collision, and debated in a council of the Church. The Church decided for the Augustinian doctrine; the humane view was declared a heresy, and has been out of favor ever since with the Orthodox sects. But when, from the bar of Orthodoxy, we appeal to the common sense of mankind, that judgment is reversed. In the court of common sense, true goodness is a natural growth: the more of individuality, the more of nature there is in it, the more genuine. Unless the original nature and deepest heart of the individual are expressed in it, however respectable, and however virtuous in its kind, it is not the highest style of goodness. It may be a good substitute where the genuine article is not vouchsafed, but good only as an artificial product is good in the absence of the natural. Still the natural is better. We rejoice when art can in any degree supply or redeem the deficiency of nature; but we rather rejoice in nature. A forced goodness is better than none. Nay, there may be even more merit in it than in natural goodness, because of the effort it costs. But there is not the beauty in it that there is in the natural, and therefore not the attractiveness and life-giving power. There is all the difference between them that there is in literature between a work of genius, the gift of inspiration, and a work elaborated by assiduous toil, — the same that there was between the two wives of the patriarch Jacob: "Leah was tender-eyed, but Rachel was beautiful."

It is seldom that canonical holiness is found in combination with an opulent, genial nature; still less, with humor and love of fun. But the possibility of such a combination is shown in one remarkable example at least, in which the saintly character appears completely redeemed from that ghostly unreality which attaches to most of its calendared representatives; an ecclesiastic whose goodness was not of the ecclesiastical type, but thoroughly and richly humane. St. Philip Neri, founder of the order of the "Oratory," was a man of exalted piety and boundless beneficence, — a man whose lengthened life was a life-long sacrifice, a pouring forth of himself in ecstatic devotion Godward, and in ceaseless charities manward; but withal so entirely natural, so genial, so sparkling with exuberant mirth, so constitutionally averse from all cant and pharisaism, that he often affronted the traditional standard of priestly decorum with his uncanonical deportment, his humorous disregard of conventional proprieties. The oddest freaks are recorded of him; and, while he figures as a saint in the calendar, he lives as a humorist in popular tradition. He encouraged the desponding penitent to confess, by pretending to expect something worse than the fact. "Is that all? Would I had done nothing worse!" He hated nothing so much as the reputation of a saint. One day, in the house of the Marchesa Rangoni, the Spanish ambassadress inquired of him, how long he had renounced the world. He replied that he was not conscious of having renounced the world at all, and soon began to speak of a jest-book in his possession, and to recount some of the droll things contained in it.

At the request of his friend, Angelo da Bagnarea, he called on a nobleman who had desired his acquaintance, but who was rather scandalized at his jocose manner, and afterward confided to Angelo that he had not been much edified by the interview. Whereupon Angelo requested Philip to repeat the visit, and to put on a graver deportment. "What would you have?" said the impracticable devotee. "You want me to play the serious, that people may say, 'That is Father Philip,' and tell fine stories about me. Depend upon it, if I go again I shall only make matters worse." He would never engage in spiritual conversation with distinguished strangers, whom curiosity and the reputation of his piety attracted to his cell.

At times a humorous fit would seize him in public, and tempt him to practical jokes. Standing, one day, in the midst of a crowd at the door of a church, awaiting the exhibition of some relics, his eye caught the flowing beard of a soldier of the Swiss Guard. Following the impulse of the moment, he grasped it with both hands, and began to stroke it with droll caresses, much to the amazement and amusement of the bystanders.

He was often known, when walking the streets, to take off his spectacles, and put them to the eyes of people who passed. He would dance and caper in the public squares, and say occasionally to lookers-on, after executing some extraordinary feat of agility, "What do you think of that?" He was much delighted on hearing some one whisper to his neighbor, "See that crazy old fool!"

As an instance of his moral independence and the deep sincerity of his nature, it is related, that, when the Sacred College with mistaken policy attempted to enforce the due observance of the rite of confession, by posting the names of delinquents in that kind, Philip said, "I will go, and read the list, that I may ascertain who are the brave men who will rather incur such reproach than dishonor themselves and blaspheme God by a hypocritical and forced compliance."

Not less entertaining than the pranks recorded of him is the effort of his ecclesiastical biographers to qualify and excuse these evidences of a genuine human nature underlying the saintly fame. The Church could not choose but canonize, after his death, a man of such transcendent and well-established sanctity; but he often scandalized the Church, while living, by the freedom of his manners. The same fear of scandal is evident in most of the memoirs which recount his life. What was pure, unadulterated fun they ascribe to excessive humility.* So fearful was he of being too highly esteemed

* It is reckoned as penance and mortification (*per mortificarsi*) by the Italian biographer from whom most of these anecdotes are taken. Vita di S. Filippo Neri, Fondatore, &c. Scritta dal P. R. Giacomo Bacci. Edizione Terza. Roma, 1831. From the Protestant side there is an excellent sketch in "Herzog's Real-Encyclopädie."

that he was willing to appear "a fool for Christ's sake." The "Acta Sanctorum" maintains a prudent reserve on the subject; but tradition, and the annals of the brotherhood which he established, have transmitted the genuine lineaments of one of the truest and noblest spirits that have ever sprung from the bosom of the Church.

The world in general cares less for piety than it does for force: it demands the strong man rather than the good. The types of character known respectively as "hero" and "saint" represent, not only different systems of religion, but different stages of moral culture in Christian lands and times. On the ordinary level of human experience, the hero is the more popular character of the two. With how different a sound the two titles strike the common ear! what different feelings they awaken in the breast! The one attracts with magnetic power, — it stirs the blood, it sets the whole nature aglow: the other looks pale and cold, — it seems something spectral, whose commerce and uses are not of this world. The reason is, that the former appeals to the animal nature; the other, to the spiritual. The appeal to the spiritual leaves men unmoved, because the spiritual is undeveloped. With the heroic we can all sympathize: the feelings which it touches are common to all. We cannot all sympathize with the saint for want of the saintly in ourselves: we have not yet attained to apprehend him. The saint will be our hero when we reach that plane of moral life on which he stands; and the heroes of our present idolatry will then no longer satisfy our more advanced sense of the true and the good. We outgrow our idols with growing insight: the models of our childhood are not the models of our youth, and the models of our youth have ceased to charm our riper years. In literature the authors and passages that filled our souls at one period leave us unmoved at another. The tumid phrase, the stormy sentiment, the coarse ideals, which gratified our inexperienced judgment, we now reject; and have learned to prize instead, those calmer, chaster models which once repelled. Most men are children in moral culture; their tastes are crude, their judgment green, their idols such as fit and please the undeveloped mind, — great in their way, eminent in their kind; but that way how imperfect, that kind how poor, compared with the higher models of the soul! Advancing culture disabuses us of our early predilections, exposes the inadequacy of our early ideals, strips our idols of their fancied perfections, and tears them to pieces before our eyes. We outgrow the pagan in our experience: Hercules gives way to Christ.

The world's heroes are not unworthy the homage they receive on their own plane. Whatever savors of heroism is worthy of honor. All great and shining qualities, strength, valor, genius, — who can help admiring these! I rejoice that such things are; I rejoice that there is a power in man to appreciate such. Still, there is something greater than these; they do not exhaust the power that is in man. The piety which dwells in the heights of the soul, which walks and works with God in godlike beneficence, is more sublime than the valor which breasts the shock of armies, than the genius which walks in glory among the stars.

There are two things which all men reverence who are capable of reverence, — strictly speaking, only two. The one is Beauty; the other, Power. Whatever is worshipped and loved in this world is comprised under these two heads. Our idea of God and all possible excellence is resolvable into these. Power and Beauty, — man is so constituted that he must reverence these so far and so fast as he can apprehend them. And so far and so fast as human culture advances, men will see that Holiness is Beauty; and Goodness, Power.

THE END.

Boston: Printed by John Wilson and Son.